SEW MUCH BETTER

Professional secrets to sewing faster & easier

by the Publishers of

SEW NEWS
THE FASHION MAGAZINE FOR PEOPLE WHO SEW

ACKNOWLEDGEMENTS

When SEW NEWS made its debut in November 1980, the founding editors enthusiastically promised to make the entire world of sewing their beat. From that moment on, many experts have shared their knowledge on SEW NEWS' pages to bring you the kind of good, solid sewing advice you don't find anywhere else.

SEW MUCH BETTER has drawn from this collective wisdom and expertise, especially the following authors' contributions: Shirley Adams, Marta Alto, Donna Babylon, Flo Banwart, Peggy Bendel, Ann Bozzi, Kendra Brandes, Eveylyn Brannon, Gail Brown, Roberta Carr, Clotilde, Sue Green-Baker, Arlene Haislip, Mary Halstead, Rochelle Harper, Gail Grigg Hazen, Janet Klaer, Nancy Kores, Dorothy Martin, Karen Crowley Metzinger, Jane Meyer, Marti Michell, Janet Olive, Miriam Olson, Debra Prinzing, Susan Pletsch, Ann Price, Laura Rehrmann, Belle Rivers, Kathy Ruddy, Donna Salyers, Jan Saunders, Jane Schenck, Susan Schleif, Claire Shaeffer, Joyce Shotick, Anne Marie Soto, Barbara Weiland and Nancy Zieman.

Also deserving credit are the many SEW NEWS readers who submitted their personal discoveries so everyone could benefit. You'll find their contributions sprinkled throughout SEW MUCH BETTER in the form of highlighted tips.

Representing as it does the experience of so many people who love to sew, SEW MUCH BETTER is dedicated to helping you sew better, faster and easier than ever before.

SEW MUCH BETTER

Peggy Bendel, Book Editor
Ann Davis Nunemacher, Illustrator

Staff at PJS Publications, Inc.:
Linda Turner Griepentrog, SEW NEWS Editor
Jerry R. Constantino, Publisher
Terry Boyer, Production Manager
Robin Hoffmann, Promotion Manager
Mary Johnston, Production Artist
Keith Griepentrog, Production Artist
Ken Clubb, Chapter Lead Illustrations
Dan Scharfenberg, Cover Design

CONTENTS

Chapter 1

THE ESSENTIALS

An amazing variety of sewing tools, supplies and equipment is available to help you sew faster, easier and better than ever before. Yesteryear's dressmakers would certainly be envious.

For example, you can use professional-style sewing equipment such as rotary cutters and sergers at home. Thanks to the computer chip, the latest sewing machines are remarkably versatile and easy to operate. Fusible products and other timesaving notions deserve acceptance as sewing basics.

You probably already possess everything you absolutely need for fashion sewing, but why stop there? This is an excellent time to update or upgrade your sewing gear. You don't have to spend a large sum of money. Something as simple as the right kind of thread or a better type of sewing machine needle can improve your sewing, and some aids such as a grainboard or a pleater you can make yourself.

Whether you prefer shortcut sewing or custom couture, use this chapter to find out how to choose and use a broad selection of sewing paraphernalia. In addition, make a habit of checking your favorite fabric store or mail order catalog frequently for innovations that continually appear.

Above all, try something new — it could change the way you sew.

BUTTONS

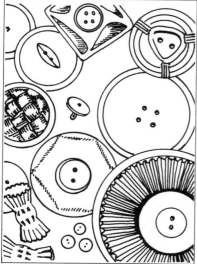

A beautiful button — one that subtly or surprisingly pleases the eye — makes a delightful finishing touch for the fashions you sew. Select from the wide range of contemporary styles available, or comb flea markets and antique stores for vintage buttons. The buttons you sew can be fashion accessories or miniature works of art in addition to being supremely functional fasteners.

TIPS FOR SELECTING BUTTONS

• When a single button closes a jacket or other garment, select a dramatic button that can assume the importance of jewelry.

• A standard blouse button is ⅜" to ½" in diameter, while a standard jacket button measures ⅝" to ¾". However, you don't have to be a slave to the button size specified by a pattern. A button ⅛" smaller or larger will make little difference.

• Keep buttons in proportion to the garment. If there are many buttons, use small, simple buttons. On the other hand, the fewer the buttons, the larger and more visually important they should be.

• Consider the option of using many small buttons 1" to 1½" apart (Figure 1) or

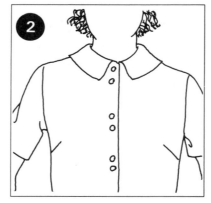

sewing two small buttons closely together in place of one large one (Figure 2).

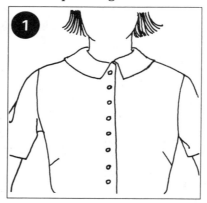

• In general, place buttons 3½" apart on a garment; large buttons can be spaced farther apart.

• If you need to respace buttonholes on a garment front, begin with one positioned at the bustline to prevent gaping (Figure 3).

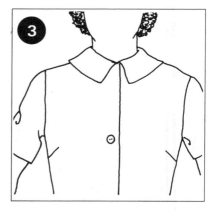

• Don't be too concerned about matching button color perfectly to blouse fabric. For a nice blend, use white buttons on light-colored fabrics and gray buttons on dark-colored fabrics.

• An easy rule of thumb when choosing buttons for a multicolored print fabric is pick the darkest color for the button.

• You can study ready-to-wear fashions for button ideas, but look only at the best lines. Many clothes sold in department stores have cheap or ill-chosen buttons.

• When buttons have textures or colors that contrast with the garment fabric, they create high fashion impact. However, take care not to overdo it. A good general rule is don't let the buttons for daytime wear be seen before you are.

• To customize large, wooden buttons, stencil or paint designs on them. Remove the varnish from the button, apply the design motif, then restore the varnish finish so the custom design will survive washing and cleaning.

• Check the button care requirements to be sure they're compatible with the care requirements of the garment's other components. Not all buttons are washable, and not all buttons are dry cleanable.

• Purchase a spare button when using novel buttons. If a button pops off and becomes lost, you can replace it easily and avoid having to replace all the buttons on the garment.

 ELASTIC

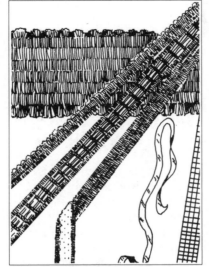

Do you find selecting the right elastic a problem? You'll know exactly which kind to choose when you understand the importance of elastic fiber content, the different types of elastic constructions and the many special-purpose elastics available.

FIBER CONTENT

Elastic has two prime components, a stretch fiber and a non-stretch fiber. Stretch fibers include rubber and spandex. Generally, the more stretch fiber, the greater the elasticity.

Rubber has moderate holding power, high elongation (stretch) and is unaffected by chlorine. It can discolor from laundering and perspiration. Perhaps the biggest drawback is it can break when stretched and lose its elasticity.

Spandex is more resistant to perspiration, and light damages it less, but it will yellow. Although many spandex fibers should neither be bleached nor exposed to chlorine, some elastics with spandex fibers are suitable for swimwear. Check the package information to be sure.

The five non-stretch fibers used in elastics are polyester, nylon, cotton, rayon and acetate. Of these, polyester and nylon are the most versatile. They are shrink-resistant and can be washed, dried and dry-cleaned without becoming lifeless. Body oils, chlorine and salt water won't affect them.

Cotton is soft and absorbent. Although it withstands many launderings at high temperatures, it shrinks and can't be dry cleaned repeatedly. It has good recovery and is excellent for sleepwear and lingerie. It's also a good choice for swimwear since chlorine won't harm it.

Rayon and acetate elastics should be washed by hand in cold or tepid water, then air dried. Avoid dry cleaning. These elastics shrink, especially when exposed to hot water and hot dryers. Since rayon and acetate elastics weaken and stretch when wet, do not use them for swimwear.

BASIC CONSTRUCTIONS

The three basic elastic constructions are braided, woven and knitted. In addition, there are specialty elastics with unique constructions.

Braided elastic (Figure 1) is lightweight, slightly ribbed,

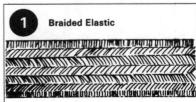

1 Braided Elastic

has good tension and is thinner than woven elastics. Since braided elastic narrows when stretched, use it for casing applications in waistbands, leg openings, necklines and sleeve edges.

Knitted (Figure 2) and woven

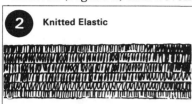

elastics do not become narrow when stretched, so you can either insert them into a casing or sew them directly to the fabric. Knitted and woven elastics are softer than the braided types, so they're a good choice when the elastic will be next to the skin.

SPECIAL CONSTRUCTIONS

Among the specialty elastics are non-roll woven flat (Figure 3) and non-roll woven rib (Figure 4) which have lateral ribs to prevent them from twisting.

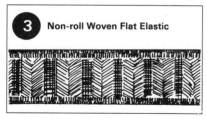

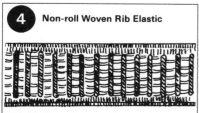

Other non-roll elastics have a special mesh construction. Use non-roll flat and mesh elastics in garments made from light- and medium weight fabrics; on heavier fabrics, use non-roll rib elastic. Either insert these elastics into a casing or stitch them directly to the fabric.

All of the following specialty elastics can be applied directly to a garment:

• Elasticized skirt belting has rubberized ribbing on one face of the elastic to help hold a blouse in place.

• Pajama elastic has a soft texture, light tension and sometimes a plush backing. Cut it 2″ −3″ shorter than the relevant body measurement.

• Lingerie elastic (Figure 5)

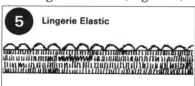

has one picot edge. Apply it to the garment's right side with the lacy picot edge at the bottom, or to the wrong side with the picot edge at the top. Usually the ½″ or ¾″ width is applied at the waist, and the ¼″ or ⁵/₁₆″ width is used around the legs.

• Soft stretch elastic, which has a very light tension and is often made of acetate, is particularly good for baby clothes. When applied directly to fabric, this narrow elastic does not recover its original length, so you may prefer the option of using it in a casing.

• Transparent elastic (Figure 6), almost invisible and very

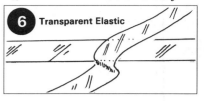

soft, is suitable for lingerie and exercisewear. It's chlorine-safe, so you can use it for swimwear. You can also stitch it into sweater and sweatshirt seams to eliminate rippling, or use it to finish the neckline and sleeve edges of a child's garment.

• Elastic waistbands (Figure 7) come in attractive colors for

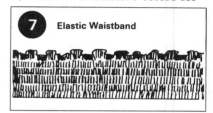

skirts and pants. Some of these decorative elastics have a stitching guide ¼″ from one edge.

• Plush back elastic (Figure 8) has a soft backing that's

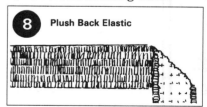

especially comfortable next to the skin. Cut this elastic about 2″ shorter than the relevant body measurement.

• Mesh elastic (Figure 9) is

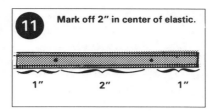

9 **Mesh Elastic**

softer, lighter in weight, and less bulky than most elastics. Use a narrow size for light-weight fabrics and a wide size for heavier fabrics. To simulate shirring, stitch through the mesh along the top and the bottom, then space several rows of stitching evenly in between.

• Round or oval cord elastic stretches softly. Use it to make shirring or rows of gathers, insert it in a fabric casing, apply it directly to fabric or insert it in a thread casing made from zigzag stitches (Figure 10). You can also use round cord elastic to make button loops for wedding dresses.

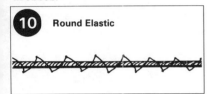

10 **Round Elastic**

TIPS FOR DIRECT APPLICATIONS

• When elastic is applied directly to fabric, it rarely returns to its original length. This makes it difficult to decide how long to cut the elastic.

To solve this frustrating sewing problem, cut a 4″ length of elastic and a fabric scrap 8″ x 2″. Mark off 2″ in the center of the elastic (Figure 11).

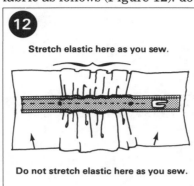

11 Mark off 2″ in center of elastic.

1″   2″   1″

Stitch the elastic to the fabric as follows (Figure 12): do

12

Stretch elastic here as you sew.

Do not stretch elastic here as you sew.

not stretch the elastic until you reach the first mark, then stretch the elastic as much as possible as you stitch to the second mark, then stitch to the end without stretching the elastic. Remeasure the stitched-and-stretched segment.

To determine the amount of elastic needed, divide the relevant body measurement (for example wrist, ankle or waist) by the new measurement of the stitched-and-stretched segment, then multiply by 2 (the original measurement of this elastic segment).

• When stitching elastic directly to a garment, use a straight, zigzag, multiple zigzag or serger stitch. Stitch type does not affect elastic recovery.

• To avoid damaging the elastic in direct applications, use a ballpoint or universal needle.

TIPS FOR CASINGS

• Make casings ⅛″ to ¼″ wider than the elastic.

• In general, for a casing cut the elastic the same length as the body measurement plus 1″ for overlapping and finishing the ends. However, cut soft stretch elastics shorter than the body measurement. When in doubt, pin the elastic around the body and wear it for a while to test for comfortable fit.

• To prevent elastic from rolling and twisting inside a casing, distribute the fabric fullness evenly and stitch in the ditch at each vertical seamline (Figure 13).

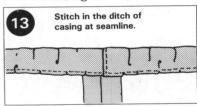

13 Stitch in the ditch of casing at seamline.

• Use a precut bias tricot strip to make a lightweight, non-bulky casing for elastic.

• To insert elastic easily in a casing, anchor the seam allow-ances of all vertical seams with glue stick or machine basting before stitching the casing (Figure 14). After stitching, use a bodkin to thread the elastic through the casing.

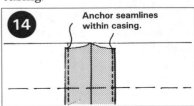

14 Anchor seamlines within casing.

GLUE

No matter what kind of sewing you do, there's a glue for you, and you'll be surprised what a timesaver it can be. Glue has always been indispensable for crafts, but it's often overlooked for sewing projects. If you've never used glue for sewing before, here's how to choose and use the best glue for your needs.

TYPES OF GLUE

Three types of glues are of interest for sewing: glue stick, white glue and permanent fabric adhesive. Each has different properties and uses.

Glue stick comes in a lipstick-style container which makes it easy and convenient to apply. Most glue sticks are white glues, although some are clear or nearly clear. All glue stick adhesives dry clear, and all wash out, so they are not permanent glues.

White glue comes in a bottle or a syringe-style applicator. All brands of white glues are basically the same polyvinyl acetate formula, but they do differ in viscosity and sticking strength; the thicker the glue, the less moisture it contains and the less it will soak through fabric. Some brands are formulated especially for use with fabric, so be sure to read the label.

White glues dry clear, are non-toxic and odorless. They reach full bonding strength in about 24 hours, but even then they will not hold up under continual stress and will break down when exposed to freezing temperatures. Also, white glues soften when exposed to water. Although some white glues will hold through one or two launderings, they are not permanent glues.

A few permanent fabric adhesives are available which, when fully cured, withstand machine washing and drying. These come in tubes and are often sold as a mending aid. They may require pressing to set the bond, and some brands are limited to use only on natural fiber fabrics and natural fiber blends as they are not safe for synthetics. It's a good idea to read the package directions carefully before use.

TIPS FOR USING GLUE STICK

• In general, glue stick is best for quick, temporary jobs. Try using a glue stick instead of basting.

• Use glue stick for positioning braid, ribbon or other trims that will be stitched later by hand or machine.

• Use glue stick to position pockets or zippers before sewing.

• Do give the glue time to bond properly to prevent the pocket, zipper or trim from sliding as you sew.

• Don't worry if the glue has bonded before you sew. Glue stick will not gum up the machine needle.

• Use glue stick to hold buttons in place for sewing.

• Before sewing a lapped seam, apply glue stick to the overlapping edge for perfect positioning.

• Use glue stick to "baste" a seam when matching plaids. Apply the glue along the stitching line only if you plan to press the seam allowances open later.

• Keep glue stick in the refrigerator. This prevents the adhesive from becoming too soft and spreading too thickly.

TIPS FOR USING WHITE GLUE

• White glues can be used in many ways, from holding appliqués to putting up hems for a garment fitting. Just remember that white glue will wash out — some sooner than others.

• To attach underlining to fashion fabric, use dots or a thin line of white glue along the raw edges, away from the stitching line. Allow to set.

• Use white glue as a temporary fray retardant. First, dilute the glue slightly with water. Then, use a small paint brush to apply the diluted glue sparingly to raw edges of a fabric.

• Most people use too much glue. The key to achieving a good bond with white glue is to apply it thinly to one layer of fabric, then wait a few minutes to let it set before putting the other fabric layer on top. This allows the glue to form a skin which keeps the moisture from soaking through the fabric.

TIPS FOR USING PERMANENT ADHESIVE

• Permanent fabric adhesives can be used in place of needle and thread. These glues can be used alone to hold something in place or can be stitched over when completely dry.

• Be sure to read the package instructions before using. It's a good idea to test the glue first on a fabric scrap.

• Use a permanent adhesive to put up hems or attach hook and loop fasteners.

• Use permanent adhesive to apply bias tape, secure belt edges or position appliqués.

• Use permanent adhesive to apply glittering sequins and beads.

GRAINBOARD

For perfect pressing and accurate cutting, make a versatile grainboard, a padded surface covered with a fabric grid. It makes a remarkable work surface for straightening the fabric grainline before and during layout, as well as for construction pressing and blocking purposes.

HOW TO MAKE A GRAINBOARD

Purchase a 36" x 54" piece of plywood, ¼" to ½" thick. If you have a permanent place for the finished grainboard, heavy ¾" thick plywood is even better.

Pad the plywood with an old wool blanket or use inexpensive wool remnants. Pure wool fabric is best as it absorbs moisture better than blends.

Wrap the wool padding around the board, mitering the corners and fastening with staples or carpet tacks on the underside. Two thicknesses make a nice, soft padding and pinning surface. Be sure the fabric is smooth and taut, without wrinkles or puckers.

Purchase a grainboard cover of 100% cotton printed with 1" squares. Press it to remove all wrinkles, but don't launder or preshrink it.

Smooth the grainboard cover right side up on the padded board, with the printed outside edge even with the edges of the board.

Beginning in the center of each side, wrap the cover to the underside and tack or staple in place. Continue working toward the corners, following the numbered sequence shown (Figure 1) — tack the center of one edge, the center of the opposite edge, the center of each side edge, then work from the centers to the ends. Be sure to keep the printed grid lines straight; use

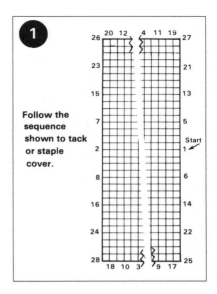

Follow the sequence shown to tack or staple cover.

a yardstick and T-square to check your progress. The cover should be smooth and taut, but not too tight or the lines will be distorted.

Press the installed cover, using a damp (not wet) press cloth to shrink it slightly.

Iron dry, and the grainboard is ready to use.

TIPS FOR USING A GRAINBOARD

• Place the completed grainboard on a flat surface at a comfortable standing height for you. A chest of drawers or table with casters is ideal because it can be moved easily.

• Use the grainboard during all steps of garment construction to respect the fabric grainline. This make sewing easier and gives you a finished garment that hangs perfectly on your body.

• To establish fabric grainline, first preshrink the fabric using an appropriate method for the fiber content. In a woven fabric, pull a crosswise thread and cut away any uneven edges along the thread (Figure 2).

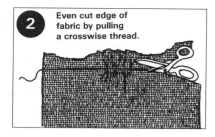

Working on the grainboard, fold the fabric in half lengthwise. Pin the fabric layers together both along the selvages and across the cut crosswise edges. If the fabric ripples and does not lie flat, the fabric is not perfectly on grain.

• To fix off-grain fabric, steam-press the fabric using a dry iron and a damp press cloth which holds lots of moisture. Press, lift, and repeat, overlapping the just-pressed area each time you move the iron. Don't slide the iron.

Once you have steam-pressed an area, lift the press cloth and press gently to dry the fabric. This sets the fabric grain and the garment will hang perfectly for its lifetime.

• It's not possible to change or reset the fabric grain on permanent press fabrics or synthetic fabrics with heat-set finishes.

• Once the fabric is grain-perfect, use the grainboard for pattern layout and cutting. The cloth cover helps to prevent fabric slippage, particularly when working with silky or slick fabrics.

• To pin pattern to fabric, push the pins straight down and into the padding of the grainboard.

• Complete all construction marking before removing the cut-out garment sections from the grainboard. A chalk wheel makes marking on a padded surface easy.

• Use the grainboard for pressing as you sew. The wood base along with the natural fibers in the padding and cover help absorb moisture and enhance pressing, shaping and steaming. Also, the large work surface means garments will not hang over the edge and possibly stretch during construction pressing when you are most concerned with retaining grainline perfection.

• Finally, don't overlook the grainboard for blocking needlepoint and hand knits. It's a great place to anchor braiding and macrame projects as well.

HANDY TOOLS

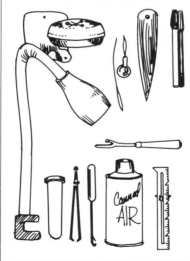

Many sewing tools once considered optional or too new to have proven themselves, now seem virtually indispensable. The following top tools of the trade are available through your favorite fabric store or mail order catalog. Chances are they'll make your sewing time more productive and more fun.

BIAS TAPE MAKER

This valuable metal pressing aid (Figure 1) for making your

Bias Tape Maker

own folded bias tape comes in four sizes: ½″ and ¾″ wide for single-fold bias tape, 1″ for wide bias tape and 2″ for extra-wide bias tape or bias hem facing.

To use, cut a bias strip of fabric slightly less than twice the width of the tape maker. Insert the fabric in the wide end, then pull the folded fabric out the narrow end, pressing the folds as you pull.

BODKIN

Reach for a bodkin (Figure 2)

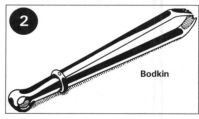

Bodkin

when inserting elastic through a casing. This tweezer-type tool has teeth to pinch the elastic and a small ring that slides down for secure hold. Just insert the rounded end in the casing and pull the elastic through. Use a bodkin also to thread cording through a casing or ribbon through eyelet or lace.

BUTTONHOLE CUTTER

You'll always get an accurate, even buttonhole opening with this wooden cutting block and razor-sharp chisel (Figure 3).

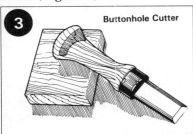

To use, place the machine-stitched buttonhole on the wooden block. To prevent accidentally cutting too far, insert a pin at each end of the buttonhole, just inside the bar tacks. Put the chisel between the rows of stitching and hit the end sharply to cut open the buttonhole. For small buttonholes, position half the buttonhole on the block; cut. Reposition, then cut the other half.

CANNED AIR

A quick blast of compressed air (Figure 4) helps clear lint

from a sewing machine's bobbin case and throat plate or a serger's knives and loopers.

It's packaged with a narrow extension tube to direct the air into hard-to-reach places. Be sure to purchase a brand of this aerosol spray not harmful to the environment so you can feel free to use it after sewing every garment or more frequently, as needed.

CHALK WHEEL

For easy construction marking without mess, the tip of this chalk dispenser (Figure 5) has a tiny wheel which

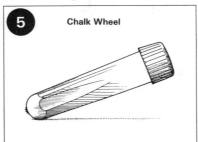

releases a fine line when you run it across fabric. It's very accurate because the tip can get right next to a ruler. The chalk powder is available in four colors and washes or brushes away.

LAMP

Supplement the general room lighting when you sew with a flexible-neck sewing lamp (Figure 6). Attach it to a sewing cabinet or table and position the concentrated light directly where you need it. Use it when sewing at night, working on dark fabrics, threading serger loopers and for any close work (hand or machine).

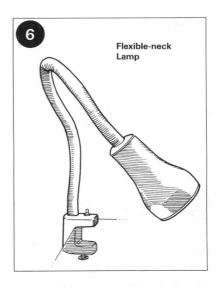

MAGNETIC PIN HOLDER

The curved top of this pin holder (Figure 7) makes it easy

to pick up pins when you need them, while the magnet inside holds the pins securely until you're ready to use them.

Keep a magnetic pin holder where you cut, where you sew, and where you press. Pass the holder over the floor to pick up any dropped pins, and use it to hold any small steel tool such as seam ripper, needle threader and scissors.

MARKING PENS

Marking pens with disappearing ink (Figure 8) are another fast, accurate way to mark fabric. Pens with purple ink are air-soluble (marks evaporate within 48 hours depending upon humidity), and those with blue ink are

Marking Pens

water soluble (marks vanish with plain water). Use blue ink pens only on fabrics which will not water spot.

To use, mark lightly. You may find it easier to mark directly through the pattern tissue with a row of dots, rather than drawing a continuous line. Remove the marks before pressing or laundering since heat and some detergents will set the ink permanently.

NEEDLE THREADER

Once rather ordinary, now the needle threader (Figure 9)

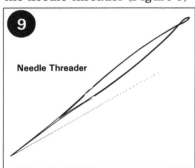

Needle Threader

is a very fine, pointed wire loop which fits completely through the eye of the needle. Use it for any kind of thread and needle, but especially when serging with special threads such as texturized stretch nylon, nylon mono-filament, pearl cotton and ribbon.

POCKET CURVE TEMPLATE

Shape perfect patch pockets every time with this template (Figure 10) which has four

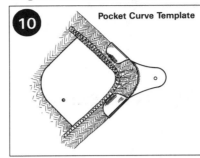

Pocket Curve Template

different curves and a two-sided clip for molding smooth, even edges.

To use, line up the template edges with the pocket seam-line on the wrong side of the fabric. Fold the seam allow-ance over the template; slide the clip in place to hold the fabric for pressing.

POINT TURNER

This wood or plastic tool (Figure 11) helps avoid fabric

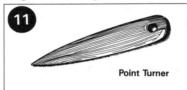

Point Turner

damage when turning sharp corners and curved edges right side out.

Use the pointed end for pushing out corners of collars, lapels, cuffs, waistbands and pocket flaps as well as when removing basting threads. Use the rounded end to push out a curved edge, hold a seam open for pressing or creasing fabrics that can't be pressed with an iron.

SEAM RIPPER

This ever-handy sewing tool (Figure 12) removes basting

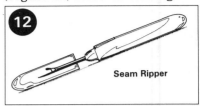

Seam Ripper

threads and stitching mistakes. Most seam rippers have a sharp, curved blade for cutting threads, a long prong with a point for removing threads and a short prong with a safety ball to protect the fab-ric from damage. To use, slip the point under the stitches and carefully cut the thread with the blade.

SEE-THROUGH RULER

A ruler (Figure 13) that lets

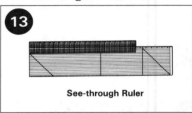

See-through Ruler

you see what you're measuring is a must. Newer rulers feature markings in two colors to show up on light or dark fabrics, a lip on one edge so the ruler functions as a T-square, bias markings and a metal edge. Use it for pattern alterations, checking grain-lines, as a straight edge for construction marking and as a guide for a rotary cutter.

Another necessity, this 6″ ruler (Figure 14) has a sliding

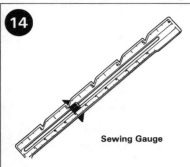

14

Sewing Gauge

marker. Use it to measure hems, mark circles, mark scallops and space tucks, pleats and buttonholes with precision.

NEEDLE NOTES

I fasten a small self-stick note on the side of my sewing machine. Each time I change the needle — whether for size or purpose — I write down the needle size and date and cross off my previous entry. This eliminates the guessing game of what needle is in my machine, and I don't have to try to read the tiny sizes engraved on the needle shank.

C. Fenstemacher,
Nipomo, CA

POINT PERFECTION

I make my own mini-point turners from tongue depressors. The blades are ¾″ wide and can be trimmed down to make a perfectly-shaped point. Use fine sandpaper to smooth any rough spots caused by trimming.

A. Guskea,
Corry, PA

HOUSEHOLD DISCOVERIES

It may surprise you, but there's something in every room in your home (including the bathroom) useful for sewing. Throwaways, household staples and specialty items — they're all here on this list of creative sewing aids you'll find around the house.

THROWAWAYS

• A soap sliver is one of the best fabric markers you can find (test on a scrap first and avoid using soaps with oils or creams). Also use soap to lubricate the needle point when hand sewing, to tame threads that snarl and to rub over difficult-to-stitch fabrics so machine stitches won't skip.

• A dried-out ballpoint pen, when used with dressmaker's carbon paper, is a fine tool for transferring appliqué and embroidery designs.

• A stiff, plastic, credit card holder, when placed on top of bulky or fragile fabrics, enables them to slide easily under a sewing machine presser foot.

• Shoe boxes store elastics, zippers, trims, tools and more. Label similar size boxes and stack them.

• Shoe box tops hold spools of thread, neatly organized by type and/or color.

• Large manila envelopes (used) store patterns that refuse to fit back into their original envelopes (Figure 1). Tape the pattern envelope on the outside for easy identification of the contents.

1

• A thermometer case, aspirin bottle or match box is a good size for storing hand sewing needles. Take one along for emergency repairs when you travel.

• Film canisters, pill bottles, baby food jars and margarine tubs sort and store buttons, snaps, hooks and eyes and other assorted little findings.

• An old mascara brush removes lint and fuzz from the sewing machine.

• Dry cleaning bags can preserve patterns. Press a layer of plastic bag between each pattern section and a sheet of tissue paper.

• An empty spray bottle, filled with water, is handy near the pressing area for misting. Fill a second bottle with a 50/50 vinegar/water solution for setting and removing creases. Label the bottles clearly.

• A dishwashing detergent bottle with squirt top fills a steam iron quickly and easily.

• An old shower curtain covers the floor under the ironing board to avoid soiling large items that drag on the floor.

• An old toothbrush removes short threads when ripping out stitches. It also fluffs the nap and hides pin holes after stitching synthetic suede.

• Old mattress pads or wool blankets make excellent ironing board pads. Or, bind edges with bias tape and turn them into portable pressing surfaces for travelers and sewing teachers.

• Old diapers, cotton or linen dish towels, linen napkins and handkerchiefs make wonderful press cloths.

• Old or odd pillow cases convert into beautiful garment bags when you make a small opening at one end for the hanger hook (Figure 2).

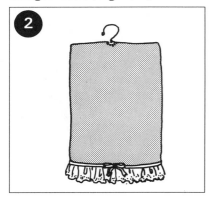

• Tubes from paper towels and wrapping paper provide wrinkle-free storage for wide laces, patterns, interfacings, fusible webs and delicate fabrics.

• An old magazine makes a seam roll substitute when you roll it tightly and cover with a towel.

HOUSEHOLD STAPLES

• A steel wool pad keeps needles sharp and rust free. Just insert the needles occasionally.

• Aluminum foil, placed under garment sections when applying a fusible product, creates more steam and saves time.

• White vinegar cleans a clogged steam iron, removes fabric folds and sets garment creases.

To clean an iron, fill it with ¼ cup vinegar and ¼ cup water. Adjust to a steam setting and heat 3 to 5 minutes. Unplug and place iron flat on a cake rack in the sink. Allow the solution to drip for half an hour, then rinse several times. Repeat as needed.

• Cornmeal removes grease stains on leather.

• Toothpicks can substitute for pins when basting fake fur fabrics, or push snags to the wrong side on knit fabrics.

• A spring-style clothes pin keeps pattern pieces clipped together until the sewing's done and you're ready to return them to the envelope.

• Wax paper is handy for adjusting or making patterns.

• Plastic-coated freezer paper extends the life of frequently-used patterns. Just press a paper backing onto each tissue.

• A dampened sponge picks up threads from floor and carpet or applies extra moisture when pressing.

• Cover fabric with a layer of tissue paper to eliminate stitching problems as long as you stitch with the paper's grain. To determine the grain, tear the tissue paper from top to bottom and again from side to side. It tears more easily and cleanly with the grain.

• Denatured or rubbing alcohol removes fusible residue from the iron soleplate and the right side of fabrics, as well as glue or sticky build-up on sewing machine needles.

• Hair clips or paper clips

"baste" leathers, pretend leathers and open-design laces (Figure 3).

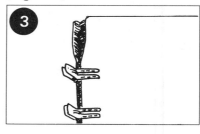

• Hair spray coats the cut end of thread for easy needle threading.

• Clear nail polish renews worn gripper snaps on jeans. Coat both sides of the snap and let dry; repeat until snap holds securely.

• An emery board or very fine sandpaper sharpens sewing machine needles in an emergency. Just stitch slowly through the board or paper.

• Safety pins or twist-ties organize buttons.

• Toothpaste eases the pain if you burn yourself while pressing.

• Waxed dental floss is strong enough to sew on buttons which have metal shanks.

• Typing paper, cut to the desired width and exact shape of the stitching line, helps when topstitching intricate seamlines or difficult shapes. Pin or tape the paper to the garment.

• Manila file folders are another pattern storage option. Stitch each end closed, using an old machine needle. Tape the original pattern envelope on the outside.

• A towel with thick, fluffy nap makes an excellent pressing surface for lace and napped fabrics.

• A scrap length of 2 x 4 board makes a practical pounding block for tailoring.

• A fold-out credit card case organizes your color samples and fabric swatches for ready reference when you shop.

• Typewriter correction fluid (white) makes a sewing machine needle easier to thread when you use the fluid to coat the front of the presser foot shank (Figure 4).

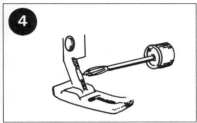

• An art gum eraser removes light soil from suede leathers.

• A mat knife cuts buttonholes smoothly and cleanly if you use it carefully.

• Pipe cleaners string matching thread spool and filled bobbin to avoid confusion (Figure 5).

• Multi-skirt or -trouser hanger stores interfacings and fabrics compactly and without wrinkles.

• Physician's examining paper, available from hospital supply stores, is convenient for altering patterns.

INTERFACING

Almost everybody who sews struggles with the interfacing dilemma. There are so many choices, it's not always easy to decide which interfacing is best for which project. And, just when you think you've figured it out, certain interfacing brands and types are discontinued, others are improved or new ones are introduced.

While there are no ironclad rules to make matters simple, there are guidelines to help. As you read the tips below, remember interfacing choice is very personal. The ultimate decision depends on your taste, your sewing experience and the fashion fabric's personality. If you like an interfacing-fabric combination, it's correct.

COLOR TIPS

• White or beige interfacings are customary with light-colored fabrics; use black or gray interfacings with dark colors.

• Because interfacing can shadow through to the right side of a garment, most interfacings designed for ultra-sheer fabrics come in a range of colors. Experiment to find the best color choice.

• White interfacing is not always best for a white garment. Often a light beige interfacing blends better with the fashion fabric and your skin tones.

• Interfacing color is very important for an unlined jacket or coat. If white interfacing is used in a dark, unlined jacket, no one will know as long as you are wearing the jacket. But, remove the jacket and drape it over a chair, and it will signal amateur workmanship. You'll wish you had chosen black or gray interfacing.

INTERFACING CONSTRUCTION

• Consider all types of interfacing constructions available: woven, nonwoven, knitted and weft insertion.

• If stretchability is a factor, choose a nonwoven or knitted interfacing.

• If looking for a stable interfacing, choose a woven, nonwoven or weft-insertion interfacing.

• Weft insertion construction is unique. While it's actually a knitted fabric, it has a crosswise (weft) thread inserted. This makes it stable crosswise while retaining the drapable quality of a knit.

FUSIBLES

• The basic issue of whether to choose a fusible or sew-in interfacing could be resolved quickly by the fashion fabric involved. Fabrics generally unsuitable for fusibles include metallics, rayon and acetate velvets, most brocades, fake furs, leather, openwork fabrics such as lace and mesh, and fabrics decorated with sequins, beads or re-embroidery.

• Test fusible interfacings on fabric scraps to preview the results. Make each sample a generous size, and follow the fusing directions carefully.

• The key to successful fusing is a combination of heat, steam and pressure to achieve a good bond. The exact combination varies from one interfacing to another, so do follow the manufacturer's directions.

• Even though the directions recommend an iron setting, it's important to note there are no standards within the appliance industry for exactly what temperature is meant by the fiber-designated iron settings. As a result, it may be necessary to adjust the iron temperature higher (or lower), or increase (or decrease) the number of seconds you hold the iron in one spot.

• Supply the necessary pressure by leaning on the iron; if this stance feels awkward, lower the height of the ironing board.

• Repeat the entire fusing routine, first on the wrong side, then on the right side of the fashion fabric. Even if not suggested in the manufacturer's directions, spend this extra time to ensure a strong, even bond.

• Most fusibles make the fabric slightly crisper.

• You may decide to use a fusible interfacing in one area of a garment and a sew-in interfacing in another area of the same garment, depending upon the fashion effect you are seeking.

STRETCH

• Do consider the stretch-ability of the interfacing. In general, the softest shaping comes from those interfacings which are all-bias or stretch in the crosswise direction.

• If you desire the traditional, crisply-tailored look, choose an interfacing that's stable both lengthwise and crosswise.

CARE

• It seems obvious, but do read the care information for the interfacing you are considering. Both interfacing and fashion fabric must have compatible care requirements.

• Don't put a dry-clean-only hair canvas interfacing in a washable garment.

• Don't put a permanent press interfacing in a silk blouse.

PINS

Silk Pin
Dressmaker Plastic-head Pin
Extra-fine Pin
Ballpoint Pin
Quilting Pin

While everyone thinks of the common pin as just that, you can hardly classify it as common anymore. Actually, there are more than 40 different kinds of straight pins, if you count all the variations in size, substance and point. Of these, dressmaker, silk, extra-fine, ballpoint and quilting pins are especially important for sewing.

TIPS FOR SELECTING PINS

• Select pins based on their length, size and metal content, or even easier, look for an identifying label on the package.

• Pins are manufactured to a standard determined by their length and wire diameter. Pin length is measured in sixteenths of an inch; a size 20 pin is $^{20}/_{16}"$ or $1\frac{1}{4}"$ long.

• Brass, steel, nickel-plated brass or steel and stainless steel are used for all straight pin sizes. Steel and stainless steel are the most common because they resist rust and corrosion the best.

• Although all quality pins are finished to resist rust and corrosion, stains can occur if pins are left in fabric for an extended period of time, especially in damp climates.

• Pins become dull or develop rough points with use. If a pin resists insertion or snags fabric, discard it immediately.

FAMILIAR TYPES

• Dressmaker pins are considered general-purpose sewing pins. They're suitable for most fabrics and are available in sizes 17 and 20. The more common is size 17.

Dressmaker pins have a thicker wire than silk pins, and extra-fine pins have a smaller diameter wire than silk pins.

• Silk pins can also be used with almost any fabric.

Because of their smaller diameter, they are especially recommended for use with finer fabrics such as silk or silk-like fabrics.

• Ballpoint pins were developed during the early 1960s when double knit fabrics were popular. Their slightly rounded point slips between knitted yarns rather than piercing them, preventing fabric damage.

• Quilting pins usually have a fine, narrow shaft and are longer than dressmaker or silk pins. Their length helps when working with thick fabric layers.

Quilting pins are also recommended for plush velvet, other pile fabrics and bulky fabrics. Weave the pins into the fabric to hold the layers together for sewing.

• Type of pin head also makes a difference. Regular pin heads are small, but glass or plastic heads are easier on the fingers as you work. They are also easier to find when dropped on the floor or when inserted in plush fabrics.

PLEATER

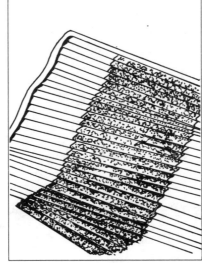

Set aside some sewing time to make a pleater, and you will have a pressing aid to help create your own pleated edgings and insertions quickly and easily. Yesterday's women made their pleaters from feed sacks and corset stays, but you can use the fusible web shortcut.

HOW TO MAKE A PLEATER

To make a 12″ square pleater with ⅜″ pleats, you will need the following fabrics: 12″ x 36″ of heavy muslin, 12″ x 36″ of paper-backed fusible web, two 12″ squares of polyester fleece and a 13″ square cotton fabric backing. You will also need an air-soluble marker.

Fuse the web to one side of the muslin. Leave the web's paper backing intact.

Beginning 1⅛″ from the top (Figure 1), mark lines across the muslin every 1⅛″. Stop 1″ from the bottom.

Peel off the web's paper backing.

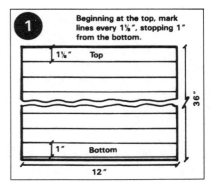

1 Beginning at the top, mark lines every 1⅛″, stopping 1″ from the bottom.

1⅛″ Top

36″

1″ Bottom

12″

Crease the muslin firmly on each marked line, and straight stitch ⅜″ from each crease on the muslin side. There should be about 27 pleats. Trim the excess fabric to ¼″ above the top pleat fold and ¼″ below the bottom line of stitching (Figure 2).

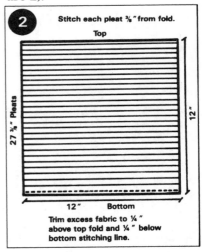

2 Stitch each pleat ⅜″ from fold.

Top

27 ¾″ Pleats

12″

12″ Bottom

Trim excess fabric to ¼″ above top fold and ¼″ below bottom stitching line.

To stiffen the pleats and edges, place the two squares of polyester fleece on the wrong side of the pleated muslin, against the fusible web. Using plenty of steam, press the pleats to fuse the inside folds together and the fleece to the wrong side of the pleats.

To apply the cotton backing to neaten the edges and cover the fleece, hand baste a ½″ pleat across the center of the backing on the wrong side. Pin the backing to the muslin pleats, right sides together, making sure the backing pleat runs the same direction as the muslin pleats. The backing should extend ½" on both sides of the muslin, but be even with the backing at top and bottom.

Stitch the top and bottom in ¼" seams, being careful not to catch any pleats in the stitching and leaving the sides open (Figure 3).

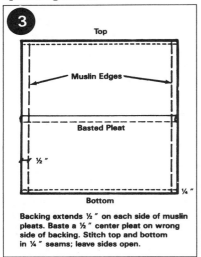

Backing extends ½" on each side of muslin pleats. Baste a ½" center pleat on wrong side of backing. Stitch top and bottom in ¼" seams; leave sides open.

Remove the basting to release the ½" pleat on the backing. Turn the pleater right side out through one of the open sides.

To bind the sides of the pleater, fold the side extensions under ¼" twice, covering the pleat edges. Slipstitch by hand or topstitch by machine close to the first fold, mitering the corners as you go (Figure 4).

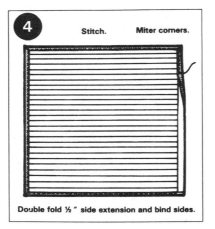

Double fold ½" side extension and bind sides.

TIPS FOR USING A PLEATER

• Use the pleater with single- or double-layer fabric strips. Try it with lace edgings, too.

• Use the edge of a sewing gauge or ruler to force the lace or fabric all the way into the back of the pleater folds (Figure 5).

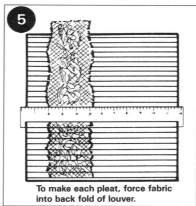

To make each pleat, force fabric into back fold of louver.

• For the fullest, prettiest pleated ruffle trim, tuck the fabric into every pleater fold.

• Skip one or more pleat folds to create fewer, more widely-spaced pleats.

• To set the pleats, moisten a press cloth with club soda or diluted white vinegar, place over the fabric in the pleater, and press. Allow the fabric to cool and dry out before removing it from the pleater.

• Use spray starch to add extra crispness when pleating cotton fabrics.

• When making long strips of pleats, use water-soluble basting tape to secure one edge of the completed pleats before removing them from the pleater (Figure 6).

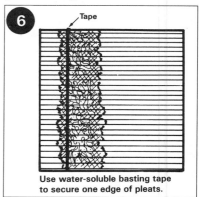

Use water-soluble basting tape to secure one edge of pleats.

• For a continuous long strip, place the last pleat made in the first pleater fold and continue pleating the strip.

PLEATER OPTIONS

• The 12" pleater with ⅜" deep folds is perfect for making trims, but you can vary the pleater size and depth as desired. Allow 3 times the depth of each pleater fold to determine the total length of muslin needed, and cut the backing ½" larger all around than the pleated muslin.

• To pleat a larger fabric area, such as a skirt, make the pleater slightly larger than the garment panels.

• Or, to pleat a large fabric area one portion at a time, modify the pleater so the sides of the pleat are free. Follow the pleater how-tos on page 19-20, but apply a seam sealant to the pleat edges before bonding the fleece. Also, instead of binding the sides over the pleats, fold the backing side extension in ⅛", then ¼" so the first fold is even with the pleat edges. Slipstitch the backing fabric fold to the fleece only, close to the pleat edges, mitering the corners as you go (Figure 7).

Using this free-pleat method, you could press the pleater folds in varying directions to create inverted or box pleats (Figure 8) if desired.

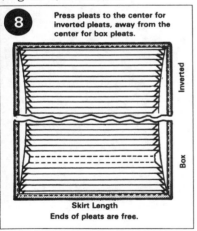

PRESSING AIDS

One of the key sewing principles is press as you sew. It's as important to know how to press a fine seam as it is to know how to sew it, and this skill often separates the amateurs from the pros.

To help you press beautifully, there are dozens of aids on the market today. They range from the basic pressing ham to the more exotic needle board. Acquire the basics first, then add others to your collection as your sewing interest grows.

DRESSMAKER'S BOARD

This versatile pressing aid (Figure 1), made of three snap-

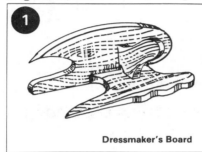

together boards, provides 12 different shapes for pressing curves, points, collars, straight seams and more. Use the board unpadded for crisp edges and seams, or add the padded covers for softer shaping as you press.

DRESSMAKER'S HAM

The most basic pressing aid is the dressmaker's ham (Figure 2), sometimes called a

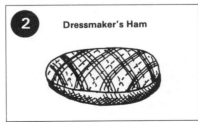

tailor's ham. Stuffed firmly and shaped somewhat like an edible ham as its name implies, it simulates various body contours. There's also a contoured ham (Figure 3)

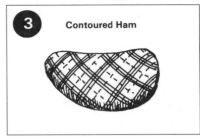

which has a more pronounced inward curve.

Select the appropriate rounded area on the dressmaker's ham to press darts, curved seams, shaped collars or fitted sleeves. Use the contoured ham in a similar way; use the inward curve for pressing lapel roll lines and fitted seams. Pressing on the ham's shaped surface helps build shape into the garment you are sewing.

Some hams are covered in one fabric, while others are covered in two. For versatility, choose a pressing ham with one side covered in cotton drill and the other side covered in wool. Use the wool side for pressing fabrics requiring low to medium heat and the cotton side for pressing fabrics requiring medium to high heat.

HAM HOLDER

To use a dressmaker's ham effectively, use a molded stand (Figure 4) to prop it in a pressing position. With a holder like this, you can stand the ham on either rounded end, on its side or tilt it as needed.

If you don't have a ham holder, it's possible to impro-

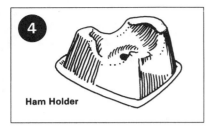

Ham Holder

vise with kitchen utensils. A mixing bowl can help hold a ham on end, and a loaf pan can stand the ham on its side.

NEEDLE BOARD

This bristled board (Figure 5) allows you to press velvet

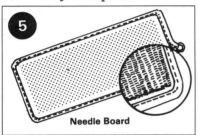

Needle Board

and other plush fabrics face down without crushing the texture. Standard needle boards are made with tiny steel needles; newer boards have a nylon bed.

POINT PRESSER & CLAPPER

The point presser (Figure 6)

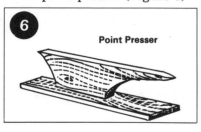

Point Presser

and the clapper (Figure 7) are also available as a combina-

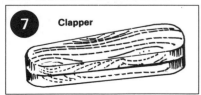

Clapper

tion tool (Figure 8). Use the

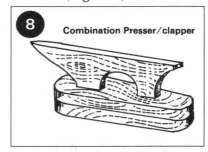

Combination Presser/clapper

point presser for crisp corners and details; cover it with a towel for softer shaping. Use the clapper to flatten seams, creases and edges after steam pressing; pound the area firmly to force out heat and moisture and set the shape.

PRESS CLOTHS

When pressing on the right side of fabric, a press cloth protects the fabric from scorching, shine and water spots. Dampened, a press cloth helps create additional steam for construction pressing or applying fusible products.

A sheer, cotton press cloth is essential and useful for many fabrics. This type of press cloth also helps create maximum steam when misted with a spray bottle, and its see-through quality allows accurate pressing. Fold it and use it doubled if extra fabric protection is needed.

You may need various other press cloths for special purposes. For example, a nonwoven press cloth controls heat, moisture and pressure on synthetic fabrics, and a bristled press cloth facilitates steam penetration as well as prevents flattening of napped and pile fabrics. A tailor's heavy-duty press cloth treated with beeswax and paraffin

helps press sharp pleats and creases, and gives professional results for final pressings.

PRESSING MITT

This small cushion (Figure 9)

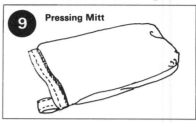

Pressing Mitt

slips over your hand, onto the end of a sleeve board or inside a garment to press enclosed areas which are hard to reach.

PRESSING PAD

This thick pad (Figure 10)

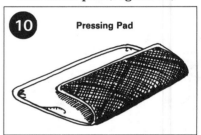

Pressing Pad

covers the ironing board to prevent raised details from becoming flattened. Use it also to cover a table top as an auxilliary pressing surface, and to press serged seams, zippers, buttons and button-holes, pockets, hems and embroidered decorations. One side has a heat-reflective fabric face for more effective fusing.

SEAM ROLL

This firmly-filled, flattened cylinder (Figure 11) is ideal for pressing long seams, zipper applications and hard-to-reach tubes such as pants legs and jacket sleeves. But one of the seam roll's biggest advantages

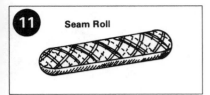

Seam Roll 11

is the rounded shape prevents seam allowance edges from leaving imprints. As is true for pressing hams, the most versatile seam rolls are covered half in cotton drill, and half in wool.

SLEEVE BOARD
The sleeve board (Figure 12)

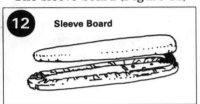

Sleeve Board 12

helps when pressing sleeves, legs and other garment areas too narrow to slip over the end of a standard ironing board. Double sleeve boards have one tapered side that's smaller than the other, making them extra-versatile.

You can use a sleeve board as a small, portable ironing board and set it up next to your sewing machine for construction pressing. You can also place the sleeve board on top of the ironing board to let the ironing board support the garment weight as you press an area.

SOLEPLATE COVER
This iron accessory (Figure 13) slips over the soleplate of the iron to protect fabric from scorching and iron shine. You can use a soleplate cover instead of a press cloth for a clear view when working on the right side of a fabric.

Soleplate Cover 13

Other advantages of a soleplate cover include protecting heat-sensitive fabrics (the cover reduces the heat that effectively reaches the fabric) and dark-colored fabrics. The cover also protects the iron from fusible residue stains.

TIPS FOR PERFECT PRESSING
• Before starting a project, test the iron heat setting on a fabric scrap. Linens use the highest setting and synthetics the lowest.

• When the iron is too hot, the fabric puckers. When the iron is too cool, pressing is ineffective.

• Remember, while pressing you're actually molding the garment into shape. Raise the iron to reposition it. Don't slide the iron back and forth.

• Avoid over-pressing. Pressing with too much heat, moisture or pressure will flatten the garment and make it look homemade.

• Press a dart first on a padded surface to embed and smooth the stitches into the fabric. Press along the dart fold, stopping ½" from the dart point.

• To avoid impressions on the right side from a dart, place a strip of brown paper bag under the dart fold as you press it on a dressmaker's ham.

• Press from the wide end of a dart to the point to create a curved shape.

• To press a dart point, use the small end of a dressmaker's ham. Gently press until the point is eased into the fabric.

• Split darts in heavy fabric along the dart fold to within 1" of the dart point (Figure 14). Press open to eliminate some bulk.

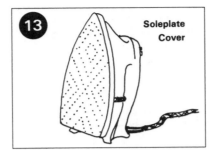

14 Do not cut.

• Finish pressing a dart from the right side, using a press cloth. Press over a dressmaker's ham.

• After trimming facing seam allowances and clipping the curves, place the facing wrong side up over a dressmaker's ham. Gently press the facing seam open.

• When pressing shaped princess seams or other curved seams, press over a dressmaker's ham. Let the seam cool down and dry completely while draped over the ham.

• Press all plain seams open before joining them to another garment section.

• Clip the seam allowances along curves before pressing.

• Gently open seams with your fingers, then lightly press with an iron.

• Press zippers flat under a damp press cloth.

• Use the small end of a dressmaker's ham to shape a sleeve cap and ease the fullness of a set-in sleeve to fit the armhole (Figure 15). The

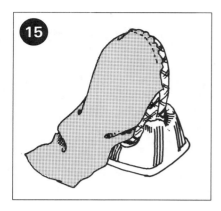

small end of a ham has the shape of a human shoulder.

• Do not press a sleeve cap from the right side after setting the sleeve into the bodice. This could very easily flatten the roll of the cap.

• Use the large end of a dressmaker's ham, which is shaped like a human neckline, for pressing shape into the undercollar of a jacket. After fusing interfacing to the undercollar and stand area, fold the collar along the roll line. Pin the collar around the ham (Figure 16). Hold the iron

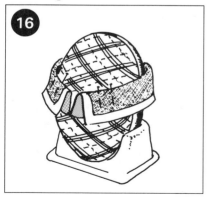

1″ above the roll line and steam. Allow to cool down and dry completely. When unpinned, the collar will retain its neckline shape.

• To press hems, use a press cloth on the right side of the garment. Lightly and carefully pat and shape the hem.

• Once a garment is finished, a complete pressing is the final step. Be certain nothing is left undone. If you've pressed the garment as you sewed, this last step will take very little time and yield beautiful results.

✂ ROTARY CUTTER

A rotary cutter makes it a snap to whiz around pattern curves and slice seamlines, and it literally shaves your sewing time in half. Resembling a pizza cutter in design and function, the rotary cutter joins scissors and shears on the list of essential sewing tools.

It's no wonder these time-saving cutters have found their way into the hearts of those who sew. Rotary cutters cut virtually any type of fabric quickly and easily without distorting pattern cutting lines. Up to six or eight layers of fabric can be cut at once, and the fabric lies flat throughout the entire process.

Among fans of rotary cutters are dressmakers who cut a lot of fabric, those who suffer from arthritis and those whose hands tire easily. Why? The rotary cutter's blade does all the work while the fingers mostly glide, applying just a little pressure. Some brands can be adjusted to control the amount of pressure exerted; this allows you set the cutter for lightweight or heavyweight fabrics.

CUTTER FEATURES

Rotary cutters are available in two basic sizes, and for sewing you'll probably want one of each. The standard cutter has a 1″ blade, and the heavy-duty, large cutter has a 1½″ blade.

Because of its size, the large model cuts fast and cuts multiple fabric layers easily. The standard model pivots more easily and is better for maneuvering around small curves such as necklines and armholes. All cutter models have a guard cover which conceals the blade when the cutter is not in use.

A guide arm is available as an accessory for some models and as a built-in feature on others. The guide arm attaches to the handle and allows you to cut strips of fabric accurately. You can also use the guide arm to cut wider or narrower seam allowances of consistent width without taking the time to mark and measure.

COMPANION MAT

To set yourself up for rotary cutting, you'll need a special mat (Figure 1) to cover the

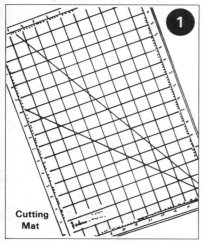

Cutting Mat

working surface. The mat protects the working surface from cuts as well as prolongs the life of the cutter's blade.

Mats come in various types, and some are softer in composition than others. A pliable mat is convenient if space is limited because you can roll it up for storage. If you have the space, a rigid plastic mat provides a nice, firm cutting bed. Some mats have a textured surface on one face to help control fabric slippage and accommodate push pins; the smooth surface on the other face is marked off in a grid with superimposed bias lines.

Mat sizes range from 6″ x 15″ to 40″ x 72″. The 18″ x 24″ or 24″ x 36″ size is convenient for fashion sewing, as it will accommodate 45″ wide fabric folded in half lengthwise. If possible, purchase a mat large enough to cover the working surface you use for pattern layout and cutting.

OTHER COMPANION TOOLS

Nice to have for rotary cutting is a transparent plastic ruler (Figure 2) marked in a

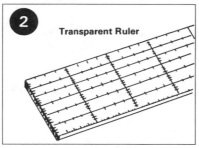

Transparent Ruler

grid to use as a measuring and cutting guide. Some of these rulers have one metal edge to prevent blade nicks; others have a lip which clips onto the edge of the mat, making it easy to square off the fabric.

Also nice to have are weights. Although you can insert straight pins or push pins through pattern and fabric into the mat, using weights saves time. A few, strategically-placed weights are really all you need.

The newest weights for sewing fit common pattern curves, right angles and straight edges (Figure 3).

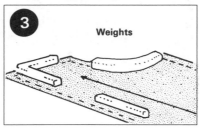

Weights

There are also round weights with gripper tacks on the bottom and felt-bottomed lead weights designed specifically for sewing purposes.

TIPS FOR ROTARY CUTTING

• Begin by placing the rotary cutter 1″ in from the fabric edge. Pull the cutter toward you, off the edge of the fabric.

This initial clip keeps the fabric from bunching in front of the blade. It also provides a smooth start for the forward cutting motion.

• As you cut, hold your head directly over the blade. If your head leans to the right or left of the blade, the cut will follow to the right or left of the cutting line.

• Use a ruler as a cutting guide for straight edges. For curved shapes, use a French curve or hipline curve ruler as a cutting guide.

• Change blades frequently. A dull blade won't cut as efficiently as a sharp one. A dull blade also scars the cutting mat more easily because you'll have to press harder to make a clean cut.

• Be careful not to run the rotary cutter off the mat. Treat the blade as you would a pair of shears. The extremely fine, sharp edge can be damaged if you drop the tool, run over a pin or pivot too sharply.

• In addition to using a rotary cutter to cut out garment sections, use it to trim exposed edges on synthetic suede garments.

• It's easier to cut out silky fabrics with a rotary cutter than with shears.

• Cutting bias strips is easy with a rotary cutter which has a guide arm. Use a grid-marked ruler to keep strip size consistent and to guide the cutter blade.

• Engage the safety guard when the rotary cutter is not in use. Always store the cutter in a safe, high place away from children.

SEAM SEALANT

A small bottle of seam sealant not only qualifies as a sewing trouble shooter, but also prevents many sewing problems from occurring in the first place. This clear liquid, which dries clear, has the unique ability to lock fabric yarns and sewing threads so they won't ravel. You'll find it useful before, during and after you sew a garment.

TIPS

• Test a drop of seam sealant on a fabric scrap or hidden seam allowance to be sure it won't discolor the fabric or add too much stiffness.

• If the sealant's plastic squeeze bottle releases a larger amount of liquid than you like, remove the bottle top. Use a toothpick or a fine paint brush as an applicator, dipping it into the bottle to pick up a small amount of sealant.

• Allow seam sealant to dry thoroughly before continuing to sew on the fabric section. If you're in a hurry, set a hand-held blow dryer on low and aim at the wet sealant.

• If a fabric seems to ravel away right before your eyes as you cut, apply seam sealant to the raw edges.

• Keep seam sealant handy when serger sewing so you can dab the thread chain with seam sealant at the end of a row of stitches (Figure 1). Trim

excess chain after sealant dries. With this technique, you don't need to bother weaving the thread chain back into the stitches.

• Seal cut buttonhole edges immediately after cutting the buttonhole open.

• If you cut a buttonhole too far, add a dot of seam sealant to each end (Figure 2). No one will notice your mistake.

Seal here.

• Apply a thin line of seam sealant along the raw edges after stitching and slashing for a continuous lap opening on a sleeve (Figure 3) or placket.

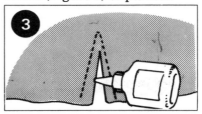

• A dot of seam sealant helps strengthen enclosed points which are trimmed closely, such as lapels and collars.

• Use seam sealant to finish the raw ends of ribbon ties. It's neater and much easier than trying to turn and slipstitch the ribbon ends.

• After trimming the fabric behind a lace appliqué, use seam sealant to protect the exposed fabric edges (Figure 4).

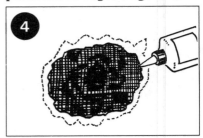

• If a machine appliqué has sharp corners, treat the corner points to a drop of seam sealant immediately after zigzag stitching the area.

SERGERS

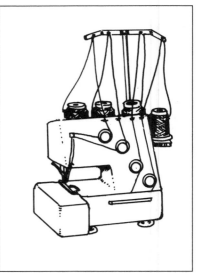

Sewing has definitely entered the serger age, and some say using this unique, compact sewing machine can make or break your fashion look. What a serger does best is make neat, narrow, thread-bound seams and edges like those found in ready-to-wear fashions. Because a serger is so specialized, you still need a conventional sewing machine for fashion sewing. A serger doesn't replace the conventional machine, but rather supplements it.

You may want to know more about sergers, especially if you're considering adding one to your sewing room. Shopping for a serger can be enlightening as well as confusing, but don't be intimidated. The serger is a different type of machine, so you must become familiar with new territory. This overview will help you understand what sergers have to offer.

SPEED

A serger is actually a home version of an industrial machine. It finishes the seam allowances and sews the seams like a high-speed factory machine.

In fact, a serger sews the seam, cuts the excess seam allowance away and overcasts the raw edges all at the same time and at the fast rate of up to 1,700 stitches per minute. This concept is almost unbelievable if you don't have a serger.

CONVENIENCE

When you have a serger, you can avoid certain sewing aggravations. For example, the steps for finishing seams with a conventional machine are more time consuming and pro-

duce much rougher results.

Also, a serger will not:
• Unthread its needle when you begin to sew.
• Thread jam.
• Eat the fabric, even on a corner of a difficult-to-handle fabric such as sheer chiffon.
• Require you to reach back and pull the fabric taut. With a serger, you can keep both hands in front of the needle to guide the fabric while the serger does all the work.

SERGER TIPS

• You acquire new sewing habits when you own a serger. For example, you must fit the garment before you sew since the serger cuts off the excess seam allowance and leaves little margin for alterations. Baste first on a conventional machine, try on the garment to test the fit, then serge. This is one of many reasons why it's convenient to have a conventional machine and serger set up side-by-side.
• Sergers use more thread than conventional machines. A serger may have 3, 4 or 5 sets of thread guides, but to give you an idea, a 3-thread serger uses about 20 percent more thread than a conventional sewing machine using a triple-action overcast stitch. However, although sergers use more thread, this really adds only pennies to the cost of a garment.
• Learning to thread a serger seems impossible at first, but it's actually easier than it looks. Most sergers have color-coded thread guides, excellent threading diagrams on the machine and illustrated instructions in the handbook.

• When you purchase a serger, it will already be threaded. To change thread color, merely cut the threads, tie the new threads onto the old, and pull the threads through the machine. This is the quick way.

When you purchase a serger, be sure to remove all the threads and thread the machine several times from scratch in the dealer's presence. This is the slow way, but you'll overcome any fear of serger threading and be prepared to handle thread breakage at home.
• Serger tension dials are adjusted often — every time you change the fabric, type of thread or style of stitch. You'll be happy to know serger tension dials are much less temperamental and much more useful than the tension adjustment on a conventional machine.
• Serger tensions are changed most often to create different stitch types and to accommodate different thread types. They're also used to improve stitch quality. All sergers have either color-coded or numbered tension dials to prevent you from getting lost.

LET'S SHOP

All serger brands are quite similar. Ask yourself these simple questions when considering a serger purchase:
• Does the manufacturer have a good reputation?
• Does the dealer have a good reputation?
• Is service available locally?
• How many stitch features

does the serger have? How many meet my needs?

• Is it easy to adjust the serger for these different stitches?

• Does the dealer offer serger classes, and if so, when?

✂ SERGER THREADS

If you're interested in creative serging, you'll want to know about the rainbow of decorative and novelty threads available. Which special threads become your favorites depends on personal taste, the effect you are trying to achieve and the types of thread that work best on your serger model. The following tips about thread types and how to serge with them suggest countless possibilities.

METALLIC

Once available only in gold and silver, metallic threads now come in an almost unlimited color range. These shiny threads are formed by twisting a thin, metallic fiber around a core of sturdy nylon, cotton or polyester fibers. Edgings on eveningwear are a natural place to showcase these glittering threads.

Because the exposed metal fibers might irritate the skin, plan garment construction so these threads don't come into contact with the body. Metallics are somewhat fragile and can break easily, something to remember when testing the stitch settings before you serge.

PEARL COTTON

Needlework buffs will recognize pearl cotton as a low luster embroidery and crochet thread. Although most commonly available in limited-yardage crosswound balls and skeins, pearl cotton is available on large cones for serger use.

Two of the best weights for decorative serging are #8 (fine) and #5 (medium). Both sizes form lovely braid-like edgings which are especially attractive on jackets.

Crochet thread is similar to pearl cotton in appearance, weight and color availability, although it has a duller finish, is more tightly twisted and comes wound into balls only. It, too, makes a raised, braid-like edging when serged.

RAYON

Lustrous rayon threads range from very fine to a heavy, buttonhole twist weight and add a touch of class to fine garments. Colorfast and washable rayon threads come in a wide range of colors including pastel, fluorescent and variegated forms. The amount of thread on the spool varies from brand to brand.

RIBBON

Some serger models will accommodate narrow ribbon in their loopers. Be sure to test first to see if your serger will feed ribbon properly.

In general, a ribbon must be soft and pliable to serge well. Silk or rayon knitting ribbons, ribbon thread and embroidery ribbon are some possibilities. Decorative ribbons sold for garments are usually too stiff for serging.

TEXTURIZED NYLON

Texturized nylon is a whole new family of threads introduced for serger use. In its resting state, this non-twisted, crimped nylon fiber thread resembles yarn, but when serged into a seam or edge this thread stretches taut to form a fine, strong stitch. Offered in a good color selection, including variegated types, texturized nylon can be purchased in large cones for serging.

When you serge edges with a short stitch length, this thread fills in the spaces between stitches for a soft, pliable, braid effect. It's perfect for soft, rolled edges or pretty, decorative edges, especially in garment areas that come into contact with the skin.

TOPSTITCHING THREAD

Topstitching threads, sometimes labeled buttonhole twist, are widely available. Fortunately, many thread companies offer a full line of topstitching thread to complement their all-purpose thread so you can find a good color match if necessary. Because it's strong, this type of thread is a practical choice for decorative serging on garments that will see a lot of wear.

Most topstitching thread comes in spools with limited yardage — from 10 to 50 yards. However, a few manufacturers do offer this heavyweight sewing thread in larger amounts specifically for serging.

YARN

Although they stretch and can be tricky to use, two-ply knitting yarns in sport, fingering, baby or sock weights can be serged for a napped, braid-like texture. The sky's the limit on color options, and if you know how to knit, you'll love using yarn leftovers to decorate the fashions you sew.

STYLE TIPS

• Since decorative serging looks best accenting key areas of the garment, look for designs with simple lines (Figure 1).

Accent key areas of simple styles with decorative serging.

• Decorative thread and rolled hem serging create dramatic piping at collar, cuff, center front and princess seams (Figure 2).

Create dramatic piping with rolled hem serging.

• Flatlocking with bright, decorative threads or yarn across the chest of sweatshirts and along the side seam of sweatpants has a sporty appeal (Figure 3).

Flatlock sporty details with bright thread.

• If you desire the refined, elegant look of piping, use a fine thread such as rayon to create rolled hem edges.

• Use rolled hem serging and a contrasting thread such as texturized nylon on the stretchy ribbed neckline and ankle bands of a jumpsuit to create a lettuce-edge effect (Figure 4).

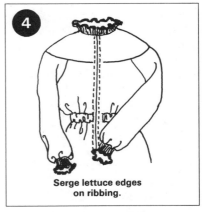

Serge lettuce edges on ribbing.

• For the look of braid, use a basic serger seam stitch to create a mock flatlock seam or lapped decorative seam using pearl cotton or crochet thread.

• There are many options, so use your fashion sense and serger knowledge to find the best combination of thread, serger stitch and fashion effect.

SERGER THREAD TIPS

• Choose thread with care requirements compatible with the fabric's. If the garment will be laundered, select a sturdy thread that will withstand repeated machine washing. If the garment will be dry cleaned, the thread must be dry-cleanable.

• Cone thread manufacturers label threads with a set of numbers such as 100/2, 50/2 and 40/3. The first number is the thread size — the higher the number, the finer the thread. The second number is the number of plies or strands twisted together to make the thread.

• Since serger thread guides and looper eyes are larger than the eye of a standard sewing machine needle, thicker threads can be used on a serger than on a conventional machine.

• Decorative serger threads must pass through the thread guides and the eye of the upper or lower looper, or in some cases, the eye of both loopers. Heavy threads with fine, tightly-twisted strands usually pose no problem, but thick, heavy threads and untwisted yarns with slubs usually will not feed evenly.

• Some thin or lightweight serger threads can be used in both the needle(s) and the looper(s) for a stitch rendered totally in decorative thread.

• To aid in threading texturized nylon thread, use a wire needle threader or tie a leader of regular thread to a strand of the nylon thread.

• Usually you have to loosen the tension on texturized nylon thread so it can fluff up after it's serged.

• If a decorative thread will show on the right side of a garment only, use the decorative thread in the upper looper only. If the thread will be seen from both sides of a garment, use the decorative thread in both loopers.

• Follow this basic formula to solve the mystery of how much thread is required: Measure the length of garment seams and edges that will be serged; measure in inches. Divide by 36 to determine the yardage.

To determine the total amount of thread needed, multiply by 6 yards of thread for every one yard of decorative stitching in the garment, or multiply by 7 if using very thin thread. Add at

least 10 extra yards of thread for testing the stitch before you serge.

• Test-serge on fabric scraps, using the same number of fabric layers you will serge when sewing the garment. Include any interfacing layers in the test.

• Set the serger stitch length to .4 mm. If stitches back up on the presser foot and won't allow the fabric to feed through, the stitch length is too short for the thickness of the thread. Lengthen the stitch until a satisfactory stitch forms.

• For heavy threads, remember this basic tension rule – the thicker the thread, the looser the tension should be. Gradually loosen the tension controlling the decorative thread until a satisfactory stitch forms.

If you've loosened the thread tension completely and still haven't formed a proper stitch, check your machine to find the thread guide that squeezes the thread; remove the thread from this guide. Or, remove the decorative thread from the tension dial.

• You may need to increase the tension on lightweight thread such as thin, slippery rayon.

• If a thread is not wound for serger use, unwind the thread carefully and evenly by hand onto an empty serger thread spool.

If the thread still does not feed properly, have an assistant unwind the thread as you serge or put the thread in a jar, stop serging frequently and unwind the thread yourself. However, do not unwind

too much thread in advance; the thread will tangle as a result.

Paper bobbins intended for use with weaving shuttles are another option. The shortest bobbins measure 4″ and easily fit a serger.

• Check your favorite fabric store for decorative serging threads. Also, check mail-order sources, often a treasure chest of hard-to-find specialty threads.

SEWING MACHINE

Selecting a sewing machine is an important decision, and everyone wants to know which is the best one to buy. The answer is there is no universal "best," but here's how to find the machine that will make you happy.

BASIC QUESTIONS

Take into account your sewing skills, needs and dreams when shopping for a new sewing machine. The answers to fundamental questions such as these will help you make a wise decision:

- What do you expect from a sewing machine?
- Do you need utilitarian and/or decorative stitches?
- Do you want a machine you can update with new stitch programs or attachments?
- Do you sew a little or a lot?
- What fabrics will you be sewing?
- Do you own or plan to buy a serger?
- How much can you spend?
- What dealerships and repair services are available in your area? Are they also available elsewhere if you move?

Common sense tells you never buy the first machine you see. Shop around. Make a list of at least three machine brands and dealerships, and visit all before choosing. If someone pressures you or says a certain deal is available that day only, forget that machine. The store is trying too hard to sell it.

HANDS-ON TIPS

- Watch a salesperson's demonstration, but don't stop there. It's very important to use the machine yourself.
- Take a selection of fabrics with you to every store and try the same swatches on each machine. Don't use the stiff demonstration cloth that makes every stitch look good.
- Let the salesperson guide you on details such as stitch selection and thread choice, but insist on doing the sewing yourself.
- The fabric swatches you bring along should represent a variety of weights and textures.

- Test a medium weight woven cotton to feel how evenly and smoothly it feeds through the machine. Let the feed dogs move the fabric (hands off for this); stitch forward, then in reverse for a few inches.

A quality machine should sew straight without veering to one side or the other. However, you should know sewing in reverse rarely if ever works as well as sewing forward.

- To see how a machine handles bulk and multiple thicknesses, sew a seam on a thick or dense fabric. All machines have a limit to the amount of fabric they can accept, and you need to know that limit. Determine which of the machines you are considering balks at bulk first.
- It can be revealing to see how well a machine sews on fine fabrics. Test a knit such as tricot to see if the machine skips stitches or if the fabric slides. Try a thin fabric to see if the feed dogs hold it firmly as you sew.
- Bring a fabric that always seems to give you problems. You may find a machine that gives you the solution.
- See if the machine fits you. Dials should be easy to read, the foot pedal or knee lever should feel comfortable to use, the light should shine on the working area, and it should be easy for you to control the machine at different speeds.
- If the machine is portable, lift it to see if you really can carry it.
- Wind a bobbin to see if this routine sewing task is easy or cumbersome. Check if the

bobbin winds evenly with no loose spots.

- Don't wind the bobbin through the eye of the needle no matter what the salesperson tells you. The slubs on threads create inconsistencies in bobbin winding that can cause tension problems.

DETAILS WORTH NOTING

- Be wary of salespeople who tell you metal machines are better than plastic machines. It's not necessarily true. Both metals and plastics vary in quality.
- Whether a machine has a rotary or oscillating stitch formation system should not be a key factor in your decision. Each system has pluses and minuses.
- Computerized machines offer the advantage of a variety of stitches. But whether you select stitches by computer or mechanical means, don't become so mesmerized by the

CLEAN MACHINES

An empty dishwashing detergent bottle, thoroughly cleaned and dried, makes an excellent source of forced air to clean dust and lint from my sewing machine. By squeezing the empty bottle, I get a short burst of air for cleaning – much cheaper than buying canned air and with no propellants to harm the atmosphere.

C. Fenstemacher,
Nipomo, CA

gadgetry you forget what's most important is the quality of the stitch.

• Beware of oversimplified features. For example, it seems like an advantage when a machine makes all buttonholes with the same stitch length, but you should be able to override the computerization manually to adjust the machine for different fabrics.

• Don't be misled by "universal" or "automatic" tension. All machines must have some type of device for you to adjust the thread tension. However, better machines use heavier metal for tension springs and discs so the thread tension remains more consistent. Also, some models locate the tension adjustment in a more convenient place than others or have a system that's easier to understand.

OPTIONS TO CONSIDER

• Make sure decorative and utility stitches are useful to you before you pay extra for them. Many stitch options are nice to have primarily if you sew children's clothing, craft items or a wide variety of fabrics.

• Reverse-cycle stretch stitches are generally useful for reinforcing stress points in garment areas such as crotch and armhole seams. You can also use them for sewing durable but flexible seams on knits.

• If you don't own a serger, look for a serpentine or multiple zigzag stitch. It looks like a broken zigzag stitch and can be used to overcast raw edges.

• A free arm makes hemming pants, attaching cuffs and other types of tubular sewing less awkward. However, make sure your sewing machine cabinet can accommodate a free-arm model; otherwise plan to purchase a new cabinet. If you're used to sewing on a standard flat-bed model, you may find it uncomfortable to sew in the limited free-arm space.

• Look for a machine with a standard high, low or slant shank that will accept interchangeable attachments. As new items come on the market, you can add them to update the machine.

• An often-overlooked feature is flexible needle position. Because you can move the needle to the right or the left as needed, you can keep more of the fabric in contact with the feed dog when sewing narrow seams or when edgestitching. Also, a flexible needle position feature is often necessary to adjust attachments such as a rolled hem presser foot.

• Check if there's a way to lower the feed dogs or otherwise inactivate them for darning, embroidery, outline quilting or other forms of creative sewing that require you to move the fabric freehand.

CHECK THE EXTRAS

• Ask for the owner's manual, and see if you can understand it. You might check the section on making buttonholes, for this is something you will do often as you sew.

• Instructional lessons must be hands-on for you to really learn. Ask if you make samples during the dealer's lessons or if you just sit and watch an instructor.

• If possible, meet the instructor. Determine if the instructor seems knowledgeable and makes you feel comfortable.

• Ask if parts and attachments are in stock or must be special-ordered, and if they continue to be available after new machine models are introduced.

• Ask to see the warranty, and note any exclusions. In general, parts are warrantied but labor expense can be three times the cost of parts. Many labor guarantees are backed only by the store, not the manufacturer.

NEEDLE ORGANIZER
To separate my sewing machine needles into sizes, I color code them with nail polish by putting a blue dot of color below the shank for size 11, a red dot for size 14, etc. When the needle is in the machine, I can spot its size at a glance.

R. Paese,
Orlando, FL

BOBBIN BEATERS
To keep unruly bobbins from cluttering my sewing basket, I corral them in a travel toothbrush holder. The see-through plastic container keeps them neat, and I can see which color I need at a glance.

J. King,
Sun City Center, FL

SEWING MACHINE ACCESSORIES

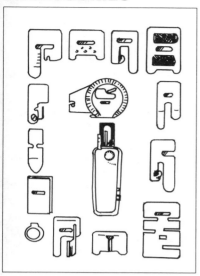

There are more than 40 sewing machine accessories available, some of which you probably already own. Your first impression of these extras might be to wonder which ones are indispensable sewing aids and which ones are cute but somewhat impractical gadgets.

The accessories guide that follows shows you the variety of special presser feet and other attachments which are available and describes the purpose each serves. Use the guide to identify the accessories you have but have not yet used and to discover possible purchases which will improve your workmanship or save you time.

GENERAL TIPS

• Most presser feet can be used interchangeably among brand name sewing machines. The secret is to know which kind of shank your machine has — the shank is where the foot attaches — and which other brands have the same shank style.

• Most sewing machines fit into either the low (Figure 1), high (Figure 2), super high (Figure 3) or slant (Figure 4) shank categories. Check your

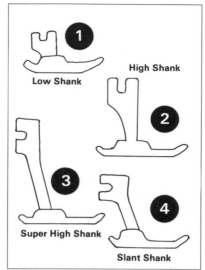

Low Shank

High Shank

Super High Shank

Slant Shank

machine manual or consult your local machine dealer if in doubt about your model.

• Some low shank models require an adaptor to allow you to use other brands' presser feet.

• If you have a very old machine with an unusual shank, custom feet can be ordered by mail or through a local dealer.

• Some newer machines have feet that snap onto an ankle (Figure 5). For best results,

Ankle snaps on here.

purchase the corresponding ankle when you buy a snap-on foot.

• In general, a presser foot that's hinged will ride over uneven fabric layers and bulky

seams easily. However, on some sewing machines a stationary foot without a hinge will bring the fabric into better contact with the feed dogs for smoother sewing.

• When you have a choice between a plastic or metal presser foot, consider that generally a transparent plastic presser foot makes it easier to see the work.

ACCESSORIES GUIDE

Alphabet stitcher (Figure 6) moves fabric to create zigzag-stitched letters in capital script. Change the cams to change the letter stitched.

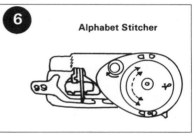

Alphabet Stitcher

Binder foot (Figure 7) has a shaped front lip which scrolls bias binding or an unfolded bias strip as you sew and wraps it around the garment edge. This foot can also be used to apply piping to an edge and to apply decorative binding as a band trim to the fabric surface.

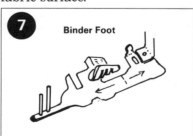

Binder Foot

Braiding or cording foot (Figure 8) has a small slot in front to hold narrow braids and cords in position as you sew. Use this foot with a straight, zigzag or decorative stitch.

Button foot (Figure 9) has short, open toes which hold sew-through buttons so you can attach them with a zigzag stitch. Most button feet have a groove to hold a pin or needle so you can also make a thread shank as you sew. Use this foot not only for sewing on buttons, but also for sewing on snaps, hooks and eyes.

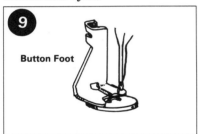

Buttonhole attachment (Figure 10) allows you to make zigzag- stitched buttonholes on a straight stitch machine and keyhole buttonholes and eyelets on any machine. You insert a template to control the buttonhole length and style.

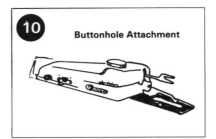

Buttonhole foot (Figure 11) for low shank machine has one long toe marked in ⅛″ increments to help you measure the buttonhole length as you sew. It also has grooves on the underside and a small knob in the back to hold cording for corded buttonholes.

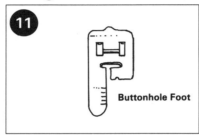

Buttonhole foot with slide (Figure 12) determines buttonhole length based on the diameter of the button inserted into the slide.

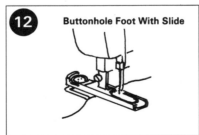

Cording foot (Figure 13) with multiple small holes in front allows fine cords to pass side-by-side under the foot for decorative effects.

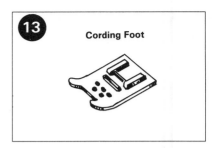

Darning or free-form embroidery foot (Figure 14) moves up and down with the sewing machine needle so you don't need to stretch the fabric in an embroidery hoop for free motion stitching.

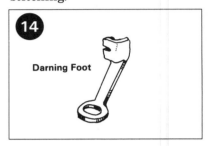

Edgestitcher (Figure 15) has slotted grooves in front to position fabrics and edgings so they barely overlap. In addition to simple edgestitching, this foot can be used for joining laces, insertions and ribbons. It can also be used when sewing tucks ¹⁄₁₆″ to ¼″ deep or as a stitching gauge for narrow French seams.

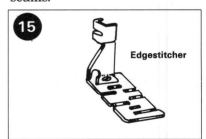

Embroidery or satin stitch foot (Figure 16) has a fan-shaped or rectangular groove on the underside to allow smooth feeding of raised satin, appliqué and embroidery stitches.

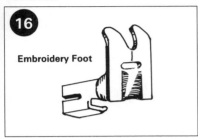

Embroidery Foot

An open toe embroidery foot is similar, but is shorter than the standard embroidery foot. A Teflon® foot is an embroidery foot with a non-stick coating on the underside which glides over sticky fabrics such as vinyl and leather for smoother sewing.

Even feed foot (Figure 17), also called walking foot, dual feeder or plaid-matcher, helps top layer of fabric feed at same rate as bottom layer of fabric. This device makes it easier to sew on fabrics that stick, stretch, creep or slip, and it helps retain the plaid or stripe match you planned during pattern layout.

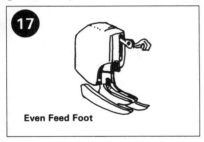

Even Feed Foot

Felling foot (Figure 18) has widely-spaced toes which guide the fabric layers when stitching standing fell and flat-felled seams. Use it also to make narrow, machine-stitched hems.

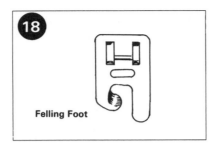

Felling Foot

Fringe or tailor tacking foot (Figure 19) has a raised central bar over which the needle zigzags to form a loopy stitch. Use this foot to make fringe, thread casings and tailor tacks.

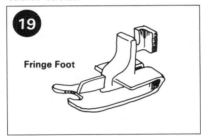

Fringe Foot

Gathering or shirring foot (Figure 20) gathers the fabric evenly for large-scale work on lightweight fabrics. Use it to make ruffle trims or multiple rows of shirring on a garment. The gathers formed are not adjustable, but rather stitched into place. To control the fullness of the gathers, you must adjust the stitch length and tension. Some gathering feet have slots which allow you to gather a fabric strip and join it to a garment section at the same time.

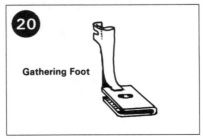

Gathering Foot

Gauge foot (Figure 21) has a small ruler which can be adjusted to the right or left side for precise topstitching and edgestitching up to 1″ from a seam or edge.

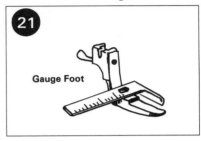

Gauge Foot

Hemming foot with adjustable gauge (Figure 22) automatically controls the position of topstitching from $\frac{3}{16}$″ to several inches away from hems and other edges.

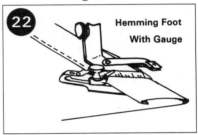

Hemming Foot With Gauge

Hemming foot for blindstitching (Figure 23) has a fabric finger which fits into the fold of fabric prepared for blind hemming; the guide lifts the fold slightly away from the underneath fabric layer to build a slight slack into the stitches for the look of a hand-sewn hem.

Hemming Foot For Blindstitching

Hemming foot for rolled hems (Figure 24) automatically scrolls the fabric to turn under the raw edge twice. Rolled hem feet vary in size from ¹⁄₁₆″ to ⅞″; purchase the foot according to the hem depth desired. Some rolled hem feet can scroll and stitch the hem as you sew on lace edging.

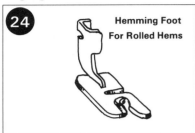

Lingerie or knit foot (Figure 25) has an automatic lever which has a serrated underside to grip fabric firmly when the needle enters the fabric, then release the fabric on the needle's up stroke. This foot, which reduces skipped stitches and puckered seams, is particularly useful on lightweight fabrics such as sheers and tricot knits.

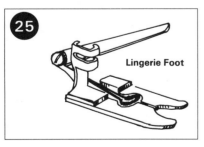

No-snag or special zigzag foot (Figure 26) has curled up toes for catch-free sewing on loopy surfaces, sweater knits, loosely-woven fabrics, and other highly-textured surfaces.

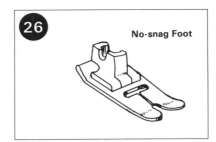

Overedge or overcasting foot (Figure 27) has a central metal bar or wire to hold fabric flat as the needle zigzag stitches over it. Use it to prevent puckers and curling on fabrics that roll such as tricot and lightweight knits.

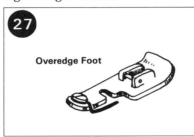

Pintuck foot (Figure 28) for use with a twin needle has multiple grooves on the underside to sew uniform, evenly-spaced pintucks sized from 1 mm to 4 mm deep.

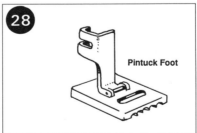

Quilting foot (Figure 29) has a single toe or two very short toes and an adjustable rod to use as a stitching guide. Use this foot to stitch parallel to a seam or edge or to stitch parallel rows accurately when quilting, topstitching or embroidering with decorative stitches.

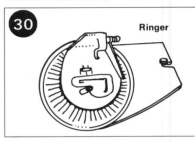

Ringer (Figure 30) pivots fabric so you can stitch decorative motifs in a circle.

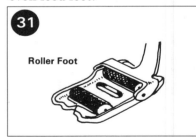

Roller foot (Figure 31) has two rollers to improve the feeding of fabrics that stick, stretch, creep or slip. It's a less expensive alternative to the even feed foot.

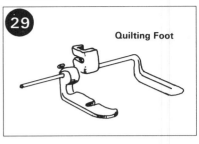

Ruffler or pleater attachment (Figure 32) stitches the fabric into tiny pleats. Adjust the fabric fullness by changing the stitch length and a lever on the attachment. Like the gathering foot, this device saves time when ruffling long strips of lightweight fabrics and allows you to create a ruffle as you apply it to a garment edge, but the ruffler is capable of making deeper pleats than the gathering foot for fuller gathers.

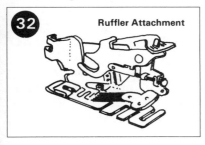
Ruffler Attachment

Straight stitch foot (Figure 33) is narrow, with two toes of different length and width. This foot holds fabric very securely to help eliminate skipped stitches and puckered seams.

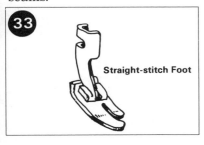
Straight-stitch Foot

Sun-stitch foot or circular stitcher (Figure 34) has an adjustable bar which pivots the fabric and helps you sew circular stitch patterns with a radius of ½″ to 2½″.

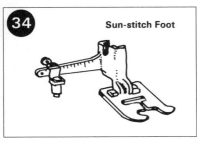
Sun-stitch Foot

Topstitching foot or top-stitching edge guide (Figure 35) is similar to the hemmer foot for blindstitching. It has a plastic lip which guides fabric

under the foot and can be used for topstitching, edgestitching and blindstitching.

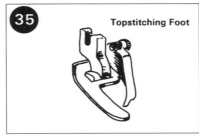
Topstitching Foot

Tucker (Figure 36) has an adjustable gauge in front to help you stitch tucks up to 1″ wide.

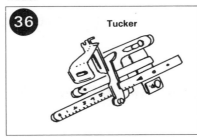
Tucker

Welting or piping foot (Figure 37) has a single channel on the underside to guide corded piping, welting or pre-gathered lace edging.

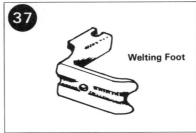
Welting Foot

Zigzagger attachment (Figure 38) makes it possible for straight stitch machines to form zigzag stitches. Templates for this attachment allow a straight stitch machine to produce a limited selection of embroidery stitches.

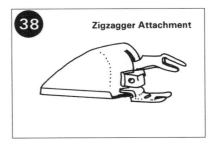
Zigzagger Attachment

Zipper foot (Figure 39) with adjustable slide allows you to change the foot's position in relation to the needle as needed to stitch next to a raised edge such as when covering cording, inserting welting or piping in a seam and applying a zipper.

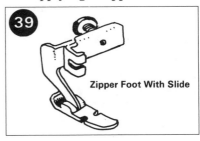
Zipper Foot With Slide

Zipper foot (Figure 40) for applying invisible zippers has two grooves on the underside which fit the zipper track. Some invisible zipper brands will only fit their own brand of zipper foot.

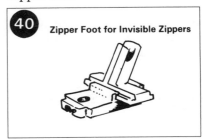
Zipper Foot for Invisible Zippers

Zipper foot (Figure 41) with single sole has a small indentation on each side for the needle. You can adjust the position of the sole to the right or the left of the needle when applying a zipper or sewing corded trims.

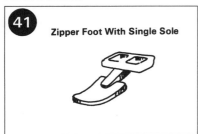

Zipper Foot With Single Sole

Zipper foot (Figure 42) with a ski-shaped sole has a small indentation at each end with an ankle hinge in the center. To position the needle on the right or left side of the zipper foot, you must turn the foot around.

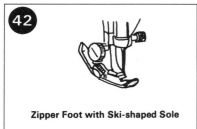

Zipper Foot with Ski-shaped Sole

✂ SEWING MACHINE NEEDLES

Are you confused by the many needle types and sizes available today? Does this leave you guessing which needle to use for a project, or do you ignore the problem by using the same kind of needle for everything you sew? If you answered "yes" to any of these questions, acquire some needle knowledge and watch your sewing improve.

Today it pays to know your needles. About 30 years ago, all sewing machines for the home were standardized to use a common needle length, the 15 x 1 or 130/705 system. Prior to this time, needles differed considerably in length and shape, and you had to use a specific brand and style for a machine.

In theory at least, today all sewing machine needles are designed to fit all machines with the exception of some sergers, older sewing machines and industrial models. However, there are some subtle differences among needles in terms of length and design. This is especially important to know when you have stitching problems. The solution might be as simple as switching to another brand of needles.

NEEDLE ANATOMY

Look at the parts of a needle (Figure 1). The various components — shank, shaft, groove, eye, scarf and point — are designed with a purpose.

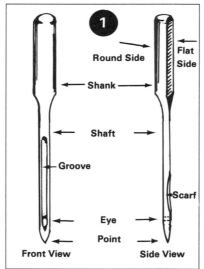

From the side view, you can see the scarf, an indentation about ¼″ long directly behind the needle's eye. The scarf is where the upper and lower threads link to complete a stitch. Needles with a well-designed scarf virtually eliminate skipped stitches because the needle thread makes a loop large enough to be caught everytime by the shuttle hook carrying the bobbin thread.

The shank is the portion of the needle inserted into the sewing machine. Most needles have a rounded shank in front and a flattened shank in back so you won't make the mistake of inserting the needle backwards.

NEEDLE SIZE

The size of a needle depends upon the diameter of the shaft; you'll find the needle size engraved on the shank. There are two size labeling systems. In both systems, the lower the number, the finer the needle.

The American system arbitrarily numbers needles from a very small 8 to a very large 18. The European system numbers needles from 60 to 110 according to the shaft diameter in fractions of a millimeter; for example, a size 60 needle is .6 mm. To cover all bases, most needles are labeled according to both systems, such as 90/14.

The size of the needle is critical to machine sewing because the needle shaft must make a hole in the fabric large enough for the thread to pass and form a stitch. For this reason, the best general guide for choosing needle size is fabric weight. Usually lighter weight fabrics require a lower number needle, and heavier fabrics require a higher number needle.

NEEDLE TYPES

Needle type is determined primarily by the point and secondarily by the size and shape of the eye, shaft and scarf. Six types of needles (Figure 2) cover most sewing situations:

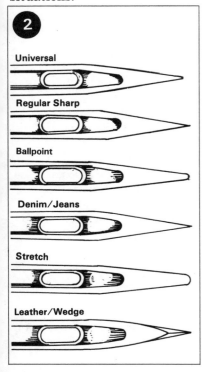

- A universal point needle is considered an all-purpose machine needle, and you can use it to sew a wide variety of knitted and woven fabrics. The needle point is very slightly rounded. Since this is the needle type you'll find most useful, stock several sizes so you'll always have a fresh needle on hand.
- A regular sharp point needle is considered the standard machine needle and sews medium weight woven fabrics. Because this needle penetrates the fabric yarns, it's important the point is free of nicks or burrs to prevent fabric

damage. Do not use a regular sharp needle on knits.

- A ballpoint needle has a rounded point which several machine manufacturers recommend for sewing on knits. On some brands, the label "SES" indicates a fine ballpoint needle for sewing delicate knits, and the label "SUK" indicates a medium ballpoint for heavier knitted fabrics.

A ballpoint needle slips between the fabric yarns rather than piercing them, eliminating fabric damage and skipped stitches. Some ball point needle brands shave the flat side of the shank to position the needle point closer to the shuttle hook, a feature that eliminates skipped stitches on some older machines.

- A denim/jeans needle has an acute point, slender eye and stronger shaft for sewing tightly-woven fabrics such as denim, twill and canvas. Use this type of needle when a fabric is so dense it deflects a regular sharp needle and causes crooked stitches.
- A stretch needle has a more rounded point than a ballpoint needle for smoother sewing on highly elastic fabrics such as power net and spandex knits. Compared to the universal point needle, the stretch needle has a smaller eye, a shaved shank for easier stitch formation and a small hump above the eye on the flat side of the shank.
- A leather/wedge needle has a unique three-sided point which cuts cleanly through tough fabrics such as medium to heavyweight leathers and vinyls. Do not use it on

synthetic suedes, however, as they are damaged by the large holes left behind.

SPECIAL NEEDLES

In addition to the familiar needle types above, the following specialty machine needles (Figure 3) are engineered for unique sewing purposes:

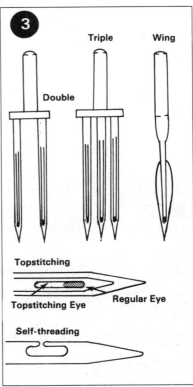

- Double and triple needles with a single shank make parallel rows of stitches for topstitching and other decorative effects. With a special presser foot, you can use these needles for pintucks.

Multiple needles come in different sizes and different needle spacings, so select them according to the exact effect you wish to achieve. Above all, use these needles only on a zigzag machine which has a large throat plate opening.

Although you set up the machine for straight stitching, a zigzag-style stitch forms on the wrong side of the fabric as the multiple needles share a single bobbin thread.

• A wing needle purposely creates large holes in a crisp, woven fabric for creative hem-stitching and French hand-sewing by machine. Also available for more elaborate effects are a double wing needle and a combination needle with one wing needle and one regular needle.

• A topstitching needle accommodates a heavy thread because it has an eye that's large in relation to the needle size; in comparison, a standard eye size abrades heavy threads. Avoid using a topstitching needle with regular sewing thread because the thread floats within the large eye and stitches form poorly.

• A self-threading needle has a slotted eye. The advantage is easy threading, but the disadvantage is the needle shaft is more fragile.

• Proper stitching results when fabric, needle and thread relate to one another. For example, use a fine thread and small size needle for thin, lightweight fabric.

• For best results, use the smallest size needle that works well.

• Some needle packages have a small, built-in magnifier to make it easier for you to read the size engraved on the needle shank.

• Change to a new needle after sewing every two garments, after hitting a pin or whenever you notice a stitching problem.

• Synthetic fibers tend to dull needles more quickly than purely natural fibers.

• A bent needle or needle burr can not only damage the fabric you are sewing, but also the machine. The price of a new needle is a fraction of the total cost of a garment or a machine repair, so don't delay replacing a faulty needle.

• To check a needle's condition or suitability, sew some sample stitches on a fabric scrap before starting to sew a garment.

• If your sewing machine is more than 30 years old, you may have to try several different needle brands to find those that work for your machine.

• Double and triple needles form stitches which are more elastic than regular straight stitches. This quality makes multiple-needle topstitching a practical as well as attractive hem treatment for knit garments.

• When using a multiple needle, adjust the needle position carefully so the needle won't strike the throat plate.

• If you change needle types, store the used needle in the original package so it is correctly identified for future use.

NEEDLE SELECTION GUIDE

FABRIC TYPE	NEEDLE TYPE	NEEDLE SIZE
WOVENS:		
VERY LIGHTWEIGHT (LACE, VOILE, CHIFFON)	SHARP	60/8
LIGHTWEIGHT (CREPE DE CHINE, GEORGETTE, TAFFETA, LAWN, ORGANDY, BATISTE, HANDKERCHIEF LINEN)	SHARP OR UNIVERSAL	65/9
LIGHT- TO MEDIUM WEIGHT (GINGHAM, CHALLIS, SATIN, PERCALE, PONGEE, BROADCLOTH)	SHARP OR UNIVERSAL	70/10 OR 80/11
MEDIUM WEIGHT (FLANNEL, LINEN, POPLIN, CHINTZ, PINWALE CORDUROY)	SHARP OR UNIVERSAL	80/11 OR 90/14
HEAVYWEIGHT (DENIM, TWEED, BURLAP, SAILCLOTH, GABARDINE, WIDE WALE CORDUROY)	SHARP OR UNIVERSAL	90/14 OR 100/16
VERY HEAVYWEIGHT (DUCK, WORK DENIM, CANVAS)	DENIM/JEANS	100/16 OR 110/18
KNITS:		
LIGHTWEIGHT (TRICOT)	BALLPOINT OR UNIVERSAL	80/11
MEDIUM WEIGHT (INTERLOCK, JERSEY, SINGLE KNIT)	BALLPOINT OR UNIVERSAL	80/11 OR 90/14
HEAVYWEIGHT (DOUBLE KNIT, FAKE FUR, VELOUR)	BALLPOINT OR UNIVERSAL	90/14
2-WAY STRETCH (SWIMWEAR KNITS, SPANDEX)	STRETCH	90/14
NONWOVENS:		
VINYLS	WEDGE POINT	100/16
MEDIUM WEIGHT (LEATHER, SUEDE)	WEDGE POINT	90/14
HEAVYWEIGHT (LEATHER, SUEDE)	WEDGE POINT	100/16

SEWING MACHINE REPAIRS

If you're ready to sew but the sewing machine refuses to cooperate, don't panic and don't give up — you can probably fix the machine yourself. About 70 percent of sewing machine repairs are minor adjustments even a novice can make. When something's wrong, chances are you don't need a professional repair person.

Most machine mishaps fit into one of three categories: noise, stitch or power problems. Use the tips below to become an ace trouble shooter.

NOISE PROBLEMS

• A squeak usually signals lack of oil. To lubricate a sewing machine, use special sewing machine oil, not an all-purpose, household oil.

Because of the constant motion and high speed, the bobbin area on some machines requires more frequent lubrication than other parts. Check the machine manual for specific oiling points on your model.

Most sewing machines should be oiled with the take up lever at its highest position (Figure 1). The take up lever is the arm that moves the needle thread up and down as you sew; when you oil the machine with the lever in its highest position, you are aligning the parts needing oil with the designated oiling ports.

• Taps or thuds as you sew indicate some sort of

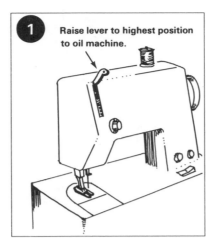

Raise lever to highest position to oil machine.

obstruction — thread, lint or a foreign object — probably in one of the machine's moving parts. The obvious solution is to dislodge and remove the obstruction.

Remove the throat plate and any brackets for easy access, and use a blast of canned air, a brush or a pipe cleaner to get rid of the debris. Don't compound the problem by jabbing around with potentially damaging seam rippers or scissors.

Thread might be trapped around the spool holder or in the tension control; it might be wrapped around the hand-wheel (Figure 2). Thread can

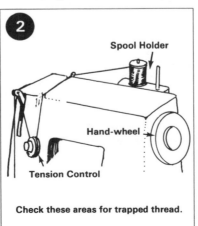

Spool Holder

Hand-wheel

Tension Control

Check these areas for trapped thread.

also become jammed in the bobbin area, causing threads to wrap around each other.

Lint usually builds up slowly, but it can eventually form felt. Look under the throat plate, around the feed dogs and in the bobbin area (Figure 3). Foreign objects such

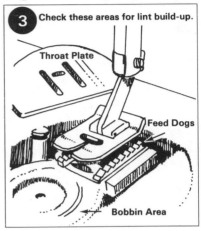

Check these areas for lint build-up.

Throat Plate

Feed Dogs

Bobbin Area

as pins or the points of broken needles can lodge in the same areas.

• A grinding or odd noise might indicate a broken or cracked part. In this situation, take the machine to a repair shop. Ask to have the defective parts returned to you to assure you they have been replaced. In some localities, this is the law.

STITCH TENSION PROBLEMS

The newest and best machines seldom require tension adjustments, as suggested by product descriptions such as self-adjusting, universal or automatic tension. But dated models might require a different tension setting for every fabric and stitch, and even on new machines, special sewing techniques or unique fabrics may require a tension setting other than a standard one.

A perfect stitch with balanced tensions on the needle and bobbin threads looks just about the same on both sides. The two threads lock in the center of the fabric layers (Figure 4). If your

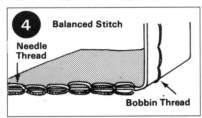

machine isn't making a stitch like this, you need tension relief. Even if you have not yet encountered tension-related stitching problems, understanding how thread tension works will help you use a machine to its fullest potential.

• Familiarize yourself with the tension dial on the machine to learn how to change the setting. Most tension assemblies include two concave discs and a tension screw or dial (Figure 5). When

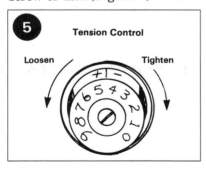

the tension screw is tightened, the discs move closer together creating a greater pull on the thread.

The tension dial may be marked with numbers, be unmarked or have "+" and "-" indicators. For numbered tension dials, turn toward the lower numbers to loosen and the higher numbers to tighten the needle thread tension; for those without numbers, turn left to loosen and right to tighten; and for those with "+" or "-" indicators, turn toward "-" to loosen and toward "+" to tighten.

• If the needle thread tension is too tight, the needle thread will lie on top of the fabric (Figure 6). You might be

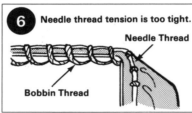

able to see the bobbin thread between each stitch, or the bobbin thread might loop on top of the fabric. Remedy by loosening the needle thread tension.

• If the needle thread tension is too loose, the bobbin thread lies in a straight line and the needle thread might loop on the underside of the fabric (Figure 7). Remedy by

tightening the needle thread tension.

• Always attempt to balance stitches by adjusting the needle thread tension first. If this fails to produce a balanced stitch, the bobbin thread tension might require adjustment. Some experts say to go to a professional repair person for this, but others say you can do it yourself if your machine model has a removable bobbin case.

If you choose to do it yourself, remove the bobbin case from the machine. The bobbin tension is regulated by adjusting a screw at the rear of a flat spring on the underside of the case (Figure 8). Turn the

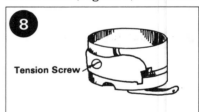

screw clockwise to tighten the bobbin thread tension, and counterclockwise to loosen it.

Because this screw is very small, a ¼ or ½ turn corrects most problems.

Some bobbin cases have a small hole at the end of a metal finger (Figure 9). You

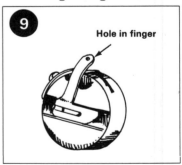

can increase the tension on the bobbin thread simply by threading it into this eye. It's an easy way to adjust the bobbin tension and lets you return to the original tension very easily if desired.

• Generally, the same tension adjustment that produces a balanced stitch on one fabric works for another fabric. However, you may have to adjust the tensions when sewing on very thin or very thick fabrics and very soft or very hard-surfaced fabrics. Other times tension adjustments may be necessary are when sewing with one thread weight in the needle and a different weight in the bobbin, or when sewing an unusually small or large stitch width or length.

• If you can't tell whether or not the stitch tension is balanced, stitch a sample seam on fabric scraps. Hold each end of the stitched seamline between the thumb and forefinger; pull sharply. The threads should break evenly. If they don't, the thread which breaks first is the tighter of the two. If neither thread breaks, both needle and bobbin thread tensions might be too loose.

• Satin stitching, used for appliqué and machine embroidery, is defined as zigzag stitching with a very short stitch length. To give satin stitches a smoother look from the right side, loosen the upper tension so the threads lock on the wrong side (Figure 10).

• For better buttonholes, which are simply two parallel rows of satin stitching, also loosen the upper tension.

• When topstitching with a

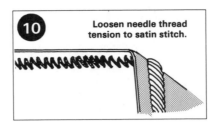

Loosen needle thread tension to satin stitch.

heavy thread such as buttonhole twist, the friction among thread, needle and fabric often results in loopy stitches or even thread jamming. Slightly tighten the upper tension to pull the heavy needle thread back up through the fabric. The stitch will then lock correctly between the layers of fabric and look balanced (Figure 11).

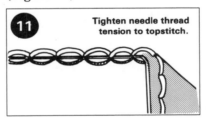

Tighten needle thread tension to topstitch.

• Other times it helps to sew with a tightened needle thread tension: when making a decorative shell hem with blindstitching, when gathering with elastic thread in the bobbin and when using a gathering foot to ruffle fabric.

• Make tension work for you when basting with a long machine stitch. Loosen the needle thread tension so the stitches loop on the wrong side and the bobbin thread lies in a straight line (Figure 12). The

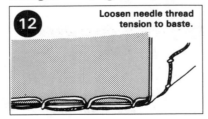

Loosen needle thread tension to baste.

loosely-locked stitches will be a cinch to remove later by pulling the bobbin thread.

• Other times it helps to sew with a loosened needle thread tension: when making gathering stitches since looser tension makes the stitches easier to pull up, when sewing with a twin needle if you want to avoid drawing up the fabric into a ridge and when making tailor tacks.

• If the tension seems too loose no matter what you do, check the threading path. Make sure the thread is passing through all guides and the tension discs correctly.

STITCH PUCKER PROBLEMS

While tension adjustments are the first thing you should suspect when a machine stitches irregularly, when the problem is puckered seams sometimes the solution is much simpler.

• Puckered seams usually point to the needle, the thread or a combination of the two. Begin the search for a solution by inserting a new needle.

Next, suspect the thread. Poor quality thread will feed inconsistently through the needle; change to a better quality thread.

• If the thread is too elastic or wound too quickly onto the bobbin, it stretches while under tension; after the stitch is formed it relaxes and puckers the fabric. If using a relatively stretchy polyester thread, switch to a polyester/cotton thread or rewind the bobbin more slowly and evenly.

• If the thread is too large for the needle, it will not feed evenly; change to a finer thread or a larger needle.

• A defective bobbin can cause puckered stitches. Discard any bobbins with cracks, rough spots or rust stains. Also, use the right bobbin size and shape for your machine – even a tiny $1/16''$ variance causes stitching problems.

OTHER STITCH PROBLEMS

• Skipped stitches occur when the machine doesn't form a complete stitch with each up-and-down motion of the needle. The most likely culprit is a worn needle.

Insert a new needle and make sure it's inserted correctly – the flat side of the needle shaft goes toward the back of the machine. Also make sure the needle is pushed all the way up into the slot (Figure 13).

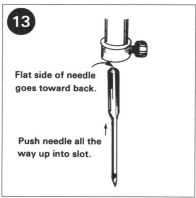

Flat side of needle goes toward back.

Push needle all the way up into slot.

• If stitches skip when sewing on knits or synthetic suede, replace the needle you are currently using with one of the types recommended for knits – universal point, ball-point or stretch needle. If you encounter skipped stitches with one of these, try one of the other two.

• If skipped stitches occur when sewing on tightly-woven fabrics such as waterproof nylon, canvas or denim, insert a regular sharp point or a strong denim/jeans needle to penetrate the fabric and form a good stitch.

• Jagged stitches suggest there's not enough pressure on the presser foot. Most machines have a dial or screw mechanism for adjusting presser foot pressure, so consult the machine manual for its location.

• Irregular stitches or a machine that causes the fabric to catch and snag as it sews point to a burr or rough spot on the throat plate. Remove the throat plate (Figure 14),

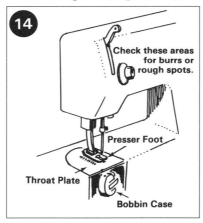

Check these areas for burrs or rough spots.

Presser Foot

Throat Plate

Bobbin Case

the bobbin case and the presser foot to check all their surfaces. Remove rough spots by rubbing them with a piece of crocus cloth, an extra-fine sandpaper available at hardware stores.

POWER PROBLEMS

• It seems obvious, but it's a common mistake: If the machine won't sew, make sure it's getting power. See if it's plugged in, and if the plug is completely inserted into the outlet. If the plug has a switch, make sure it's turned on.

Next check the circuit breaker or fuse box to make sure the electricity's on. Finally, check the plug and cord for frayed, cut or scorched areas, and check the foot pedal or knee lever to see if it's working correctly.

• If the machine is getting power but doesn't move, it may need oil. The oil can evaporate if you haven't used the machine in some time, or if you have been running the machine at top speed for an extended period (for example, satin stitching for hours).

• Another possibility for a no-sew machine that's getting power is the feed dogs may be in the wrong position. Check to see if they are in the upright position, not in a lowered or darning position.

• Some machines have rubber feed dogs which become hard or sticky with age. This deterioration causes short stitches at first, then eventually no motion at all. This is an easy repair for a professional.

• Another solution to a no-go problem is replacing a loose or slick motor belt or pulley. This, too, is a repair for a professional.

• A sewing machine motor seldom "burns out", but there are some parts called carbon brushes that wear out. These can be replaced. If a professional says your machine needs a new motor, it's wise to get a second opinion from someone else before you agree.

PREVENTING PROBLEMS

• Prevention is the best cure for sewing machine problems. Pamper your machine with regular cleaning, oiling, replacement needles and considerate use.

• To prevent needle thread tension problems, floss the tension discs frequently to remove lint or thread particles. To floss, dab a few drops of needle lubricant between the discs and pull several strands of thread back and forth to remove any debris (Figure 15).

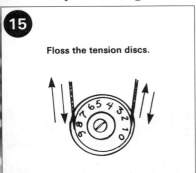

Floss the tension discs.

• Avoid layering different threads on one bobbin. Remove the old thread before winding on the new.

• Always cut off the tail of thread sticking out of a freshly-wound bobbin (Figure 16). If you don't, the thread tail

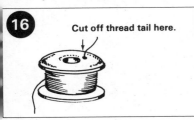

Cut off thread tail here.

can spoil the way the bobbin fits into the bobbin case.

• Avoid using old or discount thread which creates excess lint and stitch tension problems.

• Do not sew over pins.

• Take your machine to a dealer for periodic cleaning, adjusting and servicing. Some experts suggest a yearly checkup, while others suggest five year intervals.

• When you find an honest, fair repair person, tell everyone. Support the person who does quality work within a reasonable time and at decent rates.

• Sewing machines last a long time, but they do not last forever. If you spend more time and patience trouble shooting than sewing, it's time to think about a replacement.

✂ SEWING MACHINE THREADS

Once you've chosen the perfect pattern and fussed over the fabric, don't forget to include a quality thread. This small sewing notion significantly influences your sewing success and affects the finished appearance of the garment you are creating.

Just as there are a wide variety of fabrics to sew today, there are several different threads for sewing them. Learn about the types of thread available and their sewing qualities, then be choosy about the thread you use.

THREAD TYPES

• Cotton-covered polyester thread (Figure 1), an all-purpose thread, combines the best characteristics of two fibers.

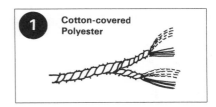

1 Cotton-covered Polyester

The cotton wrap contributes excellent sewability. This means the thread works easily into fabric, is strong enough to hold a seam for the life of a garment and resists linting, kinking and breaking as you sew. The cotton fibers also are smooth and lustrous.

The thread core, made of continuous filaments of polyester, provides strength and abrasion resistance. It also stretches with the fabric for long-lasting seams.

Cotton-covered polyester thread is uniformly strong. It's also mercerized, meaning it's passed through a chemical bath under tension and rinsed to increase its luster and ability to take dyes.

• Polyester thread, another type considered all-purpose, is notable for its strength, abrasion-resistance and its ability to stretch and recover. There are two types of polyester thread available: short-staple (Figure 2) and long-staple (Figure 3).

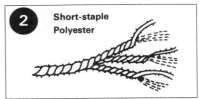

2 Short-staple Polyester

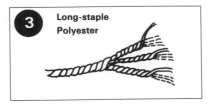

3 Long-staple Polyester

Short-staple polyester thread begins as polyester filaments that have been cut into 1½" lengths; these are then spun into thread. This type of thread appears fuzzy and has a major drawback — it tends to produce lint that could clog a sewing machine.

Long-staple polyester thread begins as longer 4" to 5" polyester filaments which are stretched, then spun into thread. This manufacturing method makes long-staple polyester thread finer, smoother and more uniform than its short-staple cousin.

• Cotton thread (Figure 4) is

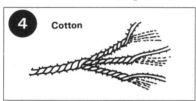

soft and mercerized, making it lustrous and sewable. Cotton thread has little or no capacity to stretch, and is recommended for use on natural fiber woven fabrics only.

Some experts recommend using cotton thread on pure silk fabrics since the soft stitches embed easily into fine fabric textures.

• Silk thread (Figure 5) is

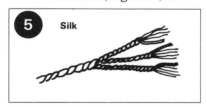

made from the only continuous filament natural fiber. While you pay extra for quality filament silk thread, you gain

a strong, highly-lustrous, elastic thread.

In addition to general sewing, silk thread is excellent for basting. It won't leave an imprint, even if you press over it. It's also good for sewing gathering stitches, as the silk thread slides smoothly through the fabric and makes the gathers easy to draw up.

THREAD TIPS

• The weight of all-purpose thread suits most sewing situations, but for better results choose an extra-fine thread when sewing delicate or thin fabrics such as chiffon or organza. Choose a heavy-weight thread for a decorative

technique such as topstitching so the thread really shows rather than sinks into the fabric texture.

• The fiber content of a thread does not necessarily have to match the fiber content of the fabric. For example, cotton/polyester or long-staple polyester thread can be used on knitted or woven fabrics made from pure natural fibers, pure synthetic fibers or natural/synthetic blends.

However, some experts recommend using cotton or silk thread on natural fiber woven fabrics only, and silk thread is somewhat contro-versial. Some experts say use

THREAD SELECTION GUIDE

THREAD TYPE	THREAD WEIGHT	RECOMMENDED USES
COTTON-COVERED POLYESTER	EXTRA-FINE	ULTRA-SHEER AND VERY LIGHTWEIGHT KNITTED AND WOVEN FABRICS SUCH AS BATISTE, CHIFFON, TRICOT, ORGANZA
	ALL-PURPOSE	LIGHT- TO MEDIUM WEIGHT KNITTED AND WOVEN FABRICS
	HEAVYWEIGHT	HEAVYWEIGHT KNITTED AND WOVEN FABRICS
	TOPSTITCHING TWIST	TOPSTITCHING MEDIUM- TO HEAVYWEIGHT FABRICS KNITTED AND WOVEN FABRICS; SEWING VERY HEAVYWEIGHT FABRICS, LEATHER, CANVAS, VINYL; BUTTONS AND BUTTONHOLES
POLYESTER	ALL-PURPOSE FINE	LIGHTWEIGHT KNITTED AND WOVEN FABRICS
	ALL-PURPOSE MEDIUM	LIGHT- TO HEAVYWEIGHT KNITTED AND WOVEN FABRICS
	TOPSTITCHING	TOPSTITCHING MEDIUM- TO HEAVYWEIGHT KNITTED AND WOVEN FABRICS; SEWING VERY HEAVYWEIGHT FABRICS, LEATHER, CANVAS, VINYL; BUTTONS AND BUTTONHOLES
COTTON	ALL-PURPOSE	LIGHT- TO MEDIUMWEIGHT WOVEN FABRICS
SILK	MACHINE TWIST, #50 REGULAR	ALL WEIGHTS OF KNITTED AND WOVEN FABRICS; BASTING; DECORATIVE STITCHING BY MACHINE
	TOPSTITCHING/ BUTTONHOLE, LINE TWIST, #30 TWIST	TOPSTITCHING, BUTTONHOLES, DECORATIVE STITCHING BY HAND

silk thread only on natural fiber fabrics, while others recommend silk thread as an all-purpose notion which has few limits.

• Silk thread seems to work better on some sewing machines than others. This might stem from the thread's twist, which depending upon the brand, has a definite "s" (clockwise) or "z" (counterclockwise) direction. If you have problems machine sewing with silk thread, try rewinding the thread from the spool onto some bobbins to reverse the twist. Thread both the needle and bobbin with this rewound thread supply.

• The rule of thumb for selecting thread color is to find a shade to match the fabric or go one shade darker.

• Match thread color to the background or the dominant color in a tweed, plaid or print.

• Dye lot numbers are printed on the end of thread spools. If you need more than one spool for a project, check the dye lot numbers to be sure all spools match.

• Thread colors are updated about every 18 to 24 months to reflect the changing fashion palette. At this time, new colors are introduced, and "slow" colors are dropped. Therefore, the best time to find a perfectly-matched thread is at the time you purchase a fabric.

• All-purpose threads are available in the greatest selection of colors — easily 150 or more. This might influence your choice of thread type when a good color match is especially important, such as when quilting, topstitching, edgestitching or appliquéing.

 # SHEARS & SCISSORS

No matter how old you are, if you reach for the sewing shears to snip out a newspaper coupon, a little voice inside says, "Don't use the good scissors."

Perhaps today that command doesn't pack the punch it once did. The chemicals used in manufacturing polyester fabrics can be even harder on your cutting tools than paper.

However, quality shears and scissors can last a long time with some care. And, today more than ever you have access to a selection of cutting instruments to save time and make construction a little easier.

TYPES OF CUTTING TOOLS

• A pair of dressmaking shears (Figure 1) is one of most

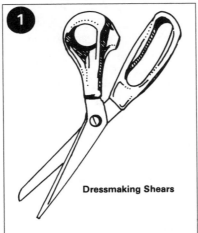

Dressmaking Shears

basic sewing investments. Shears differ from scissors in having blades longer than 6″ and one of the two handles sized large enough for two fingers.

These differences make shears well-designed for cutting fabrics on a table. Bent handles enable the blades to follow the surface of the table and keep the fabric layers flat for greater accuracy when cutting. The fact that one handle holds two fingers gives you greater power to cut.

Dressmaking shears are generally available in 7″ to 9″ blade lengths, so select a size that's comfortable for you to handle. The longer the blades, the faster the cutting and the smoother the strokes on large pieces of fabric.

• Pinking shears (Figure 2)

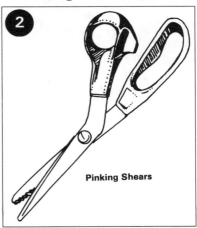

Pinking Shears

cut a zigzagged line for decorative edges or for a raw edge finish on fabrics that don't ravel easily. These shears can also be used for quick and easy notching when trimming the seams on outward curves, such as the edges of collars.

Scalloping shears are similar to pinking shears, except they cut a scalloped line. This adds a pretty touch to the edges of items such as soft, synthetic suede belts.

• Trimming scissors (Figure 3) have 5″ to 6″ blades. They're

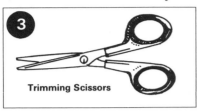

Trimming Scissors

designed for cutting out small areas, trimming seams and for detail work.

• Appliqué scissors (Figure 4) are specially designed for

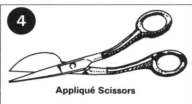

Appliqué Scissors

trimming closely while protecting fabric from damage. The "duckbill" blade enables the scissors to glide between layers of fabric with little danger of the blade points poking through. The curved handles make it easy to trim appliqués and threads when fabric is stretched in an embroidery hoop.

• Embroidery scissors (Figure 5) have narrow blades 3½″

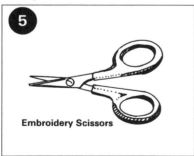

Embroidery Scissors

to 4″ long. They're ideal for fine detail work and needlework. Ornamental embroidery scissors with special decorative

designs and finishes make lovely gifts.

• Thread clips (Figure 6)

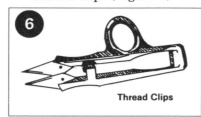

Thread Clips

squeeze together like tweezers to snip threads right next to the fabric, then the handles spring back into the open position. This timesaving tool works whether or not you slip your thumb into the handle; you can quickly grab it, squeeze it, and it will cut.

TIPS FOR BETTER CUTTING

• Invest in quality scissors and shears. These are tools you use every time you sew, so it doesn't pay to scrimp.

• When shopping, ask to remove the scissors or shears from the package so you can test them on scraps of challenging fabrics such as lightweight polyester fabric and heavy denim or wool. A quality tool should cut completely and cleanly through at least four layers of fabric from the back of the blade to the point; this is the same number of layers you often cut while sewing.

• Lightweight stainless steel blades are extremely resistant to corrosion from humidity and the salts and moisture on your hands. They do not need to be sharpened often, but they may need realignment from time to time for better cutting.

• Solid steel frame scissors and shears are made of high carbon steel; a quality pair is

chrome-plated on both inner and outer blade surfaces to prevent corrosion. However, there can be no protective coating on the very edges of the blades since this reduces sharpness. In time, some light surface oxidation will show. This harms neither the blades nor the fabrics you cut.

• To use shears to maximum advantage, take long strokes the length of the blades.

• Keep small scissors or thread snips handy by tying them to a length of ribbon (Figure 7). Wear them like a

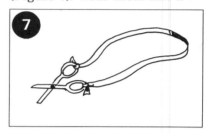

necklace when you sew.

• Shears and scissors should close with a gentle pressure. Check to see if the pivot screw (Figure 8) can be adjusted for

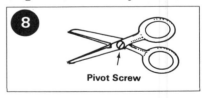

Pivot Screw

personal comfort. Some screws are fixed, but others are easy to adjust with a screw driver.

• Oil adjustable pivot screws periodically.

• After each use, wipe lint from blades with a soft cloth. Lint from polyesters and other synthetic fibers has an abrasive effect on the cutting edges.

• Avoid cutting over pins.

• Don't force a cut. If the fabric offers heavy resistance,

either the cutting tool is too light for the job, or the blades are too dull. Forcing a cut can deform the blades or spread them permanently.

• Protect scissors and shears when not in use by slipping them into a triangular case (Figure 9). Make your own

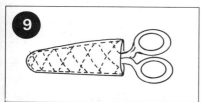

case from quilted remnants.

• Sooner or later all scissors and shears need sharpening. Most experts agree this is a job for a professional, although you can hone the blades yourself on a sharpening stone. Many fabric stores offer sharpening service. Pinking and scalloping shears can be sent to the manufacturer for sharpening.

SHEER BIAS TAPE

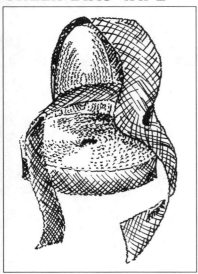

Sheer bias tape is one of those handy notions that's useful day-to-day, but also comes to the rescue when you have a sewing problem to solve. Precut from lightweight nylon tricot in two widths — ⅝″ and 1¼″ — the tape comes in more than a dozen colors. White, black and natural are particularly useful as staple sewing supplies, for probably one of them will blend with whatever fabric you are sewing.

TIPS FOR USE

• Use sheer bias tape to bind raw seam, hem and facing edges without adding bulk. The tape molds easily to the shape of straight or curved edges and does not need to be pressed into shape beforehand like standard bias tape.

• To apply the tape to a raw edge, lay the tape right side up under the presser foot and place the raw fabric edge on top (Figure 1). Pull the tape

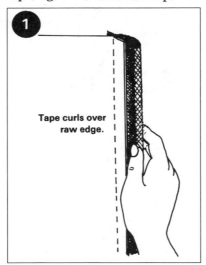

Tape curls over raw edge.

gently. It will curl automatically toward its own right side and cup over the raw edge, eliminating the need

to pin or baste before you sew.

• Do not stretch the tape too tightly. The more you stretch it, the narrower it becomes.

• Use the 1¼″ width to create a casing for elastic or a drawstring (Figure 2). The

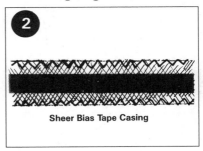

Sheer Bias Tape Casing

tape is less bulky than most self-fabric or standard bias tape casings.

• Reinforce seams subject to stress and seams on delicate or open-weave fabrics by including sheer bias tape in the stitching. For example, tape the armhole seam of a lace garment (Figure 3).

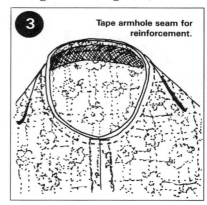

Tape armhole seam for reinforcement.

• When sewing on a stretchy or bulky fabric such as sweater knit, use sheer bias tape for facings.

• Rely on sheer bias tape as an alteration or mending aid. For example, when replacing a collar, you'll often find the original seam allowances have been trimmed too closely for easy sewing. Extend the seam allowance by basting a strip of sheer bias tape just beyond the original stitching line (Figure 4). After repairing the

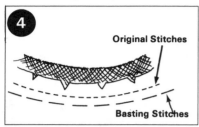

garment, remove the basting stitches. Leave the excess tape intact or trim it close to the new stitching line.

• Press carefully. If you use too much steam or high heat, sheer bias tape can melt.

✂ SHOULDER PADS

Whether shoulder pads are in or out as a fashion accessory, they're always useful for fitting purposes. In effect, shoulder pads fool the eye. They disguise sloping shoulders or the one shoulder that is lower than the other. They can even make your head-to-toe image look better.

Slip some pads into a dress or jacket and look into the mirror. Notice how much thinner and more stately you look.

While shoulder pads are a necessity in fine tailoring, you can put pads into just about any garment if you like. Here's how to choose and use these inner shaping aids.

TYPES OF PADS

• Shoulder pads for set-in sleeves are triangular in shape (Figure 1). To position them in

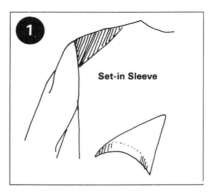

Set-in Sleeve

a garment, put the garment on and slip the pads in place. Try several pad positions until you find the one that gives you a comfortable fit and a smooth, square shoulder line. The pointed end of the pad belongs near the neckline; the wider, straighter end belongs at the armhole.

• Shoulder pads for jackets and coats have a slight curved shelf called a sleeve head which fits over the shoulder and extends ¼″ or more into the sleeve cap (Figure 2). This

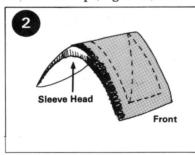

Sleeve Head
Front

pad style gives a little more shape and support to the shoulder area so the sleeve doesn't abruptly drop from the shoulder.

• Shoulder pads for raglan, kimono and dropped shoulder garments have a larger, cupped sleeve head which fits over the top of your natural shoulder (Figure 3).

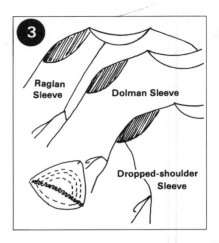

Raglan Sleeve
Dolman Sleeve
Dropped-shoulder Sleeve

SHOULDER PAD TIPS

• Shoulder pads are always fitted from the outside of a garment. Do not force pads into position, but let them go where they want to, even if they stray away from the shoulder or armhole seams. If might not look right from the inside of the garment, but it will look right from the outside where it really counts.

• To anchor shoulder pads inside a garment, pin pads in place from the right side of the garment. On the inside, sew the pad with stab stitches to the armhole seam allowances (Figure 4); tack the pad point

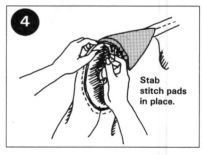

Stab stitch pads in place.

loosely to the shoulder seam allowances.

• Anchor raglan-style pads to the shoulder seam allowances only.

• After sewing shoulder pads into a garment, place the

shoulder area over a dressmaker's ham and lightly steam to shape. Use a press cloth to protect the fabric.

• To make pads detachable when laundering or dry cleaning the garment, use hook and loop fasteners. Sew the loop portion to the garment shoulder seam and the hook portion to the topside of the pad. Let the pad tails hang free.

• Cover shoulder pads for unlined garments the easy way. Cut a pair of squares from lightweight garment fabric, lining fabric or lingerie tricot. Fold a square over each pad, stitch around the edges, then serge or trim with pinking shears (Figure 5).

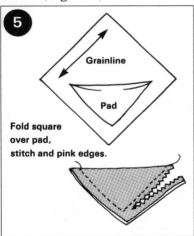

Fold square over pad, stitch and pink edges.

TUBE TURNERS

Cylindrical brass tube turners streamline the tedious, time-consuming task of turning narrow tubes of fabric right side out. Unlike comparable tools which thread or push the fabric, a tube turner enables you to pull the fabric tube through a cylinder.

Not only is this method effective, it also lets you fill the fabric tube with cording, batting, belting or another filler as you turn.

Most tube turner cylinders come in a wide range of sizes from ⅛″ to ¾″ in diameter; you can use the tubes for straps, button loops, belts, sashes and more.

GENERAL TIPS

• Use plain fabric tubes to make straps on jumpers, overalls, totes and purses, or to create sashes and belt loops. You can also press the tubes flat and use them for appliquéd stems and vines, Celtic motifs or stained glass decorative designs.

• To make a basic fabric tube, start with a strip of fabric. Cut the strip on the bias grain for appliqués or shaped decorative details; cut on the straight grain for straps, ties and belt loops.

Fold the fabric strip in half lengthwise with right sides together; stitch the long raw edges together in a ¼″ seam.

• Slide the fabric tube onto the appropriately-sized cylinder, keeping the seam straight (Figure 1). If the tube

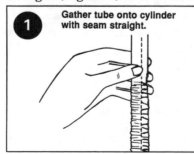

Gather tube onto cylinder with seam straight.

is longer than the cylinder, ease the fabric into compact gathers.

• Insert a wire hook into the cylinder. Holding the tube end taut over the end of the cylinder, pierce the fabric with the corkscrew tip by twisting the hook to the right (Figure 2).

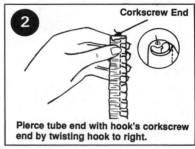

Pierce tube end with hook's corkscrew end by twisting hook to right.

• To turn the tube right side out, slowly pull the hook handle with one hand while easing the fabric off the cylinder with the other (Figure 3).

• When the tube appears at the end of the cylinder, remove the hook by twisting it to the left (Figure 4). Using your fingers, continue pulling the tube right side out.

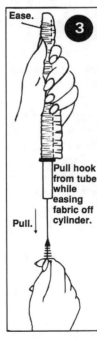

Ease.

Pull hook from tube while easing fabric off cylinder.

Pull.

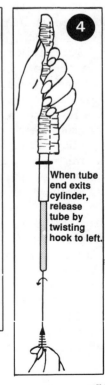

When tube end exits cylinder, release tube by twisting hook to left.

SEWING TECHNIQUES

• Tubes filled with their own seam allowances can be used for spaghetti straps, bows, button loops, frogs, and Chinese ball buttons.

To make a self-filled fabric tube, cut the fabric strip twice the desired finished width plus seam allowances; experiment to determine the correct seam allowances for a specific fabric type. Cut woven fabrics on the bias grain; cut knits on the lengthwise grain for straps or the crosswise grain for loops, buttons, bows and frogs.

• Cord-filled tubes have uses similar to self-filled tubes. Because corded tubes are strong and stable, you can weave, braid or knot them together for accessories such as belts.

To fill the tube, use cable cord, piping cord or yarn. For soft sculpture jewelry, you can use chenille stems, pipe cleaners or floral wire covered with fleece.

To make a corded tube, cut the fabric strip wide enough to fit around the cord plus ½" for seam allowances. Cut woven fabrics on the bias grain; cut knits on the crosswise grain.

Follow the general tips above, but trim the seam allowances to ⅛". Wrap one end of the cord with transparent tape to prevent the cord from untwisting. Pull the fabric about ½" into the cylinder and stop. Finger-press the seam allowances open at the cylinder end and place the cording into the tube (Figure 5). As you continue pulling the tube right side out, the cording will be drawn into the tube.

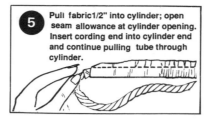
5 Pull fabric1/2" into cylinder; open seam allowance at cylinder opening. Insert cording end into cylinder end and continue pulling tube through cylinder.

• To fill a tube with stiff belting, cut a fabric strip on the straight grain the length of your waist measurement plus 6" and twice the width of the belting plus ½" for seam allowances. Cut the belting as long as your waist measurement plus 5½".

Fold the fabric strip in half along its length with right sides together and stitch the long raw edges in a ¼" seam. Press the seam open.

Position the seam so it runs along the center of the tube's length. Stitch one end into a point and trim the seam allowances; trim one belting end the same shape (Figure 6).

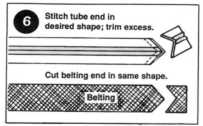
6 Stitch tube end in desired shape; trim excess.

Cut belting end in same shape.

Belting

Slip the tube onto an appropriately-sized cylinder. Slightly pinch the shaped end of the belting without creasing it and insert it into the cylinder; push the belting into the tube until the belt appears at the end of the cylinder. Using your fingers, pull the remainder of the belt from the cylinder (Figure 7).

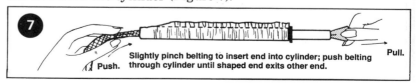
7 Slightly pinch belting to insert end into cylinder; push belting through cylinder until shaped end exits other end. Push. Pull.

If necessary, adjust the seam so it is at the center back of the belt. Finish the belt appropriately.

• To make a batting-filled tube, cut two fabric strips for each tube and one polyester batting strip the desired length and width, plus ½" for seam allowances.

Place the fabric strips right sides together with the batting on top. Stitch each long edge in a ¼" seam; trim the batting out of the seam allowances (Figure 8).

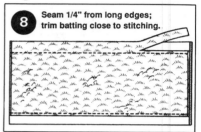
8 Seam 1/4" from long edges; trim batting close to stitching.

Insert a cylinder between the two fabric layers. Insert the wire hook into the cylinder. Holding the tube end taut over the cylinder end, pierce the fabric and batting with the corkscrew tip by twisting the hook to the right. Turn the tube right side out by slowly pulling the wire handle with one hand while easing the fabric off the cylinder with the other.

Press the tube flat. You can butt the tube edges and sew them together with a decorative machine stitch for wearable art garments and accessories.

Chapter 2

FABULOUS FABRICS

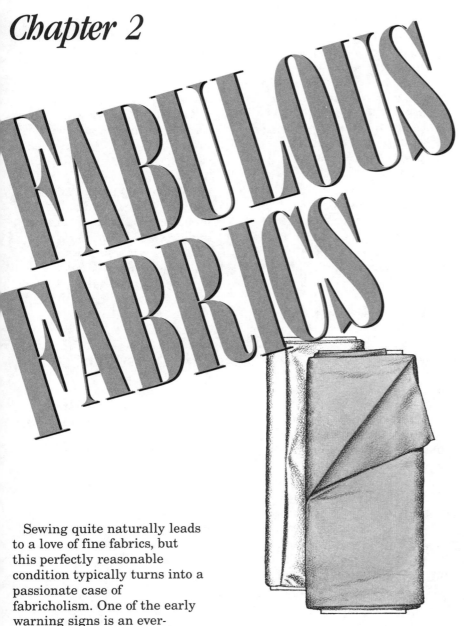

Sewing quite naturally leads to a love of fine fabrics, but this perfectly reasonable condition typically turns into a passionate case of fabricholism. One of the early warning signs is an ever-increasing collection of past purchases and assorted scraps just too pretty to toss out. Another obvious symptom is carrying swatches in your purse in an effort to coordinate new acquisitions with the stockpile.

It is, after all, the fabrics that make sewing a lifelong, creative adventure. There's always something new to sew (and collect). Therefore, discovery never ends.

Whether you're a sewing beginner or relatively experienced, now and then try some of the more exotic fabrics available for sewing. It's always a surprise to see how spectacular the simplest garment can look when you use a maverick fabric. You will gain confidence in your abilities, too. This chapter will help you go beyond the basics.

Let fabric inspire you. If you have a wonderful fabric to work with, you'll always enjoy the process of sewing as well as the finished product.

GETTING STARTED

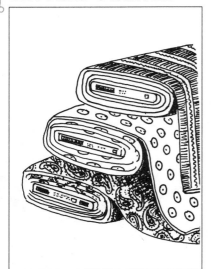

Although you're probably anxious to start sewing, it's a good idea to launch every project with a few preliminary steps. Prepare the fabric so it won't change character later on, figure out the best way to arrange the pattern pieces on the fabric, then weigh the merits of various seam finishes. By the time you sit down at the sewing machine, you'll feel confident of success.

THINK PRESHRINK

It never fails. Somehow, your favorite silk blouse slips into the washing machine and emerges smaller and several shades lighter. Or your wool coat trots off to the dry cleaner slightly soiled and returns slightly shrunken. What's a fashion-sewer to do? Think preshrink.

The rule of thumb is clean a fabric before you sew the same way you plan to care for the finished garment. This prevents shrinkage, the prime reason for pretreating fabric; removing chemical finishes such as formaldehyde and sizing is another. Because finishes often affect fabric texture, drape and sheen, it can be misleading if the garment is fitted while finishes are still present. Also, finishes can cause stitching problems.

Pretreating fabric before you sew and properly caring for custom-sewn fashions afterwards are vital for good appearance and extended wear. Let's take a look at several types of fabric fibers and how to handle them before you sew.

• Unless clearly marked "washable wool," wool fabrics require dry cleaning. If you're concerned about shrinkage, buy an extra 1/8 yard of fabric and have the entire piece cleaned before you cut.

A do-it-yourself alternative is steaming the fabric with an iron or table press. Set the iron or press on a hot steam setting, use a damp pressing cloth, and steam sections of single-layer fabric until they're warm but only slightly damp. Prop the freshly-steamed area on an adjacent table or other surface so the weight of the fabric won't stretch the warm, damp fibers.

• Although its fine hand and soft drape makes it seem delicate, silk fabric can be washed by hand or machine. This may be one of the best reasons to sew your own silks, since by prewashing the fabric you can then launder the finished garment. You'll not only save the dry cleaning expense, but also create a garment that won't suffer from water spots. In addition, dry cleaning chemicals dry out silk fibers and shorten the life span of the fabric, while washing rejuvenates the fibers.

Even if you prefer to dry clean silks, it's a good idea to prewash the fabric to prevent shrinkage and damage from water spots. To allow for shrinkage, buy an extra 1/8 yard for every 2 yards when hand washing or dry cleaning, and an extra 1/2 yard for every 2 yards when machine washing.

To hand wash silk, add 1/4 cup of white vinegar to every 2 gallons of water to retain the color, use a mild detergent, and squeeze the fabric to remove excess water. Press the damp fabric until dry with a hot, dry iron.

To machine wash silk, use a delicate cycle, cool water and mild detergent; press until dry as above. Test either washing method first on a scrap to see if you approve of the change in color, sheen and drape that occurs.

Another option is steam-shrinking silk fabric; follow the instructions given above for wool. Be careful not to burn the silk, and test a small area first for color changes, as there will be some fading.

• In general, cotton fabric shrinks, so it's wise to preshrink cotton fabrics by machine washing and drying. Buy an extra 1/8 to 1/4 yard for every 2 to 4 yards to compensate.

Of course, hand washing and dry cleaning are always options. You may prefer them when sewing heavily-constructed or highly-detailed garments from cotton fabrics.

• You may prefer to dry clean linen, as machine washing tends to fade darker colors and makes the fabric limp rather than crisp. Hand washing handkerchief linen is an option, but be careful when handling the damp fabric; linen becomes weak when wet.

Steam-shrinking, as described above for wool, is also an alternate preparation method for linen. To allow for shrinkage with any method, buy an extra ⅛ yard for every 4 yards required.

• Blended fabrics containing more than 30 percent synthetic fibers shrink very little, but pretreat them to remove the fabric finishes. In general, blends can be laundered. Choose dry cleaning to control possible fading, pamper a delicate construction or preserve the texture and drape of special fabrics such as satin, taffeta or polyester crepe.

FABRIC FUDGING

Uh-oh — there's not enough fabric? Whether you're digging through your fabric stash or the remnant table, you're sure to encounter a tight squeeze occasionally when trying to fit a specific pattern on a specific cut of fabric. Before giving up, here are some strategies for saving a critical few inches here and there.

• Consider shortening the pattern. Decide how long you want the finished garment to be and how you'll finish the hem, then cut off excess pattern tissue.

• Reduce the hem allowance. For a bias skirt, use a narrow pinked-and-stitched (Figure 1) or serged (Figure 2)

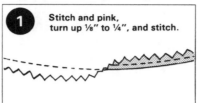

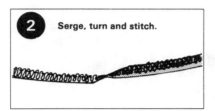

hem which requires minimal hem allowance. On lightweight silky fabrics, use a narrow, machine-stitched hem or serger hem. On other garments, maybe you could eliminate the hem allowance and face the hem instead.

• Use narrower seam allowances. Especially if you're sewing seams on a serger, you don't need the full ⅝", so cut out skinnier seams to save fabric.

• Eliminate seams. For example, if you can cut a straight-grain seam on a fold, you'll save 1¼" of fabric.

• Use the selvage for a seam allowance — but only if it's smooth, flat and straight and the seam is a straight-grain seam. You may be able to use this ploy for the center back seam of a skirt or jacket.

• Rearrange the pattern layout. Although there's not much margin in the yardage listed on the pattern envelope, sometimes you can save fabric by cutting the pattern on a single layer rather than on folded fabric or by folding the fabric off-center rather than using it as it comes off the bolt.

• Cut some pattern pieces on the bias grain such as blouse cuffs or jacket pockets. You may be able to fit these oddly-shaped pieces on large scraps.

To change the printed grainline from straight grain to true bias grain, fold the pattern in half, then refold so the first foldline matches the printed grainline (Figure 3).

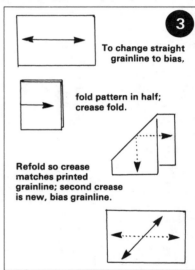

The second crease is the new, bias grainline marking.

• Cut some pieces on the crosswise grainline. Stripes and plaids lend themselves to crosswise layouts for pattern pieces such as yokes, cuffs, bands or pockets. However, don't use this strategy on too many small details or the garment will have a spotty look.

• Use a contrasting fabric. Cut some of the pattern pieces such as upper collar, under-collar, facings, neckband, belt, yoke or pocket from this second fabric. A coordinating solid or print peeking out at the undercollar and neckband on a shirt looks like designer detailing (Figure 4), however a

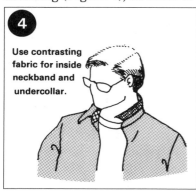

Use contrasting fabric for inside neckband and undercollar.

good rule of thumb is cut no more than three contrast pieces.

• Combine related fabrics. For example, cut the skirt of a dress from one fabric and the bodice or sleeves and collar from another. You could end up with a very creative garment.

• Eliminate a detail. It's easy to skip pockets, for

example, if you can live without them.

Another fabric-consuming detail that's easy to eliminate is a back-button closure on a blouse. Change to a pull-on style by cutting away the back facing section and adding a center back seam allowance. Stitch the center back seam, leaving a 6″ opening at the top. Narrow-hem the opening and attach the collar or facing (Figure 5). Add a button and loop closure at the neck edge.

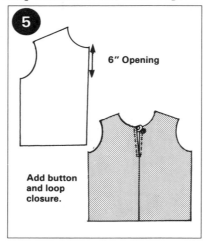

6″ Opening

Add button and loop closure.

Or, cut the back on a fabric fold and apply a placket facing to create the necessary opening (Figure 6).

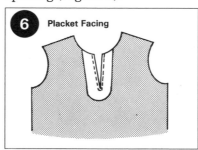

Placket Facing

• Remove a little fullness from gathered or flared skirt styles — but only if this won't spoil the look. Take a small tuck at the hemline of the

pattern piece, tapering the tuck to nothing at the waist (Figure 7).

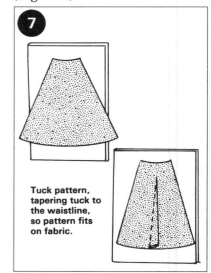

Tuck pattern, tapering tuck to the waistline, so pattern fits on fabric.

• Piece garment sections. If a jacket or coat facing won't fit, cut it in two below the roll line; don't forget to add seam allowances to both pieced sections (Figure 8).

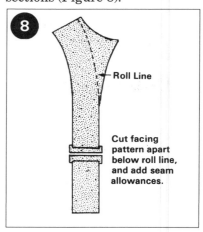

Roll Line

Cut facing pattern apart below roll line, and add seam allowances.

To piece cuffs, split the pattern at the fold and add a ¼″ seam allowance to each edge (Figure 9). You might be able to squeeze the four smaller sections out of scrap pieces.

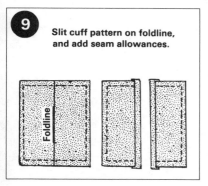

9 Slit cuff pattern on foldline, and add seam allowances.

Foldline

Piece large, flared or bias skirt sections with a seam close to the hem edge. Make sure you cut the pieced sections on the same grainline as the main sections, and add seam allowances (Figure 10).

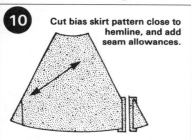

10 Cut bias skirt pattern close to hemline, and add seam allowances.

MEET YOUR MATCH

Fashion vibrates with prints, plaids, checks, florals, paisleys and jacquards, not to mention laces and bias designs which require careful layouts. Take a look at any season's ready-to-wear stock, and notice how these fabric designs match — or sort of match — at the seams. But only on the most expensive designer labels will you find the fabric design perfectly matched at the center front closing. You can do it, too, by following these simple instructions:

• Concentrate on the pattern's center front line. Notice the four different bodice patterns illustrated (Figure 11) — ignore the edges, for it's the center front line you need to note.

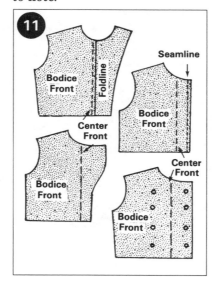

11 Bodice Front • Foldline • Center Front • Seamline • Bodice Front • Center Front • Bodice Front • Bodice Front

• Wrap the fabric around you to decide where to place the fabric's prominent motifs. For example, if you're large-busted, you probably will find an eye-catching red rose more flattering at the shoulder than at the bustline. Decide which motifs, if any, look best at the center front position.

• Pin the front bodice pattern printed side up on a single-layer of fabric so the fabric motifs are aligned as you desire. Cut out this pattern piece for the right front bodice section. Mark the center front with tiny snips at the top and bottom (Figure 12). Unpin the pattern.

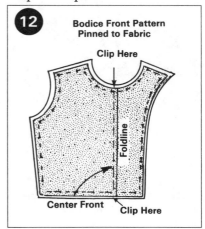

12 Bodice Front Pattern Pinned to Fabric • Clip Here • Foldline • Center Front • Clip Here

• Slide the cut bodice section on the uncut fabric until you find a place where it blends in exactly and matches perfectly at the center front line. Pin-mark the uncut fabric at the center front line, at the clip-marks on the cut bodice section (Figure 13). Set aside the bodice.

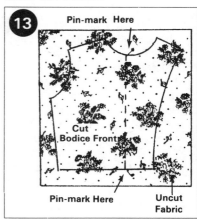

13 Pin-mark Here • Cut Bodice Front • Pin-mark Here • Uncut Fabric

• Place the front bodice pattern printed side down on the uncut fabric, aligning the pattern center front line with the pin marks. Cut out this section, which is the left front bodice, and you have a perfect match (Figure 14).

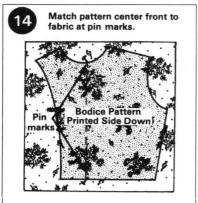

14 Match pattern center front to fabric at pin marks.

Pin marks

Bodice Pattern Printed Side Down

• Naturally, the larger the fabric repeat, the more fabric you'll need (a repeat is the area containing a complete motif). If this presents layout problems, piece some of the large waste scraps. Use this "invisible" technique also when sewing narrow imported fabrics and garments such as circular skirts which have very large pattern pieces:

COORDINATED EFFORTS

Each time I complete a garment or shorten a ready-made item, I save a small swatch of each fabric. I keep the clips in a small plastic bag in my purse and use them to coordinate other fabric and clothing purchases. There's no more guessing about what colors might go well together. This has eliminated many impulse purchases.

K. Guidry,
Mt. Vernon, WA

Pin the pattern on the fabric and cut, even though the pattern piece is too large for the fabric (Figure 15). Unpin the pattern.

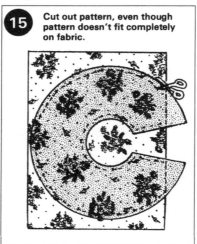

15 Cut out pattern, even though pattern doesn't fit completely on fabric.

Press under ⅝" seam allowance the each of each cut-out garment section requiring more fabric (Figure 16).

16 Press ⅝" seam allowance on edges which will be pieced.

Move the pressed-under edges around on the uncut fabric until you find a position where the fabric design matches precisely. Anchor the folds at the edges of the cut-out garment section to the

uncut fabric with double-faced basting tape (Figure 17). Be

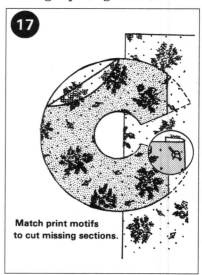

17

Match print motifs to cut missing sections.

sure the basting tape doesn't extend beyond the folds at the edges of the cut-out section. Pin the pattern back onto the fabric to cut the missing area.

With the basting tape still holding the fabric layers together, unfold the ⅝" seam allowance and stitch on the pressed crease (Figure 18).

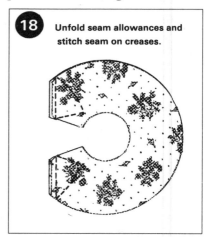

18 Unfold seam allowances and stitch seam on creases.

Remove the tape and press the seam open. The seam will be barely detectable.

STRIPE SMART

Whether you choose a fresh, lively stripe or a more subdued style, you'll find sewing with stripes isn't difficult. In fact, success is mainly a matter of selecting an appropriate type of stripe and pattern style, then devising a strategic layout.

• When choosing a stripe to sew, keep figure flattery in mind. The wider the stripe and the bolder the colors, the broader you will look. Use this to your advantage to fill out a small bust or make slim hips look more proportional. If you can't afford the possibility of a wider look, however, choose small-scale stripes which create no strong optical illusions.

• When learning to sew stripes, choose a simple pattern with few pieces. Look for easy skirts, pants and pullover tops. If you're more advanced, you may prefer a more detailed pattern so you can cut cuffs, bands, pockets, yokes, front panels and other small pieces from a contrasting stripe or on the true bias grain for a customized treatment.

Some patterns are illustrated in striped fabrics to show their suitability, but occasionally a pattern envelope indicates a style is not suitable for stripes. This is usually because the shape of the seams prevents a good match or results in a haphazard look; this no-stripe warning may be due to features such as princess seams, eased areas, horizontal darts or slanted French darts.

• The wider the stripe repeat, the more fabric you'll need for pattern layout. As a rule of thumb, multiply the size of the repeat by the number of main pattern pieces to determine how much extra fabric you'll need.

• To avoid creating stripe mismatches later, make any fitting adjustments on the pattern pieces before layout.

• All stripes are either even or uneven. Even stripes are easier to lay out, but uneven stripes are often worth an extra effort because they create exciting, unregimented garments.

To decide whether you have an even or uneven stripe, fold the fabric through the center of one stripe repeat. Fold back one corner at a 45-degree angle on the true bias grain. If you see matched chevrons, it's an even stripe (Figure 19).

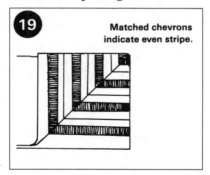

Matched chevrons indicate even stripe.

If you see mismatched chevrons, the stripe is uneven. The stripe may be uneven because the color bars are different widths (Figure 20), follow a different color sequence on the right and left halves of the repeat (Figure 21) or both.

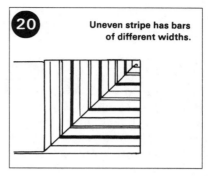

Uneven stripe has bars of different widths.

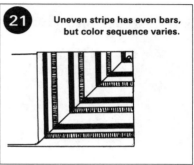

Uneven stripe has even bars, but color sequence varies.

Sometimes it's difficult to spot an uneven stripe this way. If in doubt, lightly press a fold through the center of the stripe repeat and open the fabric (Figure 22). Examine

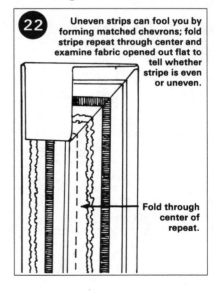

Uneven strips can fool you by forming matched chevrons; fold stripe repeat through center and examine fabric opened out flat to tell whether stripe is even or uneven.

Fold through center of repeat.

the fabric to see if right and left halves are symmetrical. If so, it's an even stripe; if not, it's uneven.

• To lay out even lengthwise stripes, fold the fabric through the center of a repeat and smooth the fabric layers so the stripes stack perfectly.

Position pattern seamlines (not cutting lines) so stripes match at the most important places: any center front or back seams or closures, at the front armhole notches on set-in sleeves, at side seams on skirts and pants and at the seam joining the upper collar to the lapels on a tailored jacket collar. Also, if possible position pattern pieces so straight hemlines (Figure 23)

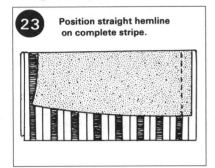

23 Position straight hemline on complete stripe.

and seamlines of details such as yokes, cuffs or patch pockets (Figure 24) fall on a complete stripe.

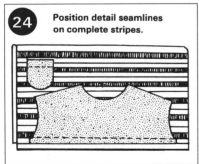

24 Position detail seamlines on complete stripes.

• To lay out uneven lengthwise stripes, in general fold the fabric through the center of the most prominent stripe and use a "with nap" layout in which all the pattern pieces

are aimed in a single direction. If the pattern has a fold at centers front and back, lay out all the pattern pieces printed-side-up and the stripe repeat will flow around the garment in the correct sequence.

However, if the pattern has a seam or closure at center front or back, lay out the pattern on a single layer of fabric with the prominent stripe at center front. Flip the pattern piece over to cut the second side, positioning the pattern center front on the same prominent stripe (Figure 25). The stripe

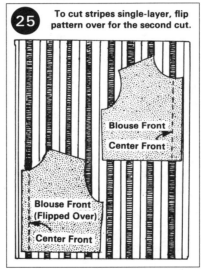

25 To cut stripes single-layer, flip pattern over for the second cut.

Blouse Front
Center Front

Blouse Front
(Flipped Over)
Center Front

repeat will be uninterrupted from left to right on the finished garment.

• To lay out even or uneven crosswise stripes, simply stack the stripes on both fabric layers. Use a "with nap" layout for the uneven stripe.

BE A SEAM SPECIALIST

A plain, pressed-open seam is a traditional sewing technique and probably the first method you learned.

However, you can't use it exclusively. Depending upon the fabric of the moment and the fashion effect you are trying to achieve, you'll need a variety of seams and seam finishes in your sewing repertoire. Then, you can sew a more decorative, more durable or less bulky type of seam as needed for a more professional look.

• A plain seam with raw edges finished on the serger (Figure 26) is a practical, all-

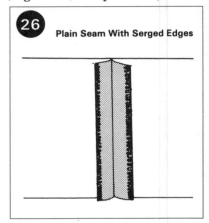

26 Plain Seam With Serged Edges

purpose method. It's especially good for fabrics that ravel or for bulky fabrics.

• A plain seam with zigzagged raw edges (Figure 27) is another all-purpose

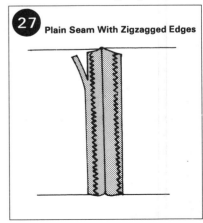

27 Plain Seam With Zigzagged Edges

option that's especially suitable for fabrics that ravel. Use a short stitch, zigzagging near but not on the raw edge of the seam allowance; trim the raw edge close to the stitches.

• A plain seam with hand-overcast raw edges (Figure 28)

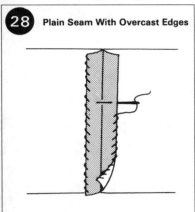

28 Plain Seam With Overcast Edges

is a fine finish for delicate fabrics. Make the hand stitches about ⅛" deep and ¼" apart, being careful not to pull the thread too tightly.

• A plain seam with Hong Kong finished edges (Figure 29) is a pretty and practical

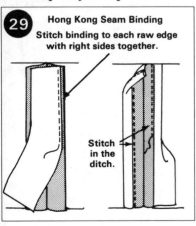

29 Hong Kong Seam Binding
Stitch binding to each raw edge with right sides together.

Stitch in the ditch.

technique for unlined garments or for fabrics that ravel. For the binding, cut bias strips from lightweight lining fabric or use precut sheer bias tape. Right sides together, stitch the binding to the raw edge in a ¼" seam, fold the binding over the raw edge and press. Finish by stitching in the ditch of the binding seam from the right side. Trim any excess binding.

• A topstitched plain seam (Figure 30) is attractive on

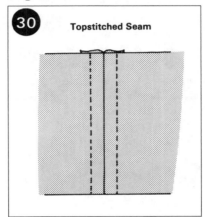

30 Topstitched Seam

leather, synthetic suede, melton and other fabrics which do not ravel. The topstitching, ¹⁄₁₆" to ¼" on each side of the seamline, holds the seam allowances flat on difficult-to-press fabrics and adds strength and stability to the seam.

• A welt seam (Figure 31) begins as a plain seam, but the seam allowances are pressed to one side. Trim the underneath seam allowance in half, then topstitch the overlapping seam allowance close to the edge. The strong,

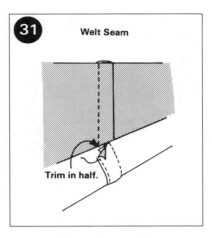

31 Welt Seam

Trim in half.

stable seam is lightly padded by the underneath seam allowance for a decorative effect.

• A lapped seam (Figure 32)

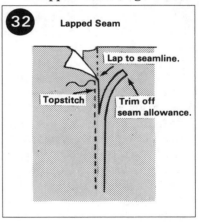

32 Lapped Seam

Lap to seamline.

Topstitch

Trim off seam allowance.

is a good choice for medium to heavyweight fabrics which do not ravel, such as leather and synthetic suedes. To sew, trim off the seam allowance on the overlapping edge. Matching the seamlines, topstitch ⅛" from the overlapping edge. If desired, topstitch a second time ⅜" from the overlapping edge.

• A serged seam (Figure 33)

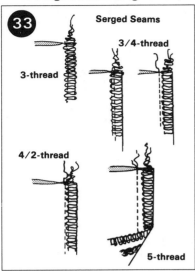

is the fastest and easiest seam method. Sew a sample to see if the seam your serger makes is sturdy enough for the garment you are sewing. Also, check to see if this seam leaves a ridge when pressed to one side on lightweight fabrics. Use an elastic thread such as texturized nylon for a stretchy serged seam on knits.

Exposed decorative seams, which are simply serged seams sewn on the right side of a garment, are a popular ready-to-wear technique. To duplicate this detail, adjust a serger for a short stitch, use decorative thread in the loopers, and place the wrong sides of the fabric together so the seam forms on the right side.

• A French seam (Figure 34) is traditional for sheers and laces, but can be used to make neat, narrow, durable seams on other lightweight fabrics, too. Sew a French seam twice

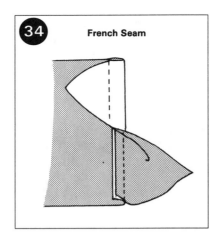

— first on the right side, then on the wrong side — so all the raw edges are enclosed. If desired, sew the first stitching on a serger to trim the raw edges evenly and efficiently before they're enclosed by the second stitching.

• A mock French seam (Figure 35) plays a similar

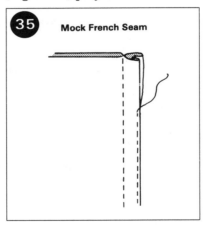

role, but is easier to sew than the classic French seam. Begin by sewing a plain seam, then fold under each seam allowance ¼″ toward the seamline; edgestitch the folds together.

• A flat-felled seam (Figure 36), the familiar jeans seam, is another sturdy technique which encloses the raw edges.

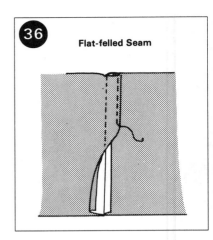

To sew, place wrong sides together and stitch a ⅝″ seam or, for thick fabrics, cut 1″ seam allowances and sew a wider seam. Trim the underneath seam allowance to ¼″. Fold the raw edge of the overlapping seam allowance under ¼″; press. Topstitch the overlapping seam allowance close to the folded edge.

• Double-stitched seams (Figure 37) can be sewn with

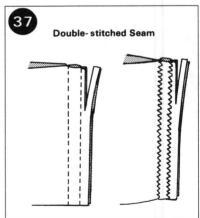

two rows of straight or zigzag stitches spaced ¼″ apart. Trim the excess seam allowance close to the second stitching for a neat, narrow seam on sheers and lightweight fabrics. On knits, stretch the fabric as you sew this type of seam.

BOILED WOOL

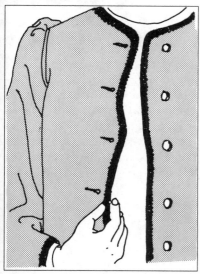

What's more timeless than a short, fitted, boiled wool jacket topping an ankle-length skirt? The classic elegance of this famous fashion ensemble — or any of its many variations — can be yours at less than half the ready-to-wear price when you sew it yourself.

Boiled wool, a one-of-a-kind fabric that's surprisingly easy to sew, isn't actually boiled. It's knitted from fine merino wool, then shrunk under carefully controlled conditions of heat and humidity so the fibers felt together. This makes the fabric so luxuriously dense it has the stability and texture of a woven fabric, yet it retains the comfort and flexibility of a knit. Another apparent paradox: boiled wool is wind- and water-resistant, yet it breathes, making it suitable for year-round wear.

Boiled wool, 60″ wide, is available in two weights. The medium weight, 16 ounces per yard, is suitable for shaped and detailed garments such as jackets, skirts, tailored coats

and capes. The heavier weight, 24 ounces per yard, is suitable for jackets, coats and other outerwear with simple, unstructured lines. Dyed-to-match wool foldover braid is available for a decorative edge finish like that found on ready-to-wear boiled wool jackets.

SEWING TIPS

• Preshrink boiled wool before cutting. If you plan to dry clean the finished garment, have a dry cleaner steam-press the fabric, or do it yourself with a good steam iron and a press cloth. Do remember to move the iron across the grain of the fabric only, since the knit structure is easily distorted.

If you plan to hand wash the finished garment, purchase an extra ¼ yard to allow for shrinkage. Use a cold water washing product and block the fabric like a fine knit. Allow it to dry flat, away from sunlight.

• Ready-made boiled wool jackets have no linings, facings or interfacings, making them more like a sweater than a tailored jacket. Since this cuts down on the work and materials required, it's an idea worth copying at home.

• Sharp dressmaker's shears and pinking shears are a must for cutting this dense, thick fabric.

• Use extra-long pins during layout and construction.

• There is no right or wrong side to boiled wool, and you can position pattern pieces so the grainline arrow runs either lengthwise or crosswise on the fabric.

• Staystitch all edges to prevent stretching.

• Stitch seams with a narrow zigzag stitch to build in a small of amount of stretch. Or, use a straight stitch and stretch the fabric slightly as you sew.

• To compensate for the fabric thickness, it may be necessary to adjust the pressure on the presser foot and use a slightly longer-than-normal stitch length. Test-stitch on a scrap of boiled wool.

• Use a size 80/11 ballpoint or universal point sewing machine needle.

• Because boiled wool is a knit that has been processed to compact the stitches, it doesn't ravel. Elaborate raw edge finishes are unnecessary, but pink the seam allowances to prevent the edges from pressing through to the right side.

Or, if desired, topstitch ¼″ on each side of front and back princess seams, then trim all seam allowances to ⅜″ (Figure 1).

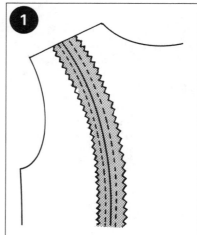

• Press seams open and do not clip curves. The fabric will flex smoothly around a curve when steam-pressed.

• Avoid overpressing and iron shine damage by using plenty of steam and a wool press cloth. To avoid seam edge impressions, press seams open over the edge of a dressmaker's ham or seam roll.

After pressing, apply pressure with a tailor's clapper to set the press.

• Stitch buttonholes over a backing of tear-away or water-soluble stabilizer.

• Prevent stretching and gaping by making corded buttonholes. Stitch the buttonhole over heavy topstitching thread, leaving a loop of thread at the end of the buttonhole closer to the center front (Figure 2). Afterwards,

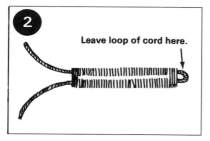

Leave loop of cord here.

pull the thread ends to hide the loop. Knot the thread ends (Figure 3) and bring them to

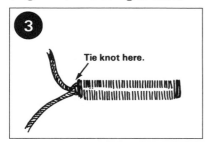

Tie knot here.

the wrong side by threading them through a tapestry needle.

• Reinforce buttons by sewing a small self-fabric circle or a small, clear plastic button on the wrong side (Figure 4).

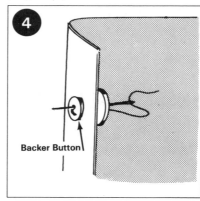

Backer Button

DECORATIVE DETAILS

• Ready-to-wear jackets are edged with dyed-to-match or contrasting wool foldover braid, but other options include synthetic suede strips, velveteen or challis bias binding and serging the edges with yarn in the loopers.

• Before applying foldover braid, preshrink it. Otherwise, the trimmed edges will distort and curl at the first cleaning.

• To apply foldover braid, pin the braid in place carefully. Steam-press to mold and shape it around curved edges, taking the utmost care not to stretch the boiled wool fabric. Baste the braid in place.

Use a zipper foot to topstitch close to the edge of the braid. Or, for a more polished look, pick stitch by hand.

• Prevent the cut edges of braid from raveling with a coat of seam sealant.

• Decorative pintucks are beautiful on boiled wool. Use a widely-spaced (3 mm or 4 mm)

double needle and a pin-tucking presser foot. Sew over cord for maximum emphasis.

• A fashionable treatment for boiled wool jackets is exposed decorative seams, especially around the armhole seam. To duplicate this detail, use decorative thread in the loopers of a serger.

• Add passementerie trim or touches of embroidery by hand or machine for ethnic flavor.

CHALLIS

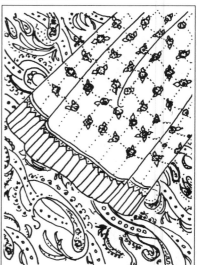

Soft, supple, lightweight challis originated in the 1830s in England. Contemporary challis has the same personality, making it a very versatile fabric.

The soft hand and exceptional drapability make challis an ideal blouse fabric, yet it has enough body for skirts and dresses. It's especially lovely when used for softly-gathered garments or designs with draped details. The attractive challis floral, paisley and geometric prints available seem flattering to most figure types and are appropriate for multi-season wear.

TYPES OF CHALLIS

Challis is manufactured from wool, cotton or rayon fibers, giving those who sew many choices. While the basic weave, weight and drapability are similar, challis tends to take on the character of the fiber used.

To give you some background for selecting challis, following are some general qualities of the three prominent challis fibers:

• Cotton is absorbent, tends to wrinkle, shrinks unless treated, is free from static electricity and usually can be laundered.

• Wool resists wrinkles, is absorbent, shrinks unless treated, requires moth proofing and usually needs to be dry cleaned although some wool challis is washable.

• Rayon is soft, absorbent, prone to wrinkles and will shrink or stretch unless treated with special finishes. Some types of rayon challis are washable, but others must be dry cleaned.

SEWING TIPS

• An all-purpose polyester or cotton/polyester thread works well on most challis types. Or, for cotton or rayon challis, use size 50 cotton thread; for wool challis, use fine silk thread.

• Select a medium size 80/11 or fine size 65/9 machine needle.

• Most challis ravels, although some ravel more than others, making a raw edge finish mandatory. Finish raw edges on seams with serging, zigzag stitching or sheer bias tape binding. Another option is using a French or mock French seam technique which encloses the raw edges.

CORDUROY

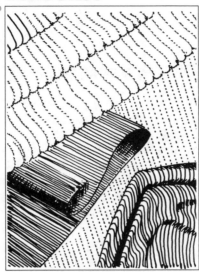

Plush corduroy has been popular for generations as a staple for sewing sportswear, work clothing, childrenswear and all types of casual fashions. Durable and washable, corduroy was used centuries ago by workers in the French royal palaces; in fact, the fabric traces its name to the phrase "cord du roi" — cord of the king. Today, it's one of the fashion classics.

TYPES OF CORDUROY

Made of cotton fibers or a cotton/synthetic fiber blend, corduroy's weave contains an extra set of yarns in vertical rows that create a pile surface on the right side. Called wales, these rows give the various types of corduroy their names. There are numerous weights, ranging from thick wide wale — sporting as few as 3 wales per inch — to fine pinwale which has 16 wales per inch. Generally, the wider the wale, the heavier and bulkier the fabric. The surface of ribless corduroy, which has wales too fine to discern, resembles velveteen.

SEWING TIPS

• Judge corduroy quality by the backing's construction and the density of the pile. The fabric back should be tightly woven and resist shifting when stretched in a variety of directions. The pile on the face should be so dense the woven backing does not show through.

• Select patterns to complement the wale type. Wide wale corduroys look best in styles with boxy, simple silhouettes and minimal details. Lighter weight pinwales work well in styles which have soft lines and some fullness from gathers or pleats.

• Avoid details such as topstitching, welt pockets and bound buttonholes unless working with a finely waled corduroy. Also avoid any design detail that creates sharp folds in the fabric, as this distorts the pile.

• Use a "with nap" pattern layout so all pattern pieces head in the same direction. This is necessary for the color to look uniform in the finished garment. Whether the nap runs up or down on a garment is up to you.

• The deeper the pile, the more likely corduroy is to shift as you stitch. Place pins fairly close together and use a medium to long stitch (10 to 12 per inch). A roller foot or even feed foot also helps solve shifting problems.

• Stitch in the direction of the pile for smoother seams.

• Grade seam allowances to reduce bulk.

• To avoid flattening the pile, press gently from the wrong side if possible. Use pressing aids such as a seam roll and a needle board.

• Corduroy ravels, so finish raw edges with serging, zigzagging or sheer bias tape binding.

• You can wash and dry corduroy by machine. Remove it promptly from the dryer and little or no ironing will be needed.

DENIM

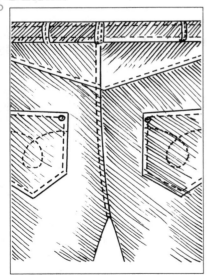

Ask any number of people what's their pet item of comfortable clothing. Chances are they'll answer a denim garment – a jacket, skirt, shirt or the all-time favorite, a seasoned pair of jeans.

One of the reasons for denim's popularity may be that denim clothes seem to take on the form and the personality of the owner, becoming distinctively his or hers. Add in the softness of well-worn denim and its durability, and it's easy to see why denim's a hit with so many.

TYPES OF DENIM

Interestingly, denim's construction makes it naturally strong and long-wearing. Like gabardine and drill cloth, traditional denim is a warp-faced twill weave fabric, meaning most of the yarns on the surface are durable, lengthwise, warp yarns. These yarns have a higher twist than crosswise weft yarns, so they have more strength and less stretch. No wonder denim wears so well and withstands countless launderings. You can recognize this type of denim by the diagonal lines on the wrong side.

When denim has tiny "V's" on the wrong side, it's a herringbone or "broken twill" weave. This type of denim has a slightly dressier look, and was developed to minimize shifting of the fabric grain during laundering.

Originally denim was woven from indigo blue lengthwise yarns and white crosswise yarns. Now, in addition to classic blue denim, there's a wide variety of colors and finishes available with fashion appeal.

Denim is often overdyed to create undertones of a second color, or stonewashed to give it a well-worn look. It may have spandex fibers to give the woven fabric a little stretch for closely-fitted garments. Printed denim has a distinctive look since the design is printed over the bicolored base weave, and there are yarn-dyed woven denim plaids and stripes.

Whether you select denim with classic or sophisticated styling, the weight of the fabric is an important sewing consideration. Denim comes in several weights, which are identified in terms of ounces per yard. Heavier denims hold up to hard wear better than lighter weights and are most suitable for simple pattern styles with few seams and details such as jeans, overalls and work-style clothes. Save more complex pattern styles such as shirts, dresses, skirts and pleated pants for use with lightweight denims.

SEWING TIPS

• Preshrink denim by machine washing and drying it. Preshrink 100-percent cotton denim at least twice and possibly three times to remove all sizing and residual shrinkage.

• To minimize fading of dark blue or black denim, presoak the fabric in one cup white vinegar and ¼ cup salt in a bathtub half full with water. Soak at least two hours.

• Flat-felled seams are traditional on denim garments. This technique not only controls raveling, but also makes a strong seam which holds up under hard wear and repeated launderings.

• Multiple rows of top-stitching in a heavy, contrasting thread are a popular detail for denim garments. For best results, use heavy thread in the needle only and regular thread in the bobbin. Loosen the needle thread tension slightly to achieve a balanced stitch, and use a topstitching/denim machine needle for better penetration through the layers of fabric.

• For topstitching like that found on ready-to-wear, lengthen the stitch so the thread sits on top of the fabric rather than sinks into the weave.

• If you can't find the right color topstitching thread, use two strands of regular sewing thread through the needle.

• Another topstitching option: use regular sewing thread in the machine needle and bobbin, and set the machine to sew with a multi-motion straight stitch (Figure 1). This creates a saddle-stitched effect.

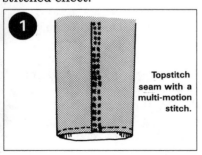

Topstitch seam with a multi-motion stitch.

• For perfectly parallel rows of topstitching on lightweight denim, use regular sewing thread and a twin needle.

• You may find these sewing machine accessories helpful when sewing denim: an edgestitch foot for even topstitching on seams or a blind hem foot to guide the needle along the raised edge of a flat-felled seam; an even feed foot to prevent the fabric layers from shifting as you sew; and a seam guide, magnetic or screw-in, to help topstitch around curves and edges.

• Denim garments can be difficult to hem, especially if you have sewn flat-felled seams which extend into the hem allowance. Instead of folding under the raw hem edge, serge it or overcast with zigzag stitches. Topstitch the hem for an authentic "jeans" look (Figure 2).

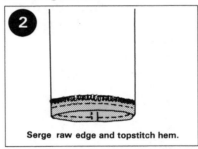

Serge raw edge and topstitch hem.

• You can stitch more easily over thick flat-felled seams if you pound them flat with a hammer. Protect the fabric with a self-fabric scrap as you pound.

• For a professional looking fly front zipper when sewing jeans-style pants, topstitch from the crotch seam to ½"

above the zipper seam (Figure 3). Make bar tacks with a short, narrow zigzag stitch.

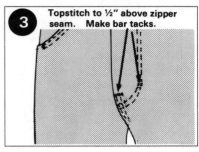

Topstitch to ½" above zipper seam. Make bar tacks.

• To make belt loops, cut a denim strip on the selvage. Press the strip lengthwise into thirds, with the raw edge folded in first and the selvage folded on top (Figure 4).

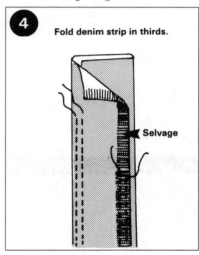

Fold denim strip in thirds.

Selvage

Topstitch two rows along each lengthwise edge, then cut the strip into individual belt loops.

DOUBLE-FACED FABRICS

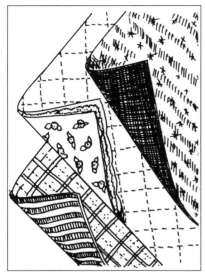

Sewing with reversible, double-faced fabrics is challenging and exciting, but definitely not difficult. These designer-style fabrics have two "right" sides – either face can be used as the outside of a garment.

TWO TYPES

There are two basic types of double-faced fabrics. One type consists of two separate fabric layers which can be separated when sewing seams. Although this group includes quilted fabrics with a layer of batting in between and coordinating fabrics that have been bonded together, the most deluxe examples are woven wools joined together with an extra binder yarn. These fabrics are ideal for making reversible garments that look exactly the same inside and out.

The other type of double-faced fabric cannot be split apart to sew seams; attempts to separate the faces damage the fabric. This group includes lightweight cottons with a different print on each side, knits with a different color on each side, fabrics with no discernible right or wrong side and a few true double cloths that have two faces woven together. Although you can use this type of fabric to create a reversible garment, only selected double-face sewing techniques can be used.

GENERAL TIPS

• You may find a few patterns designed for double-faced fabric, but you can also adapt a pattern with fairly simple styling. For best results, choose a loose-fitting outerwear pattern with wide, deep-set armholes or raglan sleeves. Consider cardigans, single- and double-breasted coats and jackets, capes, ponchos and vests.

• To take full advantage of the reversible quality of the fabric, look for details such as turned-back cuffs, patch pockets and a shawl or standing collar. Avoid styles with gathers, tucks, vents, pleats, darts and welt or in-seam pockets.

• Clutch or wrap-style closures are ideal, as are decorative closures such as toggles, ties and frogs. Buttons and buttonholes can be used, but the closure will lap in the opposite direction when the garment is reversed, and you will have to sew a set of buttons to each face.

• If adapting a pattern for use with double-faced fabric, you may need to purchase less fabric than the pattern suggests.

Modify the pattern pieces by omitting all facings. Trim hem allowances to 1″ and increase the seam allowances to 1″ to accommodate possible special construction techniques (Figure 1). Consider adding 2″

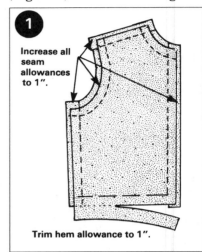

Increase all seam allowances to 1″.

Trim hem allowance to 1″.

to 3″ to the sleeve length for turned-back cuffs.

Using the modified pattern, revise the pattern layout to determine the actual yardage you need. Remember also to omit linings and interfacings.

• For speed and accuracy, cut large pattern pieces from a double layer of fabric and smaller detail areas from a single thickness. Use sharp shears or a rotary cutter.

• Quilter's long pins work well on bulky double-faced fabrics. Shorter pins tend to tear the pattern tissue during layout.

• Use a marking method that's temporary and will not leave permanent marks behind. Tailor's chalk, an air- or water-soluble marking pen and tailor tacks work well.

• Cut around notches rather than snip-marking them since you will need the full seam allowance for reversible seam techniques. Trim off the notches as you come to them when sewing a seam or edge.

SEWING TECHNIQUES

• The fastest way to sew a double-faced fabric is on a serger. Use a flatlock stitch to sew garment seams (Figure 2).

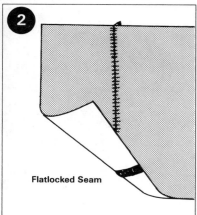

Flatlocked Seam

Finish the garment edges with a rolled hem stitch, loosening the tensions as needed to produce a flat, thread-bound edge. The effect can be dressy or casual, depending upon the thread you use.

• Topstitched construction takes advantage of the stable, non-raveling quality of many double-faced fabrics. It's a simple variation of the plain seam and ordinary turned-up hem, and you can use it for any type of double-faced fabric. This technique makes all the seam and hem allowances look like contrasting trim on one face for a dramatic "inside out" effect.

To construct this seam, stitch a standard ⅝" seam and press it open. Using a wide, slightly elongated zigzag stitch, topstitch the seam allowances to the body of the garment.

Stitch along the cut edge of the seam allowance so one swing of the needle penetrates the seam allowance and the other swing does not (Figure 3). Topstitch the hem the same way.

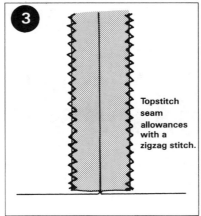

Topstitch seam allowances with a zigzag stitch.

To finish other garment edges, fold over the seam allowance 1" and press. Topstitch along the cut edge (Figure 4). Don't try to trim off

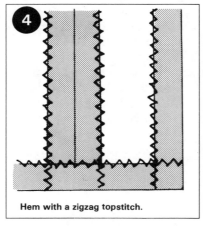

Hem with a zigzag topstitch.

the seam allowances and simply zigzag-overcast them; the garment edge will stretch and become distorted.

• Slot seam construction is a unique double-faced technique you can use when the fabric faces are separable. Although time-consuming, it creates a

reversible finish with no seam allowances visible inside or out, although probably one face will look a little neater and more polished than the other.

To sew a slot seam, trim the seam allowances to ⅝". Using a razor blade or sharp embroidery scissors, gently cut the layers of fabric apart for about 1¼" (Figure 5). Staystitch each layer if the seam is curved.

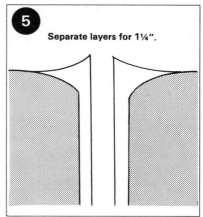

Separate layers for 1¼".

With the right sides of one face fabric together, sew a ⅝" seam. Trim the seam allowances to ⅜" and press open (Figure 6).

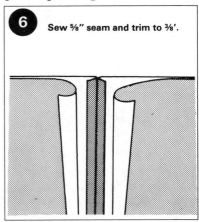

Sew ⅝" seam and trim to ⅜'.

Sew all the seams on one face of the garment this way.

To finish the seams, work from the right side of the other fabric face. Trim ⅜″ from one seam allowance. Fold the other seam allowance under on the seamline and press; trim the folded-under allowance to ⅜″ and lap over the unfolded seam allowance (Figure 7).

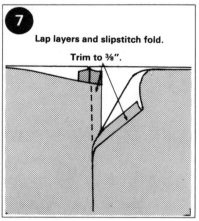

Lap layers and slipstitch fold.

Trim to ⅜″.

Slipstitch the layers together.

Finish hem and other outer edges in a similar way (Figure 8). Separate the fabric layers

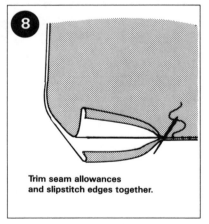

Trim seam allowances and slipstitch edges together.

for 1¼″. Trim the edge of the outer face to ⅜″ and fold under; trim the edge of the inner face to ¼″ and fold under. Slipstitch the folds together.

Finally, topstitch ¼″ from the seamlines and slipstitched edges. Where appropriate, topstitch on both sides of the seamlines to create a slot effect (Figure 9).

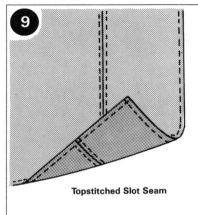

Topstitched Slot Seam

• You can adapt the slot seam method to apply a standing collar to a garment. Trim the collar seam allowance at the neckline edge to ⅜″. Separate the fabric faces for about 1″ at this edge.

Fold under each seam allowance, clipping the seam allowance if necessary when the neckline is curved (Figure 10). Finish the outer edges of the collar as described for slot seam construction, above.

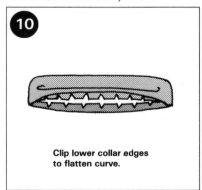

Clip lower collar edges to flatten curve.

Staystitch the garment neckline, trim the seam allowance to ¼″ and clip if necessary.

Slip the garment neckline into the "pocket" formed by the separated seam allowances of the collar. Edgestitch the collar to the garment (Figure 11), or use a felling stitch by hand.

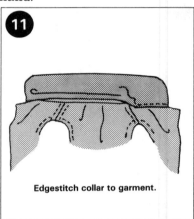

Edgestitch collar to garment.

• Strap seam construction, another option for separable double-faced fabrics, can be used throughout a garment or as a problem-solver where you can't decide what else to do. For example, a strap seam may be the only practical way to conceal the neckline seam allowance on a traditional collar.

To make a strap seam, sew a plain ⅝″ seam through all layers. If the seam is bulky, separate the fabric faces within the seam allowance to trim and grade them.

Split some leftover double-faced fabric into single-face fabric. Cut 1⅞″ wide bias strips from one of the faces. Turn under the bias strip edges ¼″; press.

Center the bias strip over the exposed seam allowances.

Edgestitch in place by machine (Figure 12), or slipstitch by hand.

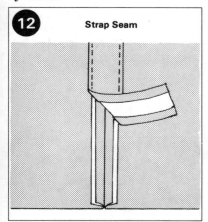

12 Strap Seam

• Adapt the strap seam method for use on inseparable double-faced fabrics by using strips of synthetic suede, flat braid or contrast bias binding for the seam-allowance-covering straps.

• Flat-felled seams are suitable for light- to medium weight double-faced fabrics with separable faces. Cut the garment sections with ¾″ to 1″ seam allowances for easier trimming and folding. If working with a quilted fabric, remove the batting from the seam allowances to reduce bulk.

• An edge-finishing option that's compatible with any type of seam technique is binding with foldover braid, self-fabric bias strips or purchased double-fold bias tape. Before binding the edges, trim off any hem or seam allowances.

• Another edge finish for fabrics with separable faces uses one face as a contrast binding for the other. Begin by staystitching on the seam line. Separate the fabric faces with-

in the seam allowance. Fold under the raw edge of one face ¼″; trim the seam allowance of the other face close to the staystitching (Figure 13). Lap

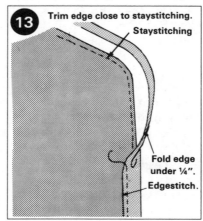

13 Trim edge close to staystitching.
Staystitching
Fold edge under ¼″.
Edgestitch.

the folded seam allowance over the trimmed edge and edgestitch or slipstitch in place.

• The quickest way to apply patch pockets on any type of double-faced fabric is to serge around the outer pocket edges, then topstitch in place (Figure 14).

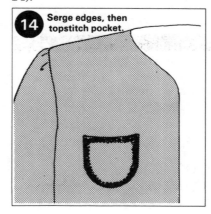

14 Serge edges, then topstitch pocket.

• To make a lined and interfaced patch pocket, first split the cut-out pocket into two fabric faces. Interface and line one of the single-face fabric layers to make a less bulky pocket.

✂ FUR

Because you sew, you can satisfy the yearning to wrap yourself in a beautiful, blatantly luxurious fur — without paying an extravagant price or worrying about environmental issues. Ingenious textile designers have created synthetic look-alikes you'd never guess came from a knitting machine. There's also the vintage fur option. Restyling or recycling a previously-owned fur from a thrift shop, flea market or estate sale can be a very rewarding way to fulfill your fashion dream.

If sewing either type of fur means venturing into unknown territory for you, be assured the techniques may differ from everyday sewing, but they don't qualify as difficult. Fur's body minimizes the need for inner construction and the deep nap camouflages any less-than-perfect details. To gain experience, why not start small by adding fur trim to a jacket, then graduate to a full-fledged fur coat?

CHOOSING FAKE FURS

There are four key qualities to think about before buying a fake fur: hand, color, sculpting and color patterning.

Hand counts because you'll enjoy a fake much more if it feels like the real thing. Brush your hand back and forth along the lengthwise nap, then crosswise. Blow into the fur to see how it responds, and pinch a fold to see whether the backing shows. A convincing fake fur has a sheen similar to naturally oiled hair and moves easily when stroked or blown into. Reject any dry, coarse, thin, stiff or bristly selections.

Exact color is a matter of taste, but be fussy about the richness and consistency. Individual yarns of the fur should vary somewhat within a single square inch. There should be several colors blending together like they do in nature.

A sculptured rather than one-length pile is very desirable. Grooves sculpted into fake furs imitate the look of real pelts which are pieced together in strips. Longer guard hairs also indicate a quality fake.

If you prefer a particular animal type, use a photo of the animal or its fur to compare to the color patterning in fake fur fabric. The best pretenders imitate an animal's natural coloring and molting pattern.

CHOOSING VINTAGE FURS

Scout sources of vintage furs with a sharp eye, for what you see on the outside may not be what you get on the inside. Do check the outside for defects or deterioration, especially at shoulders, underarms and seat, but what really counts can be seen only from the inside.

Loosen the lining for a good view. See if the skins are soft and supple. A poor buy might be cracked or have dry, brittle hair that's ready to fall out. An occasional bald spot may not be a problem if there's enough intact fur so you can work around it.

If the fur requires cleaning, get an estimate before you buy; it could cost more than the fur is worth.

Also, consider how easy your prospective purchase will be to sew. Short-haired furs such as Persian lamb, mink, squirrel or muskrat are easy to recycle since they have soft skins and do not shed. Beaver and raccoon are among the most durable furs. Sheepskin is relatively easy to sew and can be a real bargain. Rabbit and fox are very perishable furs that can be difficult to recycle.

GENERAL TIPS

• You may find a pattern designed specifically for fake fur. Consider using it for vintage fur, too.

Otherwise, adapt a simple, loose-fitting pattern, buying it one size larger to compensate for the added fabric bulk. Allow 2″ for a hem on fake fur and 1¼″ for a hem on vintage fur. Omit small pattern details such as flaps or epaulets.

• Cut facings from lining fabric to reduce bulk. Or, copy the furrier's technique of using leather or suede for facings.

• Study the fur's color patterning before layout. Determine which portion of the fur's patterning will look best at centers front and back, and if any stripes or mottled areas should be matched at the seams.

• In general, layout the pattern so the hair or nap runs down (Figure 1). However,

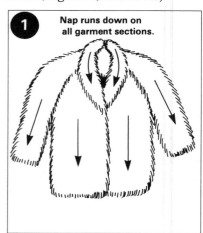

1 Nap runs down on all garment sections.

designers sometimes run the nap up, diagonally or in chevrons for creative effects and you can, too.

• Divide a collar pattern into right and left halves by adding a center back seam (Figure 2).

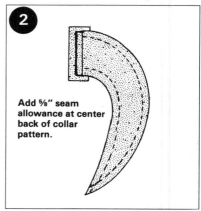

2 Add ⅝″ seam allowance at center back of collar pattern.

Then the nap will run in the same direction on both sides of the finished collar.

• Lay out and cut on a single layer of fabric, working on the backing or skin side. Hold the pattern in place temporarily with weights. Use chalk or a felt-tip pen to trace the pattern outline.

• To cut, use a single-edge razor blade and slice through the back only. As you slice through the back, hold the fabric up and pull it away from you (Figure 3).

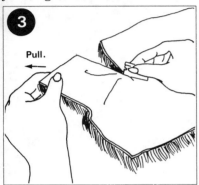

• Transfer all pattern markings with chalk or felt-tip pen.

• Many furs need no interfacing, but you can use hair canvas or a medium- to heavyweight nonwoven sew-in interfacing to support areas such as collars and facings if necessary.

• Stitch in the direction of the nap.

• After stitching seams, use a T-pin or blunt tapestry needle to free hairs caught in the stitching (Figure 4).

Free pile caught in seams.

• Press fur with your fingers or use the edge of a point presser to flatten a seam or edge. Do not press fake or vintage fur with an iron.

• Button loops can be made from braid, elastic cord or ½"-wide strips of synthetic suede which have been folded in half and edgestitched (Figure 5).

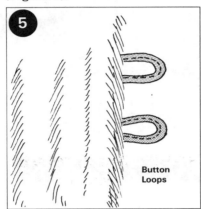

Button Loops

• For a luxurious look, choose satin lining and underline it with outing flannel. Line pockets with plush velvet or velveteen. As a finishing touch, monogram the lining with your initials.

SEWING TECHNIQUES FOR VINTAGE FUR

• To cut a new garment from a vintage fur, begin by taking the original garment partially apart. Remove the old lining. From the skin side, cut apart the sleeves using a single-edge razor blade. Cut open the shoulder seams and lay the coat body out flat.

Tape the new garment pattern pieces together with side seam allowances lapped on the seamline. For easier cutting, trace the other half of the pattern so you have a complete pattern. Lay the pattern on the skin side of the vintage fur for cutting (Figure 6).

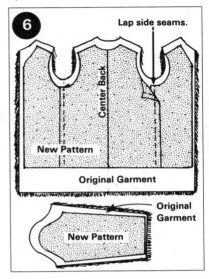

Lap side seams.

Center Back

New Pattern

Original Garment

Original Garment

New Pattern

• Fill in holes or worn spots with matching fur. Cut the damaged area into a diamond shape and use it to cut an identical patch of matching fur. Baste the patch with masking tape, then whipstitch the seam by hand (Figure 7).

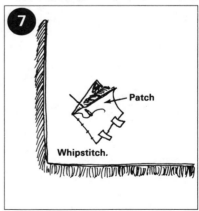

Patch

Whipstitch.

• Reinforce areas of stress such as shoulder seams and across the back with ½" twill tape. Whipstitch it by hand to the skin (Figure 8).

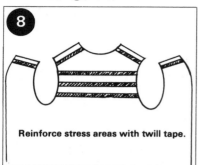

Reinforce stress areas with twill tape.

• Furriers use a special sewing machine to make a practically invisible seam which looks like ladder stitches. For a similar effect, flatlock the seams on a serger.

Or, use a wide, closely-spaced zigzag stitch; loosen the upper tension and reduce the pressure on the presser foot. Use a size 70/10 needle for lightweight furs or a size 100/16 for heavier pelts. Trim the seam allowances to ¼″ and stitch so the needle catches the skins on one swing and sews off the edge with the other swing (Figure 9). If the

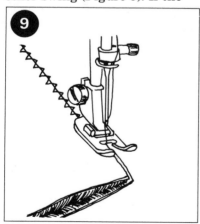

fur stretches or the skin tears, reinforce the seams with twill tape or use a longer stitch.

• Cushion fur hems to avoid wear at the hem fold. Begin by stitching ¾″ twill tape to the cut hem edge (Figure 10). Fold

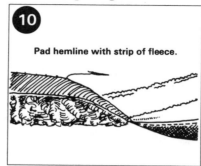

Pad hemline with strip of fleece.

the hem no deeper than 1¼″; place a narrow strip of polyester fleece inside the crease before whipstitching the hem in place.

SEWING TECHNIQUES FOR FAKE FUR

• The furrier's techniques given above can also be used when sewing fake furs. Because of the knitted backing, a fake fur will not ravel, even when you trim it closely for a narrow seam.

• Zigzag or flatlock the seams as for vintage fur, or sew a plain seam with the pile hairs clipped off for ½″ of the seam allowance (Figure 11).

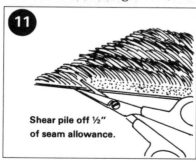

Shear pile off ½″ of seam allowance.

Use a long stitch, 7 to 10 per inch, and loosen the tension if necessary.

• For a firmer, no-sag edge, stabilize a hem midway through its depth by folding the hem allowance back on itself and sewing the hem to the backing with a catchstitch (Figure 12). Then, catchstitch the hem edge in the same way.

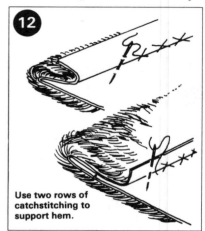

Use two rows of catchstitching to support hem.

• To make a patch pocket on fake fur, use a combination of machine stitching for strength and hand stitching for a good appearance.

To begin, trim the pocket pattern so there is a ⅝″ seam allowance around all edges (Figure 13). Cut once from

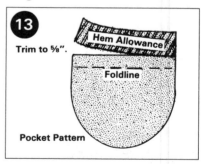

Trim to ⅝″.

Hem Allowance

Foldline

Pocket Pattern

lining fabric. Trim the seam allowance off the pocket pattern and cut once from fake fur.

Right sides together, sew the lining and pocket along the top edge (Figure 14). Cut the

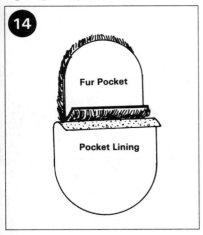

Fur Pocket

Pocket Lining

pile out of the seam allowance to reduce bulk.

With the right side of the pocket lining facing the right side of the garment, stitch the lining to the garment (Figure 15). Finger-press the seam allowance toward the pocket.

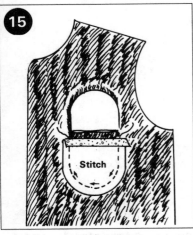

Stitch

Flip the pocket down, over the pocket lining, and whipstitch the edges to the garment (Figure 16). Free any pile caught in the stitches for a neat, practically invisible application.

Lining

GABARDINE

Looking for a long-wearing, fashionable fabric to stretch your wardrobe through several seasons? Gabardine fits the bill, lending its durable good looks to a variety of styles.

Available in several weights, gabardine has enough refinement for business suits and uniforms, yet is rugged enough for sportswear. Although wool or polyester are the most common fibers used for gabardine, this fabric can be made from others such as cotton, silk and natural/synthetic blends.

Gabardine's durability comes from its tight twill weave which has a greater number of yarns in the lengthwise direction. On the fabric surface you can see fine, diagonal ribs spaced closely together; on some gabardines these diagonals are more prominent than on others.

SEWING TIPS

• Although the surface texture has diagonal ribs, gabardine is smooth enough to use for patterns with distinctive details such as tucks, topstitching, piping, decorative seams and welt pockets. However, avoid bias cuts since the twill weave shades the fabric color in a crazy-quilt manner.

• Use a "with nap" pattern layout for uniform color shading in all garment sections.

• Pressing is probably the single most challenging facet of sewing gabardine. Press with patience.

It is better to press lightly twice than to press once with a heavy hand. Pressing with too much heat or pressure makes the fabric surface look worn and shiny.

• Press on the wrong side of the fabric whenever possible. Use a press cloth when pressing on the right side.

• When sewing wool gabardine, one of the best press cloths you can use is a scrap of self-fabric.

• Your fingers can be a useful tool when pressing

gabardine. Finger-press a seam first, to get you started in the right direction, then steam-press.

• You may find sew-in interfacings more successful than fusible interfacings. Fusible interfacings may not bond well to gabardine's tight weave, or you may need to use so much heat, steam and pressure to fuse that the fabric looks distressed afterwards. Test-fuse an interfacing sample first to check. Be sure to see if the interfacing edge shows through to the fabric's right side.

• Raw edges will ravel, so serge them or bind them with sheer bias tape.

• Machine or bound buttonholes are easy to sew on gabardine. Bound buttonholes look especially elegant, but be careful not to overpress as you sew them.

FUZZ BUSTERS

Before starting a new sewing project, I always clean my ironing board and cutting board with a lint remover. This picks up any hard-to-wipe-off fuzz from previous garments that my new project might pick up.

D. Schafer,
Renton, WA

✂ HANDWOVEN FABRICS

Although you may have to cope with an unusually narrow fabric width or find a way to cut around the occasional flaw, you'll find handwoven fabrics inspire creative sewing. Many of these fabrics are equally attractive on both sides, and all can be used to create a wide variety of stunning fashions.

TYPES OF HANDWOVENS

From time to time, handwoven fabrics are available in fabric stores, and if you like to fabric shop when you travel, you may have some handwovens among your souvenirs. The most common fabric types available include Harris tweed, Guatemalan cotton, Thai cloth, ikats and novelty weaves.

Harris tweed is a firmly-woven woolen from the Isle of Harris and Lewis off the west coast of Scotland. The yarns are spun in the island towns, then distributed to weavers in the countryside. The cloth has a finished width of 27″ to 29″, since the size of the loom is limited to the width that fits through a home's door frame. A fabric that wears well, Harris tweed is perhaps the easiest handwoven to sew and tailor.

Making Guatemalan cotton is a cottage industry in the highland villages of Guatemala. Many of these fabrics have Spanish-style stripes or ethnic motifs, and some are woven from tie-dyed jaspe

yarns. There's a full range of patterns, textures and weights available; the fabrics are 36″ wide, firmly-woven and easy to sew.

Thai cloth is handwoven cotton from northern Thailand. Available in solids and stripes, it's 32″ to 36″ wide, and another ethnic fabric that's firmly-woven and easy to sew.

The ancient technique for weaving ikats is still used in Japan, Indonesia and Guatemala. On the simplest of looms, the weaver creates a variety of patterns by resist-dyeing the yarn beforehand. Woven from silk, cotton or bast fibers by tradition, ikats vary in width from 14″ to 36″, are firmly-woven and easy to sew.

Novelty handwovens come in great variety, ranging from silk or wool suitings to one-of-a-kind fabrics with strips of leather, ribbon or bias fabric included in the weave. Frequently they are loosely woven, not particularly stable and fray easily. Some experimental fabrics created by textile artisans may have bold patterns you can't match because there is no regular repeat. Although these maverick fabrics can be a challenge to sew, the results can be so spectacular the time and effort spent is worthwhile.

SEWING TIPS

• When estimating yardage, allow extra for shrinkage, matching or balancing motifs in creative layouts and cutting around flaws. Take into account one pattern piece at a time may fit on very narrow fabric widths, and you may have to cut out on a single layer of fabric rather than folding the fabric lengthwise.

• Purchase all the fabric for a garment from one dye lot, as colors may not be consistent.

• In general, dry cleaning is the safest care method for handwovens; to preshrink the fabric, ask the dry cleaner to steam the fabric three times.

• Most cotton fabrics can be washed, although dark colors might run. To set vegetable dyes in Guatemalan cotton, Thai cloth or ikats, mix ¼ cup of white vinegar with one gallon of water; add the fabric to soak for half an hour. Rinse well, and hang the fabric to dry.

• Choose a pattern with simple lines to showcase the fabric's beauty. Avoid closely-fitted styles which can stress the fabric.

• If you have a limited amount of fabric, combine it with a compatible fabric, use it as a trim or make it into a garment which can be worn with several companion pieces.

• Attractive handwoven selvages can be cut apart from the fabric and used as handsome trims.

• Use a "with nap" layout for textured fabrics, those with directional designs and those with non-repeating motifs.

• Consider underlining the garment sections to add body or stability to the handwoven fabric. For a soft look, underline with organza, handkerchief linen or batiste. For more crispness, underline with

a fusible knit interfacing; fuse the interfacing right to the raw edge of each garment section.

• To control fraying, serge the raw edges, bind them with sheer bias tape, coat them with seam sealant or overcast them with a three-step zigzag stitch.

• Seam options include the topstitched, French, mock French, welt and flat-felled techniques.

• Alternatives to the standard hem include topstitching, binding or fringing the edge.

• When topstitching textured fabrics, a fine zigzag stitch often looks straighter than a standard straight stitch.

• Button loops, eyelets for lacing, toggles and snaps are some optional closures. If making buttonholes, stabilize the area with a patch of fusible interfacing on the wrong side.

CUTTING COOL

For an inexpensive but ever-so-handy cutting table, purchase a hollow-core door and add wrought iron support legs. For added smoothness, cover with plastic laminate. The table can be up to 1 yard wide and about 2½ yards long, so most fabrics will fit on it comfortably. It's also light enough to move next to the sewing machine if you need extra support for the volume of fabric in a project such as a wedding gown.

D. Domokur,
Akron, OH

✂ KNITS

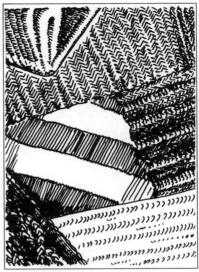

Perennially popular because they're comfortable, shed wrinkles and travel well, knits promise easy sewing, too. You'll find an abundant selection of knit fabrics any time of year, keyed to current fashion trends and ranging from stable double knits for structured fashions to light-weight jerseys for soft, drapable styles. Sweater knits make jacket sewing simple, and stretchy spandex blends make fitting and wearing knit activewear a breeze.

TYPES OF KNITS

Jersey leads the pack as a fluid, lightweight knit for bodysuits, easy-fitting pull-on pants, flared or sarong-wrap skirts and dresses with shirred or draped details. You can recognize jersey by comparing the right and wrong sides of the fabric; the right side is smoother and has vertical ribs while the wrong side has a more pronounced texture of crosswise stitches (Figure 1).

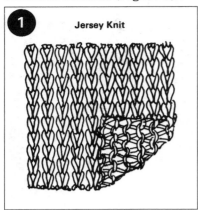

1 Jersey Knit

Most jerseys are fairly stable with minimal lengthwise stretch and just enough crosswise give for comfort.

Ribbed knit is sold precut or by the inch in tubular yardage as a trim for necklines, wrists and other garment edges, as well as by the yard in wider fabrications for body-hugging tops, skirts and pants. This very elastic fabric looks the same on the right and wrong sides (Figure 2).

2 Ribbed Knit

Double knits have a smooth surface on both the right and wrong sides (Figure 3); they're notable for their stability and excellent shape retention. You

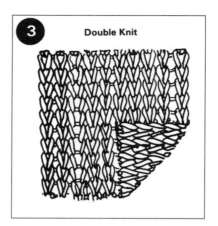

3 Double Knit

can often substitute a double knit for a woven fabric since it suits fashions with structural seaming, topstitched details and a dart-fitted silhouette.

Jacquard double knits have decorative surfaces with designs such as elaborate floral, paisley or geometric motifs knitted in. The design appears on the right side of the fabric, while the wrong side looks like a standard double knit (Figure 4).

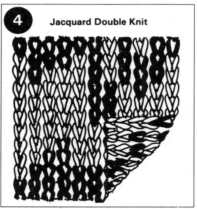

4 Jacquard Double Knit

Sweater knits look like hand knits, made as they are from bulky or novelty yarns. Add ribbing to trim the edges, and you can sew a sweater that looks like expensive ready-to-wear. Many sweater knits are

made on a raschel machine, so they resemble crocheted fabric (Figure 5) and have little or no stretch.

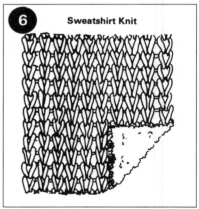

5 Raschel Sweater Knit

Interlock knits are lightweight and drapable like jerseys, but have the smooth appearance of double knits. The smooth texture makes interlocks well-suited for printing.

Sweatshirt fleece is a single knit with one brushed face (Figure 6). It's a relatively

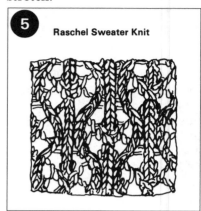

6 Sweatshirt Knit

stable knit most often used for sweatshirts and sweatpants, but also suitable for soft dresses and unlined jackets.

Two-way stretch knits with spandex fibers have notable stretch and recovery both lengthwise and crosswise. You'll find these knits available in several fiber recipes for sewing swimwear, activewear, leotards and other very close-fitting garments.

GENERAL TIPS

• Some patterns are specifically for sewing knits which have a certain degree of stretch. Since the amount of stretch varies from one knit to another, check the stretch by using the gauge printed on the pattern envelope.

• Use a "with nap" layout for uniform color shading in the finished garment.

• Lay out and cut on a surface large enough so the excess fabric won't hang over the edge and stretch out of shape.

• Interlock knits can run from one edge, something you'll need to know for pattern layout. Pull each crosswise edge to determine which edge tends to run; lay out all pattern pieces with the bottom edges headed toward this edge (Figure 7).

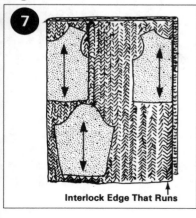

Interlock Edge That Runs

• In general, seam options for knits include plain seams, serged seams and double-stitched seams.

• Stabilize seams you don't want to stretch out of shape such as shoulder seams and front opening seams by including a strip of seam binding or twill tape in the stitching (Figure 8). Do not stretch the fabric as you stitch.

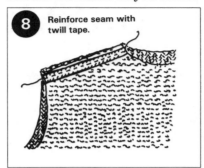

8 Reinforce seam with twill tape.

• Stabilize the buttonhole area by stitching over an oval of lightweight interfacing (Figure 9).

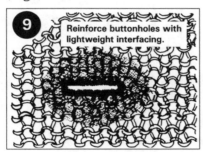

9 Reinforce buttonholes with lightweight interfacing.

RIBBED TRIM TECHNIQUES

• For good fit, ribbed trim should stretch 100 percent or more. Test by seeing if 4″ of fabric will stretch toward the 8″ mark on a yardstick or ruler. While the ribs will spread out as the fabric is stretched, the fabric should not look tortured or rippled to pass the 100-percent test.

• Do not preshrink ribbed knits; after the garment is sewn, the seams will anchor the fabric so it will not be affected by dry cleaning or laundering.

• To fit ribbing trim, pin together the cutout section and try it on. Make sure neck ribbing slips over the head and wrist ribbing allows the hand to fit through. Adjust the length of the trim if necessary before you sew.

• It's easier to apply ribbing trim while the garment is flat, so leave one side, shoulder, leg or underarm seam open. Divide the garment edge and the ribbing trim into fourths and mark the divisions with pins.

With the ribbing on top, serge or stitch the ribbing to the garment; stretch the ribbing to fit the garment edge and match the pin markers as you sew (Figure 10).

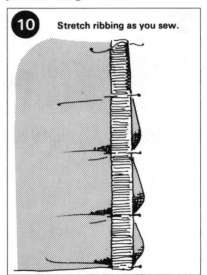

10 Stretch ribbing as you sew.

Serge or stitch the garment seam previously left open, beginning at the folded edge of the ribbing (Figure 11).

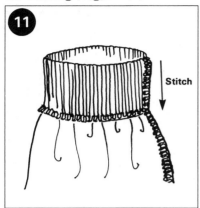

• To help stretchy seams keep their shape, use elastic thread to stay serged seams. Thread the elastic through the cording hole in the front of the presser foot, then under the foot, leaving a 2″ tail. Grasp the tail firmly but gently with your left hand to start serging (Figure 12); do not stretch the

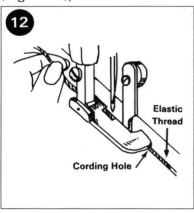

elastic while stitching or the finished seam will draw up.

If the presser foot has no cording hole, position the elastic under the back of the foot, then over the front of the foot so it's caught in the chain

of stitches but not cut by the serger knife (Figure 13).

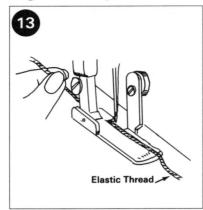

• Press with extreme care as heat and steam can distort the ribs. Try finger-pressing, or gently steam the fabric without touching it with the iron.

SWEATER KNIT TECHNIQUES

• Choose patterns with few seams or eliminate seams to simplify the sewing. Patterns with cut-on dolman or kimono sleeves make construction easy.

• On pullover styles, you can eliminate facings and hems and substitute ribbed trim.

• Serging is the best seam option for sweater knits. Set the serger for the widest, longest stitch, then test on scraps to fine-tune the adjustment. Insert a new needle, size 70/10 or 80/11, and check the knife blades for sharpness.

• Sweater knits tend to curl and frizz as they're trimmed by serger knives. Cut the garment sections with 1″ seam allowances so the knits can trim away ¾″ as you serge for smoother sewing.

• The thicker the knit, the more likely the seam will stretch and wave as you serge. Adjust the pressure foot pressure or utilize the serger's differential feed mechanism to remedy.

If this doesn't solve the problem completely, try easing the fabric in front of the presser foot as you sew (Figure 14).

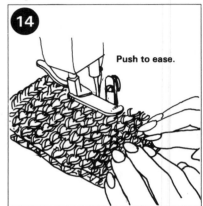

• Stabilize the extremely flexible seams sewn by 4/3- and 4/2-thread sergers by stitching over 1¼″-wide sheer bias tape. After serging, trim away the excess tape (Figure 15).

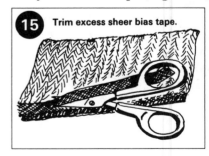

• When applying ribbed trim, do not stretch the sweater knit edge as you serge. Staystitch the sweater knit edge just beyond the serger knife cutting line so the staystitching will be trimmed away as you serge (Figure 16).

16 Trim staystitching as you join ribbing.

• An attractive edge finishing option is serging with decorative threads. Stabilize the garment edge before serging by fusing 1″ bias strips of lightweight interfacing on the wrong side.

• Or, serge over two strands of pearl cotton or crochet thread. After serging, adjust any excess fullness or stretching by drawing out or easing the encased threads (Figure 17). Anchor the

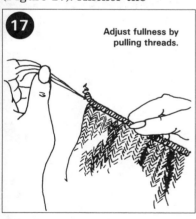

17 Adjust fullness by pulling threads.

threads by weaving through the serged stitches on the wrong side, tying a knot in the ends and tucking the tails into the stitches. Add a drop of seam sealant for security.

✂ LACE

Wouldn't it be wonderful to have a perfectly-fitted dress without any seam lines interrupting the fabric design? When sewing on most fabrics, this is wishful thinking; when sewing with lace, it's not only possible – it's relatively easy.

By using a variation of the lapped seam, lace garment sections can be joined inconspicuously no matter how intricately shaped the seams. Although time-consuming, this special method for working with lace is particularly appropriate for expensive laces such as Alencon and Chantilly, but you can also use it on other types of laces.

GENERAL TIPS

• Avoid buttonholes on lace. Instead, use thread loops and small buttons, or use hook fasteners.

• Cut facings from flesh-toned net, tulle or organza. Or, use precut sheer bias tape instead of a facing.

• An optional way to finish lace edges is to bind them with chiffon or satin bias strips.

• To add body to lace while retaining most of the sheer effect, underline the garment sections with flesh-toned net, tulle, chiffon or organza.

• To eliminate the sheer effect on all or selected portions of a lace garment, underline with satin, velvet, taffeta or lightweight lining fabric. Use a contrasting underlining color if desired.

• Insert zippers by hand.

• To press lace, place it right side down over a folded towel. Press lightly.

• Vintage lace may be less expensive than a similar new lace. If yardage is limited, combine several different laces for a designer look.

• Many lace curtains and tablecloths can be used to make beautiful garments.

LAYOUT & CUTTING TECHNIQUES

• To save time and avoid wasting lace, make a muslin test garment first to refine the fit. Remember darts and seams can be placed anywhere to improve the fit since they will be hidden in the finished garment.

• Once the fit is perfected on the test garment, mark all stitching lines. Carefully take apart the test garment, and press each section. Label the sections to indicate right and left sides. Use the test garment sections as the pattern for layout.

Or, duplicate the test garment sections on pattern tracing cloth, and use this pattern for layout. You can see through tracing cloth, a helpful feature when working with lace.

• To make lapped lace seams, cut a wide, irregular seam allowance on the overlapping side. Cut an even, narrow ¼″ seam allowance on the underlap (Figure 1). Mark the test

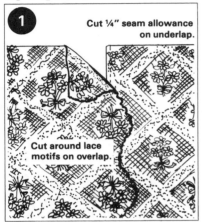

1 Cut ¼″ seam allowance on underlap.

Cut around lace motifs on overlap.

garment/pattern or tracing paper/pattern sections to indicate whether the seam allowances are overlapping or underlapping.

In general, lap seams at shoulders, sleeves, and sides toward the back of the garment (Figure 2). Lap

2 Lap shoulder, side and sleeve seams toward garment back. Lap waist seam toward hem.

horizontal seams such as waist seams toward the hem. Lap center front or back seams in either direction.

• With the lace right side up, spread the fabric out in a single layer. Most laces have a regular, repeating motif. Study the lace as if it were a print to decide how to handle the motifs during pattern layout.

• If the lace has a border on one or both lengthwise edges, you can use the border as a ready-made hem for a skirt or sleeves. Or, trim off the border for future use as an appliqué edging.

• Lay out the pattern on the lengthwise *or* crosswise grain of lace, giving you great flexibility in pattern positioning. However, motifs on adjacent garment sections should blend nicely. The motifs should look balanced on each side of the centers front and back, and horizontal motifs should be aligned to fall at the same level around the garment.

• As you pin pattern pieces to lace, leave a margin several inches wide in between to allow extra fabric for the special lace seams.

• With the pattern pinned to the lace, trace all the seamlines with thread (Figure 3).

3 Trace seamlines with thread.

• Cut out each pattern section, following the design motifs. On the overlapping seam allowances, cut around the design motifs, rather than through them – the cutting line will be quite crooked (Figure 4). Cut the underlapping seam allowances to ¼″.

4 Cut around lace motifs.

SEWING TECHNIQUES

• Match and pin the thread-traced seamlines of the cut lace sections, working with the fabric right side up and lapping the cut edges (Figure 5). Baste the garment together on the seamlines.

5 Lap at thread-traced seamlines.

Try on the garment to check the fit. It is easy to make alterations at this point, but very difficult later, after the seams have been sewn.

• To sew the seam, use an appliqué technique. Whip-stitch around the overlapping lace motifs by hand, or zigzag stitch by machine, using a medium-wide stitch (Figure 6). Remove the basting stitches.

6 Stitch seam around motifs.

• Trim the excess seam allowance on the underlapping fabric layer close to the stitches. For a really close trim, use 5" trimming scissors and the "palms-up" technique (Figure 7). Hold the scissors in

7 Trim underlapping fabric.

your right hand with the thumb in the larger handle, and hold the garment in your left hand with the wrong side up and the raw edge of the seam toward your body. Keep both palms up. Position the blade of the scissors under the seam allowance to trim close to the stitches.

• Sew darts using a similar lapped technique. Mark the dart stitching lines with thread tracing, then clip around lace motifs between the stitching lines (Figure 8).

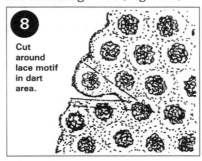

8 Cut around lace motif in dart area.

Lap the edges on the thread-traced stitching lines, baste, and appliqué by hand or machine.

READY REFERENCE

To keep yardages and notions at my fingertips as I shop for fabric, I photocopy the front and back of each of my pattern envelopes. I file the copies in a notebook that I take to the fabric store for quick and convenient reference while shopping.

D. H. Stringer,
Jackson, MS

✂ LEATHER

As fashionable as they may seem, leather garments are anything but new. In fact, leather followed the fig leaf, and archaeologists have turned up leather items dating back to the earliest caveman.

Today you can construct almost anything in leather from coats and suits to blouses, T-shirts and camisoles. This is due in part to the fact that many leathers are thinner, softer, more supple and more affordable than ever before. They sew and drape similar to the more familiar fabrics, and in some cases have fashionable finishes. Leather can be buffed, polished, foiled, embossed, beaded, printed, perforated, painted, fringed or embroidered for interest.

LEATHER TERMS

• Chamois is the underneath layer of sheepskin. Tanned and sueded, it's soft, pliable and relatively inexpensive.

• Crocking refers to color rubbing off leather. Suede leathers are more likely to crock than smooth leathers.

• Embossing involves using heat and pressure with a metal plate or roller to etch, engrave or electroplate the leather surface with a permanent texture. Designs include animal skin grains, corduroy and seersucker effects as well as abstract motifs.

• Full grain cowhide is the outer side of leather from which the hair is removed.

• Goatskin is a strong but soft leather. Cabretta is a lightweight goatskin with a fine grain and rich finish.

- Hides are the skins of larger animals such as cows, steers, horses, buffalo and deer.
- Naked leather has an unglazed finish which is tanned to look natural, without a sheen.
- Pelt is another term for hide or skin.
- Pigskin is leather with a grain texture and distinctive clusters of three marks where bristles grew. Pigskin may be buffed for a matte finish or polished for a shiny effect.
- Plonge is leather from Japanese cows fed on a beer diet. Moderately priced, plonge has few imperfections but drapes and feels like expensive, luxury leathers.
- Shearlings are sheep or lamb skins tanned with the wool intact.
- Silk suede is sueded leather that weighs only ¾ ounce per square foot and feels like silk.
- Skins are taken from smaller animals such as calves, sheep, goats, pigs and snakes.
- Splits are thin layers of thick skins. The top layer is called natural grain, while the remaining layers are simply called splits.
- Suede is the inner side of a skin which is tanned and napped. The nap always runs from the animal's neck to its tail.
- Tanning is the chemical process used to preserve skins.

GENERAL TIPS

- Find patterns with little or no easing. Kimono and raglan sleeves are easier to sew than leather set-in sleeves. Styles with seams for fitting are easier to stitch and shape smoothly than those with darts.
- Select the right pattern for the weight and suppleness of the leather. Think about the skins as if they were more traditional fabrics. How do they feel? Are they soft enough for ruffles or gathers? Do they have enough body for a jacket design?
- Select a pattern appropriate for your sewing skills. Even though leather is quite easy to sew — you don't need to worry about fraying or seam finishes — this is not the best time to make your first tailored jacket.
- Never underestimate the advantages of selecting a pattern you've used before. Among the important pluses are you've already solved the fitting problems and practiced the necessary sewing skills.
- Choose a style of leather that suits you. Maybe you'd rather make an unusual blouse or vest from one or two expensive skins than a classic jacket from several moderately-priced skins. You might prefer a casual garment to a dressy garment. Plan a look you'll love wearing.
- Leather is measured in square feet and sold by the skin or hide. Skins are small pieces measuring from 5 to 24 square feet; hides are larger, measuring about 40 to 50 square feet. A few leathers, such as python, are sold by the meter; a meter is about 39". Some skins are almost rectangles, while others have definite animal shapes.
- The cost of a leather project depends upon the number of skins required and the price per square foot. A jacket might require several skins, while a simple pullover shirt or a vest can sometimes be cut from a single skin.
- To determine how much leather you'll need, multiply the fabric requirement by the number of square feet in a yard of fabric, then add 15 percent extra to allow for flaws and the irregular shapes of skins. Here's the square footage in 1 yard of the common fabric widths:
  36" width = 9 square feet
  45" width = 11 square feet
  54" width = 13½ square feet
  60" width = 15 square feet
For example, if the pattern calls for 1½ yards of 60" fabric, you'll need 22½ square feet of leather plus 3⅜ square feet extra (15 percent of 22½ square feet), or a total of 25⅝ square feet. If the skins contain 10 to 14 square feet, you'll need two or three skins to sew the garment.
- The most accurate way to determine how much leather to buy is to take the pattern pieces to the store and actually fit them onto the skins.
- If ordering leather by mail, the catalog may include the weight of one square foot of leather. Leather weighing 1 to 1½ ounces is supple, light-weight and drapable. Leather weighing 2½ to 3 ounces is thicker and most suitable for outerwear.
- Store uncut skins or large scraps on a tube to prevent creasing.

• Always test pressing techniques on leather scraps. You may not need to use an iron; try finger-pressing, or tap gently with a mallet or tailor's clapper.

If you decide to use an iron, set it on a low temperature and use no steam; press from the wrong side, using a press cloth or brown paper to protect the leather. To avoid stretching leather, don't slide the iron.

• Steam should not be used on most leathers because it shrinks them.

• Wrinkles usually hang out of leather.

• Leather stretches and needs interfacing along most edges to maintain its shape. Select an interfacing slightly lighter in weight than you would choose for a woven fabric of similar weight.

• Non-woven interfacings are often used in ready-to-wear leather garments. Some fusible interfacings work well on leather, but be sure to test the fusing results on scraps first.

• Linings help preserve the shape of leather garments, reduce clinging and prevent leather colors from staining your skin and other garments. Select a quality lining with the same care requirements as the leather; if the leather is washable, be sure the lining is, too.

• Machine embroidery, cutwork, painting, stenciling, appliqué and patchwork can be used to accent leather garments.

LAYOUT & CUTTING TECHNIQUES

• A test garment is essential. It allows you to perfect the fit and decide if and where to add seams so the pattern pieces fit well on the skins. It also gives you a complete pattern with right and left sides to use for layout and cutting.

Use a non-woven interfacing to simulate leather's body in the test garment. After you've completed all the pattern and fitting adjustments, remove the stitches and press the individual sections for layout use.

• If you are sewing a medium weight leather, reduce the ease in a set-in sleeve pattern to no more than 1" ease.

To remove excess ease, fold a small tuck just above the circle pattern markings on the sleeve cap (Figure 1). Since a

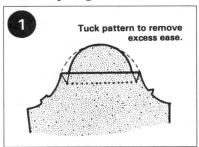

Tuck pattern to remove excess ease.

⅛" tuck will reduce the ease by ½", measure the depth of the tuck carefully. Correct the interrupted cutting line without making the sleeve cap narrower.

• Adjust the pattern to add ½" to 1" to the sleeve length and 1" to 2" to the pants leg length. Both sleeves and pants legs will shape themselves to the body and seem shorter when the leather garment is worn.

• Allow ⅝" to 2" for a hem, depending on the thickness of the leather. The thicker the leather, the deeper the hem should be.

• Substitute grosgrain ribbon for a waistband facing to save leather and to reduce bulk.

• Add seams to large pattern sections for more economical use of a leather skin. To add a seam, draw a line on the pattern to indicate the new seam. Mark one or two match points on this line. Cut the pattern apart, and add seam allowances to both edges (Figure 2).

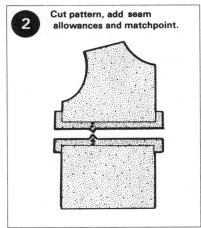

Cut pattern, add seam allowances and matchpoint.

• Be careful to position any added seams so they will look pleasing in the finished garment. For example, piece a bodice pattern above the bustline or a skirt pattern above the hipline for a yoked effect. Converting a center front or back fold to a seam is easy and adds a generally flattering vertical line.

• Few leather skins are long enough to cut pants without piecing. A traditional and attractive solution is adding a V-shaped seam just above the knee (Figure 3).

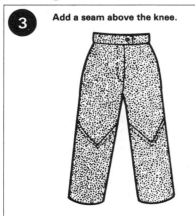

3 Add a seam above the knee.

• If using plain seams, cut out leather garments with a ½″ seam allowance for economy. A narrower seam allowance than usual is appropriate on leather since it doesn't fray, and seams can't be let out because needle marks are permanent.

• Lapped seams are often the best choice for medium and heavyweight leathers. If using lapped seams, cut out leather garments with a ½″ seam allowance on the underlapping side and no seam allowance on the overlap.

• Lay out the pattern on the right side of skins. Do not fold the skins or cut through a double thickness.

PATTERN PICKS

I hang the pieces of my frequently-used patterns over the bottom of wire hangers. To keep the pieces together, I pin the pattern envelope through all the layers. This saves wear and tear on the pattern pieces and my frustration trying to get every piece back into the envelope.

J. Villano, Eggersville, NY

• Arrange the pattern pieces according to a "with nap" layout, with all the pattern pieces aimed toward the animal's neck (Figure 4).

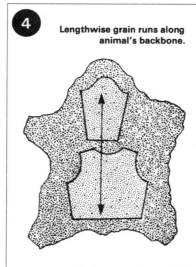

4 Lengthwise grain runs along animal's backbone.

Consider the animal's backbone as the lengthwise grainline. Position the pattern pieces to avoid any holes or flaws in the leather.

• Lay out the largest and most important pattern pieces first. Place them in the center of the skin where the leather is thickest, and cut the pattern fronts from the most attractive skin area; try to cut all the front or all the back pattern pieces from the same skin.

Place small pieces near the edges. Tip them off-grain if necessary.

• Use weights to hold the pattern pieces in place while you trace around the pattern sections with a soap sliver or dressmaker's chalk.

Avoid using pins, which leave permanent holes, and tape, which can lift off the color.

• Cut with sharp shears or a rotary cutter.

• Experiment stitching on leather scraps. Lighten the presser foot pressure as needed for thick leathers.

• To avoid splitting the leather, lengthen the stitch to 6 to 10 per inch. For thick leather, use an even longer stitch.

• A universal point needle in sizes 70/10 to 90/14 can be used on most leathers. However, if you encounter skipped stitches, change to a wedge-pointed leather needle in an appropriate size.

• Use a roller, Teflon® or even feed foot to eliminate shifting layers when machine stitching.

• Change to a straight stitch needle plate with a small opening, or alter the needle position so the leather comes into firm contact with the machine's feed dogs.

• Use quality silk, cotton/polyester or polyester thread.

• When sewing an inward curve, clip the seam allowance in several places before stitching (Figure 5).

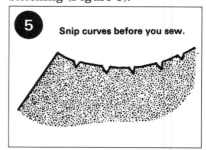

5 Snip curves before you sew.

• Prevent long lengthwise seams and any seams cut on the crosswise grain from stretching by including twill tape or a lightweight fabric selvage in the stitching.

• When stitching corners on collars, cuffs and other garment edges, round off the seamline for a smoother finish (Figure 6).

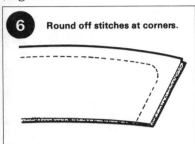

6 Round off stitches at corners.

• Stitch slowly and carefully. Needle holes cannot be removed from leather. Although they can be hidden in suede leather if you brush them with a toothbrush, unnecessary needle holes weaken the seam.

• Do not backstitch at the beginning and end of a seam. This weakens leather. Instead, tie the thread ends in a knot.

• To press a plain seam without using an iron, open the seam allowances with your fingers and tap them gently with a wooden mallet or tailor's clapper. Coat the wrong side of the seam allowances lightly with rubber cement, finger-press the seam allowances open, then tap gently again.

• Accent plain seams with topstitching 1/16" on each side of the seamline on dressy garments or 1/4" on each side on casual designs. The top-stitching not only decorates the seam, but also adds strength and holds the seam allowances flat. Practice topstitching on scraps; you may require a larger needle than the size used to sew the seam.

• To sew a lapped seam on leather, use rubber cement or glue stick to baste the overlapped edge. Topstitch 1/8" from the edge; on casual garments, topstitch again 3/8" from the edge.

• On heavier leathers, bevel the cut edges of seams and hems with a single-edge razor blade to reduce bulk (Figure 7).

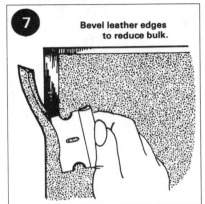

7 Bevel leather edges to reduce bulk.

To bevel, hold the blade at an angle to slice off a greater amount of thickness at the edge. Pound gently with a mallet or clapper to flatten the edge.

• Topstitch hems or glue them with rubber cement.

• If lining a leather garment, glue or topstitch the hem fold only. Leave the upper edge of the hem free so you can stitch it to the lining by machine (Figure 8).

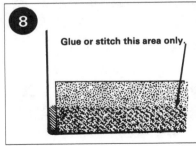

8 Glue or stitch this area only.

• Slashed buttonholes are an easy technique for lightweight leathers. Begin by marking the buttonhole length with a line. Stitch 1/8" above and below the line, pivoting at corners, to form a rectangle (Figure 9).

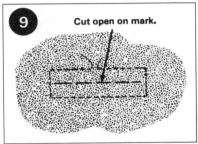

9 Cut open on mark.

Using a single-edged razor blade, cut the buttonhole open on the marked line.

• If making standard machine-stitched buttonholes, lengthen the stitch to avoid damaging the leather with too many needle holes.

• If making bound buttonholes, the window method, adapted to reduce bulk, is a good choice.

To begin, cut a window in the garment the length of the buttonhole and 3/8" wide (Figure 10). Since leather does

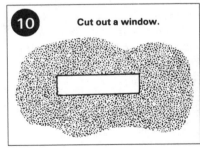

10 Cut out a window.

not ravel, you can use the cut edges as is for a non-bulky opening. However, an option on lightweight leathers is cutting through the center of the window and folding the raw edges to the wrong side (Figure 11); glue the raw edges in place with rubber cement.

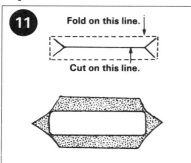

Fold on this line.
Cut on this line.

For each buttonhole, cut two welt strips, each 1″ longer than the window and 2″ wide (Figure 12). Fold each welt in

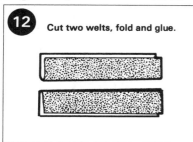

Cut two welts, fold and glue.

half along its length with wrong sides together; gently tap the folds with a mallet. Glue the welt layers together with rubber cement.

Center the welts behind the window so the welt folds meet. Glue them in place (Figure 13).

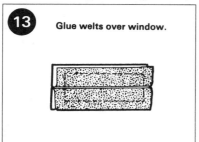

Glue welts over window.

Glue the garment facing in the buttonhole area.

Edgestitch around the buttonhole. On the facing side, cut a slit through the center (between the welts), then carefully cut out the window within the edgestitching (Figure 14). The finished

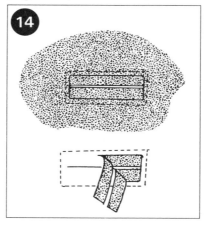

buttonhole looks the same on the outside and facing side of the garment.

✂ LINEN & RAMIE

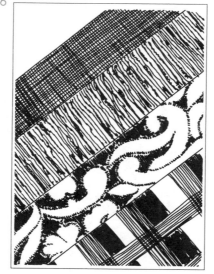

Whether crisp or soft, airy handkerchief weight or heavy suit weight, linen qualifies as a true fashion classic. It dates back to ancient Egypt, making it one of the world's oldest fibers. Made from the stem of the flax plant, it's strong and durable, with a natural luster and unique texture.

Ramie, also known as China grass, is a close cousin to linen and shares its ancient heritage. Important for centuries in China, ramie also was probably used to wrap mummies in ancient Egypt. Ramie is often blended with cotton or linen fibers for beautifully-textured fabrics.

You'll love sewing linen and ramie — or their synthetic look-alikes. They're always a wise fashion investment.

SEWING TIPS

• True linen and ramie fabrics naturally wrinkle. Some even say this is part of their fashion appeal. If you don't appreciate this quality, select a synthetic blend that has a similar look but is easy-care.

• Lining linen or ramie garments helps to reduce wrinkling.

• Avoid pattern designs with pressed pleats for ramie fabrics. The fiber is somewhat brittle and breaks from excessive folding and pressing.

• Preshrink linen and ramie fabrics.

• It's no accident the highest setting on an iron is labeled "linen," for a hot iron presses linen best. This is equally true for ramie.

When pressing either type of fiber, use plenty of steam or a damp press cloth. Spray starch is particularly useful when pressing handkerchief linen.

• Lightweight handkerchief linen works well cut on the bias for a camisole or soft blouse trimmed with lace or embroidery.

• Medium weight fusible interfacing works well on most linen and linen-look fabrics. An extra layer of lightweight interfacing may be needed in the lapel and upper collar of a tailored jacket.

• Interface the hem of a jacket for a crisper, longer-wearing edge. Cut the interfacing on the bias so the hem will lay smoothly around the body; cut the interfacing ¼" narrower than the hem allowance. Fuse the interfacing to the hem allowance (Figure 1).

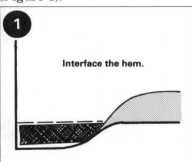

• To avoid skipped stitches, use a sharp point needle when sewing on linen and ramie.

• Linen, ramie and linen-look fabrics ravel, so serge raw edges, zigzag them or bind them.

• Linen garments will wear better and keep their new look longer if you dry clean them, although some linen fabrics are washable.

• Don't dry linen garments until they're bone-dry. They will be very difficult to press. Instead, press them while they're slightly damp.

✂ MARABOU FEATHERS

Marabou feathers make a stunning finishing touch for evening, whether you use them to decorate a gown or as an elegant wrap. Associated as they are with glamour and luxury, marabou feathers will make you look like a million dollars for far less.

Marabou feathers usually come firmly anchored to a cording in 2-yard lengths. The price varies according to the quality and thickness of the feathers. White or black feathers are always right for evening, but you can find marabou feathers in many different colors.

HOW TO MAKE A STOLE

To make a marabou stole, you will need five 2-yard lengths of feathers and 1⅜ yards of lightweight 36"- or 45"-wide fabric such as lining fabric, challis, jersey, silk faille or crepe-back satin.

Cut two 24" x 36" fabric rectangles crosswise. Right sides together, stitch the 24" ends together in a ½" seam to create one long strip. Press the seam open (Figure 1).

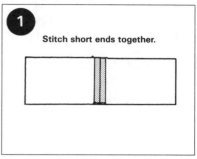

With right sides together, fold the strip in half along the long edges. Stitch the ends and long edges together in a ½" seam, leaving a 6" opening in the center of the long edge for turning (Figure 2).

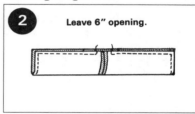

Turn the stole right side out and press. Turn in the raw edges and edgestitch the opening closed (Figure 3); you

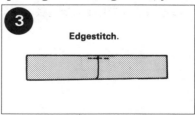

can do this by machine since the feathers will hide the stitches.

Sew the feathers in place by hand, whipstitching over the cord without catching the feathers in the stitches (Figure 4).

Sew feathers in place.

✂ OUTERWEAR FABRICS

Thanks to textile engineers, there's a whole world of high-performance fabrics designed to act as your first defense against the elements. This group of specialty textiles combines fashion with function, enabling you to be active and comfortable at the same time — even if it's windy, cold, snowing or raining.

TYPES OF OUTERWEAR FABRICS

• The most common outerwear fiber is nylon. In its various forms, it's usually very strong and easy-care.

Among the nylon fabrics you might use for shell garments are textured nylon impregnated with an acrylic coating which is breathable and highly water-repellent; fabrics with a skin-like coating to make them waterproof yet breathable and very durable; nylon which feels like cotton, yet resists wind and repels water; and breathable nylon which has a matte finish, is durable, water-repellent and wind-resistant. A tightly woven polyester/nylon blend is waterproof yet breathable for outerwear shells.

For stuff sacks, duffle bags and other accessories, you might select high-count, waterproof nylon taffeta with a urethane coating on the wrong side or heavy-duty, twill-weave, rubber-coated nylon fabric which is waterproof and abrasion-resistant.

A blend of lightweight, abrasion-resistant nylon and matte-finished breathable nylon is an extremely tough and water-repellent yet breathable and flexible fabric for rugged jackets.

• Cotton blends include a large group of fabrics with water-repellent finishes or weaves. In this category are lightweight, durable cotton/polyester blend fabrics used for running suits, outerwear linings, warm-ups and anaraks; also tightly-woven and poplin-type polyester/cotton blend fabrics which are windproof and breathable for shell garments.

• Buntings and insulations such as heavyweight polyester fleece knit retain warmth even when wet for quick-drying, easy to sew and easy-care pullovers, jackets and jacket linings.

• Knitted polypropylene absorbs little moisture yet wicks perspiration away from the skin to keep you dry and warm for garments such as tights and biking shorts. Woven polypropylene fabrics are used primarily for packs and other types of sports gear.

• Wool/nylon/spandex stretch knit is used for ski pants, ski pant inserts and winter running tights.

GENERAL TIPS

• Nylon fabrics and polyester buntings don't shrink and require no pretreating. However, cotton blend fabrics and wool blend knits do shrink, so pretreat them the same way you will care for the finished garment.

• To fit a pattern for stretch ski pants with stirrup legs, make the total length of the pants 3″ to 4″ shorter than normal. Then the finished pants will fit properly — taut from waist to stirrups.

For good fit through the torso, remove 1″ to 2″ of the length by reducing the crotch depth. Measure your crotch depth while sitting on a hard surface (Figure 1). Adjust the

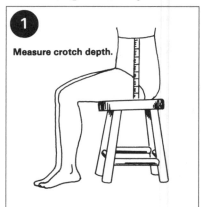

Measure crotch depth.

pattern crotch depth on the printed lengthen/shorten line above the crotch curve (Figure 2)

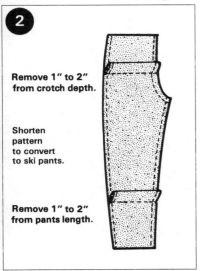

Remove 1" to 2" from crotch depth.

Shorten pattern to convert to ski pants.

Remove 1" to 2" from pants length.

or draw this line on the pattern to make the adjustment.

• Pin within the seam allowances to avoid creating holes which can cause leakage in water-repellent fabrics.

• Sear nylon fabrics to prevent raveling. Immediately after cutting out the pattern pieces, run the cut edges through the base of a candle flame (Figure 3). This melts

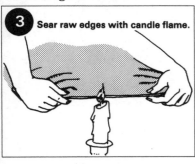

3 Sear raw edges with candle flame.

the fibers, forming a seal which is preferable to serging or other edge-finishing methods.

• As an option, cut and sear nylon fabrics at the same time with a wood burning or

soldering tool which heats up and has a wedge tip (Figure 4).

4 Sear raw edges with woodburning tool.

Trace the pattern cutting lines onto the fabric, then follow the traced lines by moving the tool at a steady pace. For best results, work on a glass surface.

SEWING TECHNIQUES

• Use quality polyester thread which retains its strength even after constant exposure to moisture.

• For most outerwear fabrics, use a size 70/10 sharp needle. However, use a ballpoint needle for tightly-woven polyester/nylon blend fabrics and wool blend stretch knits.

• In general, use a stitch length of 10 to 12 stitches per inch.

• If coated fabrics resist sliding under the presser foot, use a roller, even feed or Teflon® foot.

• To use bunting or other insulation as an interlining, cut the interlining from the same pattern pieces as used for the outer shell fabric. Machine-baste the interlining to the wrong side of the outer shell sections ½" from the edges. If one face of the interlining is unglazed, place this face against the wrong side of the outer shell sections. Stitch with the interlining

facing the bed of the sewing machine. Trim the interlining close to the basting stitches to reduce bulk in the finished seams (Figure 5). Handle both

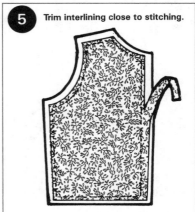

5 Trim interlining close to stitching.

fabric layers as one as you sew the garment.

• For a durable garment, choose a seam technique as strong as the fabric and able to withstand stress. Among the suitable types of seams are French, flat-felled, welt and plain seams with serged edges. You could also insert narrow piping to strengthen plain seams (Figure 6).

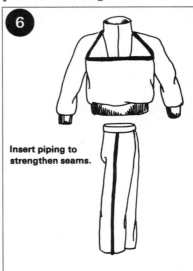

6

Insert piping to strengthen seams.

• On wool blend stretch knits, use a special stretch stitch such as a triple or overedge stitch, or use a long, narrow zigzag stitch (Figure 7).

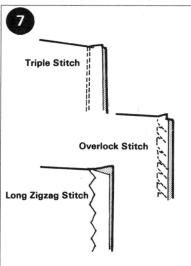

Finish each seam allowance separately with serging or zigzagging so the seam can be pressed open (Figure 8).

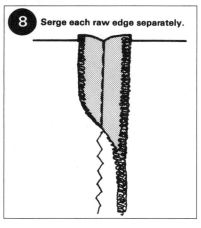

• For water-repellent and waterproof garments, seal the seams with a special liquid sealant sold in sporting goods stores.

• To apply gripper snaps, grommets and eyelets on outerwear, use a leather hole punch (Figure 9) to prepare an

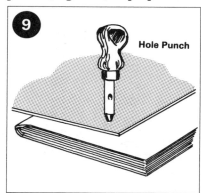

opening through the fabric layers and make the hardware application easier. Protect the work surface with a magazine.

To set gripper snaps, use a hammer and large dot snap setter with cupped anvil. The anvil holds the decorative cap that goes on the outside of the garment (Figure 10). Pliers-

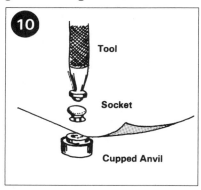

type snap setters often do not set the snaps deeply enough at the center, making them difficult to close on the finished garment.

Eyelets and grommets are packaged with tools you can use to hammer on the hardware. These give good results on outerwear.

PERMANENTLY PLEATED FABRICS

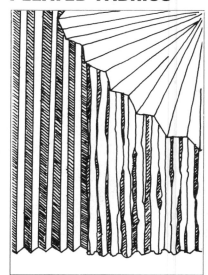

Pleating fabrics is an ancient art. Egyptians used heated stones to set pleats in heavily starched fabrics, and for centuries ruffs and other garment details for royalty were fluted with heated crimping irons. Today, manufacturers pleat fabrics by sandwiching them between two pleating papers to heat-set the folds permanently.

Pleated fabrics are available by the yard along with matching unpleated fabric, or you can have fabric custom-pleated by sending it to a pleating company. Many different fabrics can be pleated, but the permanence of the pleats depends largely on the fiber content. Generally the pleats last a long time if the fabric has a high percentage of polyester or nylon fibers; pleats in wool and silk fabrics must be pressed again with each dry cleaning. Pure cotton fabrics do not retain pleats very well.

Among the types of pleats available are traditional box and knife pleats, as well as more exotic accordion, mushroom, crystal and sunburst pleats. Whether glamorous or classic, pleated fabrics make sensational fashions. Use pleats for a slinky evening dress, an elegant gown, a simple skirt or pair of pull-on pants.

SEWING TIPS

• Although fabrics are usually pleated on the lengthwise grain, they may be pleated on the crosswise grain. Lay out pattern pieces so the grainline arrow is parallel to the pleats (Figure 1).

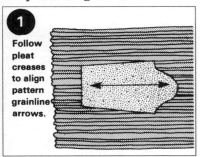

Figure 2: **Baste seam tape by hand to pleat folds.**

Use the tissue pattern as a guide to cut the tape or selvage to the correct length, and catch just the creases of the pleats in the basting stitches.

• Sew narrow serged or double-stitched seams.

• Substitute an elasticized casing for waistbands on skirts and slacks.

• A very narrow machine-stitched hem, ⅛" deep, creates a soft, rippled effect favored by many designers (Figure 3).

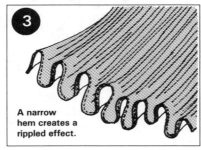

Figure 3: **A narrow hem creates a rippled effect.**

This hem is easier to sew if you machine-stitch first ⅛" below the hemline. Anchor the hem under the presser foot of the sewing machine to hold the fabric taut and trim close to the stitches (Figure 4).

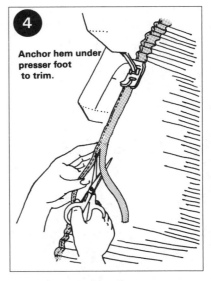

Figure 4: **Anchor hem under presser foot to trim.**

• To make a soft hem, finish the raw edge with overcasting stitches by hand, then fold under ¼" and hem loosely (Figure 5). If desired, weight

Figure 5: **Hem by hand for a soft look.**

the hem with small, ornamental beads so it drapes close to the body.

• Finish neckline edges with bias binding cut from a complementary fabric, a bias-cut organza facing or a sheer tricot bias strip facing.

• Buttonholes are almost impossible to sew on pleated fabrics, but buttons and loops can be very attractive. If the pleated fabric doesn't press flat enough to make self-fabric loops, use a complementary fabric.

Figure 1: **Follow pleat creases to align pattern grainline arrows.**

• It's more accurate to lay out a pattern on a single thickness of pleated fabric.

• Be sure pins are fine and sharp.

• Use a fine 65/9 or 80/11 universal point needle for most pleated fabrics.

• Interfacings are rarely required, but when they are, use a sew-in type. Fusible interfacings are not suitable for pleated fabrics.

• Staystitching distorts the edges of garment sections. To stabilize the edges, baste seam tape or a lightweight selvage to the edges by hand (Figure 2).

- Insert zippers by hand.
- Press lightly, using plenty of steam and holding the iron just above the fabric. Once pressed flat, some fabrics can't be pleated again.

RAYON FABRICS

Rayon, the oldest manmade fiber, enjoys renewed popularity on the current textile and fashion scene. First manufactured in the United States in 1910, rayon is no longer considered merely an inexpensive substitute for silk but a fiber prized for its own sake. The beautiful drape and soft hand of rayon fabrics make them a popular choice for dresses with sweeping skirts and blouses with ruffles and gathered sleeves. In addition, rayon's absorbency makes it comfortable for multi-season wear.

Rayon can be made by two basic processes. Viscose rayon is made of cellulose from wood pulp, while a newer method creates rayon from short cotton linters which are the fibers left on the cotton seed after ginning. Recently, viscose rayon has been improved to produce high, wet modulus rayons which are stronger and shrink less.

SEWING TIPS

- Rayon fabrics are sensitive to heat. Take care to avoid high temperatures when pressing. To prevent shine on dark rayon fabrics, press on the wrong side, using a sole-plate cover on the iron or a press cloth.
- Test a sample first when using fusible interfacings to make sure the required heat, steam and pressure do not damage rayon fabrics.
- Finish raw edges to prevent raveling. Use serging, zigzagging or sheer tricot bias binding.
- Check the care requirements for every rayon fabric. If washable, launder gently since rayon fibers become weaker when wet. If dry-cleanable, do not allow the fabric to become damp; the fabric will shrivel and shrink.
- Although rayon is notable for its ability to take dyes, the sun can fade some of the darker colors. Some rayon fabrics become weakened if they're exposed to too much light.

SHEERS

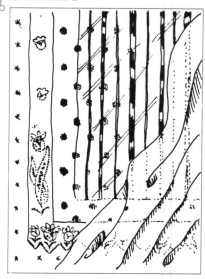

It's no wonder sheer fabrics enjoy a special place in fashion from one year to the next. They drape, they flow, and they send an unmistakable message of femininity.

But before you set out to sew sheers such as chiffon, voile, organdy, organza and georgette, brush up on special handling techniques which take textile transparency into account. You'll need a strategy which covers seam finishes, interfacings, notions and hemming techniques. In addition, basting – an optional step with many other types of fabrics – often becomes a necessity with slippery sheers.

GENERAL TIPS

- Flowing, loosely-fitted patterns are generally more appropriate than fitted fashion designs.
- Use a fine 65/9 or 70/10 needle, fine lingerie thread and a short stitch length to sew delicate sheers.

• Increase the presser foot pressure if necessary so light-weight sheers feed more smoothly.

• On slippery sheers, taut sewing might be required for a smooth, unpuckered seam. Start with one hand in front and the other hand behind the presser foot to hold the fabric gently taut as you stitch (Figure 1).

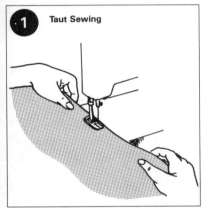
1 Taut Sewing

• Avoid interfacings if possible, since they spoil the fabric's see-through quality. To reinforce areas of stress on fragile sheers, use self-fabric or organza, or use nonwoven interfacings designed especially for sheers.

• If the pattern calls for elastic, transparent elastic is most compatible with sheer fabrics.

• Clear nylon snaps are more suitable closures for sheer garments than metal snaps.

• Push pins and a cardboard cutting board help control slippery sheers for pattern layout and cutting. To begin, align the fabric selvages and the crosswise grainline with the printed grid lines on the cutting board; anchor the fabric edges to the board with push pins 2″ to 3″ apart.

As you position each pattern piece, insert a push pin at each end of the pattern's grainline arrow. Then, use straight pins to pin the pattern to the fabric, pinning every 2″ to 3″ (Figure 2).

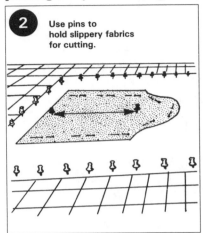
2 Use pins to hold slippery fabrics for cutting.

• Another way to control slippery sheers during layout is to cover the cutting surface with a layer of paper such as the plain, brown, newsprint-quality paper sold in arts and crafts shops or the examining table paper sold in medical supply shops. Both papers are available on rolls, making them particularly easy to use.

Pin the fabric to the paper, matching one selvage to one long edge of the paper. Pin the pattern through both fabric and paper, and cut as one.

• A pair of shears with an ultra-fine serrated edge grips slippery sheers securely as you cut.

SEWING TECHNIQUES

• Sheer fabrics often have a "wiggly" nature and call for a more secure basting method than simple pinning. While you could baste by hand, there are faster options.

One option is basting with glue stick. Test first to make sure the dried glue will not show through the fabric.

Another option is using water-soluble fabric adhesive. To use it, apply a thin line of adhesive just inside the seamline on the right side of one layer of fabric. With your fingers, lightly press the other fabric layer on top (Figure 3);

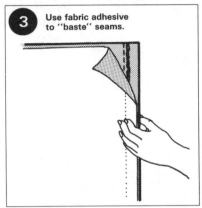
3 Use fabric adhesive to ''baste'' seams.

allow the adhesive to dry before stitching the seam. If you press too hard on the fabric layers, the adhesive will seep through the fabric.

• Make narrow seams that protect the raw edges from fraying. Suitable standard methods include serged, double-stitched and French seams. You can bind curved seams with sheer tricot bias strips.

• Use one seam method for the entire garment or use several methods in different garment areas, depending on the shape of the seam, its visibility or its potential for stress. When selecting seam methods, remember that what shows on the inside usually shows through to the outside.

• A hairline seam is a special sheer seam you can serge or zigzag; use it for enclosed seams such as those on collars and cuffs.

To sew a hairline seam on a serger, adjust the machine for a short, narrow overlock stitch. With right sides together, serge along the seamline; on loosely-woven sheers, reinforce the fabric by serging over a strip of sheer bias tricot. After serging, trim away the excess tricot (Figure 4).

Serge hairline seams on loosely-woven sheers over tricot strip, then trim excess tricot.

To sew a hairline seam on a conventional machine, adjust the machine for a tight, narrow zigzag stitch. With right sides together, lay light-weight cording such as button-hole twist or crochet cotton along the seamline and stitch over the cording. Trim the seam allowances close to the stitches (Figure 5).

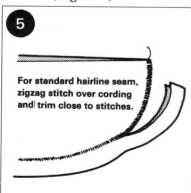

For standard hairline seam, zigzag stitch over cording and trim close to stitches.

• To hem sheers, a narrow, rolled hem sewn on a serger is by far the fastest and easiest method. If you use textured nylon thread in the upper looper, the finished hem will have a soft, "covered" appearance.

To avoid creating a bump in the hem where you serge on and off the fabric, plan ahead and leave all or just the hem area of one seam unstitched (Figure 6). Serge the hem, then finish sewing the seam.

Leave portion of one seam open, serge hem, then close seam opening.

• A narrow hem can also be sewn with a simple straight stitch. To make it easier to sew this hem on sheers, fold up the hem ⅛″ below the hemline. Baste ⅛″ from the fold with a long basting stitch (Figure 7);

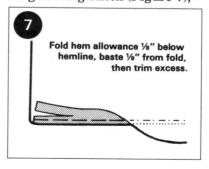

Fold hem allowance ⅛″ below hemline, baste ⅛″ from fold, then trim excess.

to prevent the fabric from becoming frayed as you begin to stitch, hold the needle and bobbin threads taut behind the presser foot for the first few stitches. Use small, sharp scissors to trim the excess hem allowance above the basting stitches.

Fold up the hem along the line of basting stitches and press. Use a short stitch, stitch the hem very close to the first fold (Figure 8). Remove the

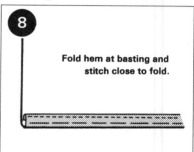

Fold hem at basting and stitch close to fold.

basting stitches, then press the hem.

• To avoid a stretched, "fish eye" look on machine-stitched buttonholes, support the fabric with a layer of nonwoven, tear-away stabilizer as you sew.

• Sew buttons on neatly with a few, tiny stitches, but do not knot the thread. Anchor the stitches with a drop of liquid seam sealant on the wrong side (Figure 9).

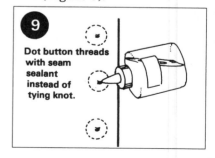

Dot button threads with seam sealant instead of tying knot.

SILK FABRICS

Silk has been revered, even called the queen of fibers, for more than 5,000 years, so you know it has some special qualities. To begin, silk is practical. As a natural fiber, silk breathes, making it comfortable to wear. It also wears well because it is a strong, tough fiber.

But silk's greatest appeal is probably aesthetic. While some synthetic silky fabrics come close, nothing looks and feels like real silk. This versatile fiber can be knitted or woven into a wide variety of fabrics. Silk crepe de chine or raw silk, because they are relatively easy to work with, are good choices for your first silk sewing project. Once you've had some silk sewing experience, you might enjoy the challenge of working with lustrous silk charmeuse or silk panné velvet.

SILK TERMS

• Raw silk is any silk yarn or fabric prior to the removal of the sericin or silk gum.

• Noil silk, often mistakenly called raw silk, comes from the short, waste fibers from the inner part of the silk cocoon. They are woven or knitted into nubby fabrics with a dull surface.

• Dupion silk fiber is created when two silk cocoons join together. The fiber is uneven, irregular and large in diameter in some areas. This type of silk fiber is used to create the slubbed textures of fabrics such as pongee and shantung.

• Wild or tussah silk comes from uncultivated silk worms who do not have a controlled diet and environment. It's strong silk, but coarse and uneven, like the tussah and honan fabrics made from the fibers.

TYPES OF SILK FABRICS

• Sheer silks include chiffon and voile.

• Lightweight silks include broadcloth, or Fuji, sometimes called shirting silk and often striped; charmeuse, which has a rich, soft satin weave with one matte-finished face; China silk or hobatai, which is thinner than broadcloth and often used for lining, inter-facing or underlining; crepe de chine, a supple, fine, lustrous woven fabric; crepe matelasse, a jacquard weave with a bubbly surface and soft texture; honan; pongee; poplin; and surah, a durable, twill weave with a distinctive diagonal rib.

• Medium or suit-weight silks include damask, a reversible jacquard weave; shantung, a ribbed, linen-look fabric; and taffeta, which has a distinctive scroop, or rustle, when made from pure silk fibers.

SEWING TIPS

• In general, the better the silk quality, the higher the price. Silk is graded by an association of silk-producing countries for even filament size, neatness and cleanliness. Once graded, silk is purchased by companies around the world and made into fabric.

• Pretreat silk fabric by laundering or dry cleaning, depending upon the care method you will use for the finished garment.

• Check washable silks for color fastness by covering a small corner of the fabric with a damp cotton cloth; press down on the cloth with a hot iron for a few seconds. If color shows on the cotton cloth, it is better to dry clean the silk fabric. If no color shows, wash the fabric by hand in lukewarm water using a mild soap.

• To control silk fabrics during layout, cover the work surface with a flannel-backed vinyl tablecloth, flannel side up.

• Silk pins, contrary to their name, are too coarse for most silk fabrics. Use extra-fine pins instead.

• Fusible tricot interfacing works well on lightweight crepe de chine, faille, poplin and broadcloth, but for the lightest weight silks, self-fabric makes an excellent interfacing.

• Interface the upper collar and outer cuffs to prevent the seam allowances from showing through.

• The front band of a silky shirt needs interfacing for strength and stability for the buttons and buttonholes.

• Silk naturally repels dirt, but perspiration, deodorant and other grooming chemicals stain silk garments. Buy or make dress shields to protect the underarm area of silk blouses and dresses.

• Use fine silk, cotton or long-staple polyester thread.

• Since most silks fray, use French or double-stitched seams, or serge the raw edges of plain seams.

SPECIAL OCCASION FABRICS

A galaxy of sparkling fabrics, from metallics in electric colors to sensational sequins, will inspire you to sew spectacular fashions for the special occasions in your life. Choose an appropriate pattern, modify some basic sewing techniques, and you'll

turn heads when you wear a glamorous entrance-maker you've sewn on your own.

TYPES OF SPECIAL OCCASION FABRICS

• Sequined fabric is made of individual sequins sewn to a knitted or woven fabric base. The sequins may be applied in an allover design, or in a patterned design.

• Metallic is the generic name for a man-made fiber composed of a metal compound; most metallic fabrics including lamé are knitted or woven. However, ciré, a popular soft and drapable fabric, is actually tricot coated with metallic, and you will find fabrics such as laces and chiffons shot through with metallic threads.

• Satin, with its shiny surface, is usually made from lustrous fibers such as silk, rayon or polyester. It comes in several weights, including firm satin peau, reversible crepe-backed satin and soft slipper satin.

• Brocade usually has woven, tapestry-style motifs and may have a raised surface texture. Some brocades have metallic threads woven throughout.

GENERAL TIPS

• Make a sample garment in muslin or other inexpensive fabric for fitting purposes before you sew. Many special occasion fabrics are too fragile for fitting alterations.

• Use a "with nap" pattern layout for all shiny, lustrous and metallic fabrics.

• Press special occasion fabrics with extra care. In general, use a dry iron and a low heat setting; test on fabric scraps first. Satins can water-spot, sequins can lose their shine and metallics can melt from steam.

• Select simple pattern styles. Even the most basic design looks dazzling when made from a glittering fabric.

• While not a necessity, a serger makes it easy to sew special occasion fabrics. See the "Guide to Serging Special Occasion Fabrics" below for appropriate machine settings and suggested sewing techniques.

SEWING TIPS FOR SEQUINED FABRICS

• While you can make an entire garment from sequined fabric, also consider using it as a garment accent. For

GUIDE TO SERGING SPECIAL OCCASION FABRICS					
FABRIC	SUGGESTED SEAM	NEEDLE SIZE	STITCH WIDTH	STITCH LENGTH	SUGGESTED HEM
BROCADE	PLAIN WITH SERGED EDGES, FRENCH	70/10 OR 80/11	4 TO 5 MM	2 TO 3 MM	FACED
METALLIC SHEERS, KNITS	DECORATIVE SERGED, FRENCH	70/10 OR 80/11	1.5 TO WIDEST	1 TO 3 MM	ROLLED, DECORATIVE SERGED
SATIN, LAME	PLAIN WITH SERGED EDGES, FRENCH	70/10 OR 80/11	4 TO 5 MM	2 TO 3 MM	TOP-STITCHED, BLINDHEM
SEQUINED	PLAIN WITH SERGED EDGES, FRENCH	70/10 OR 80/11	4 TO 5 MM	2 TO 3 MM	FACED

example, set a diagonal sequined panel into the bodice of a satin dress, or use a sequined collar on a velvet jacket.

• Increase the pattern seam allowances to 1" for easier handling.

• During layout, run the sequins down toward the hem of the garment.

• Lay out and cut one fabric layer at a time. Use weights to hold the pattern on the wrong side of the fabric.

• Cutting sequins dulls shears. Use an expendable pair, or plan to have the shears sharpened when you are finished.

• Use lining fabric for facings, and face hems, so sequined fabric will not irritate skin.

• Remove the sequins from the seam allowances by unstringing them from their threads (Figure 1). Save the

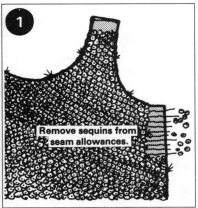

Remove sequins from seam allowances.

loose sequins for possible future repairs. Staystitch the threads on the seamline, or use fabric glue to secure the thread ends to the seam allowance.

• Serge the seams, or use a straight stitch and a zipper foot, positioning the needle to

the left of the zipper foot (Figure 2). Stitch slowly and

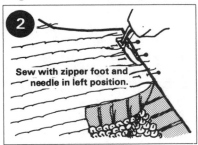

Sew with zipper foot and needle in left position.

try to avoid sewing over sequins, as they will break if the needle strikes them.

• On a conventional machine, stitch sequined fabrics with double-stitched seams or plain seams with Hong Kong finished edges.

• Remove sequins from the hem allowance and interface the hem, or face the hem with lightweight fabric cut on the bias (Figure 3).

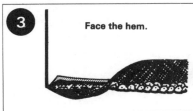

Face the hem.

• To press, it may not be necessary to use an iron. Finger-press seams and edges.

• Sew loose sequins by hand to any bare spots near the seams, edges or hems.

SEWING TIPS FOR METALLICS
• Use a "with nap" pattern layout.

• Underline fragile fabrics to add strength to the seams.

• Metallics tend to dull needles, so you may need to insert a new needle often.

• Serge or bind the raw edges on metallic fabrics that ravel.

• If the fabric is scratchy or irritating to the skin, use lining fabric for garment facings and to cut bias hem facings.

• When serging a rolled hem on metallics, some fabric yarns may poke through the stitches. To remedy, serge the hem over a strip of sheer tricot bias tape. Trim away the excess tape when you are finished.

• Take advantage of the scalloped edge on metallic laces as a ready-made hem (Figure 4).

Use metallic lace border as ready-made hem.

SEWING TIPS FOR SATIN
• Needles and pins leave holes, so place pins in seam and hem allowances only.

• Test water-soluble marking pens on a scrap first to see if they leave water spots.

• Underline fitted bodices and skirts to strengthen seams and prevent the fabric from spreading and shredding at the stitches.

• Before handling cut garment sections, serge the raw edges to prevent raveling, or coat them with a thin line of liquid seam sealant.

SYNTHETIC SUEDE & LEATHER

Synthetic suede and leather fabrics appear to be natural leather, but they're washable, colorfast and won't stretch, shrink, pill, fray, water-spot or stiffen. Such fabrics belong to a unique family of nonwoven fabrics made from polyurethane blends that are instantly recognizable for their luxurious, leather-like appearance and hand.

When the first polyester/non-fibrous polyurethane synthetic suede was introduced in the early 1970s, it became an instant hit with top fashion designers as well as sewing enthusiasts. Today there are second and third generations of this distinctive, prestige fabric. Some are lightweight and supple, while others mimic smooth calfskin. All will tempt you to sew creative fashions you'll be proud to wear.

TYPES OF SYNTHETIC SUEDE & LEATHER

• Medium weight synthetic suede feels and drapes somewhat crisply, like real leather. Since this fabric is difficult to press and difficult to ease, use fashion patterns designed for this type of fabric or modify a standard pattern to use special construction methods.

• Lightweight synthetic suede is much more supple and drapes softly, like a blouse-weight fabric. This makes it suitable for a wide range of pattern styles, including those with gathers and fitted details. Although some special handling methods apply, you can sew this type of fabric with standard techniques.

• Stretch synthetic leather, synthetic suede's "sister", looks like smooth calfskin, has moderate stretch (35 percent) and a laminated knit backing. A versatile fabric, it can be used for patterns suggesting moderate stretch knits, woven fabrics, leather or synthetic suede. Like lightweight synthetic suede, it needs some special handling but can be sewn with standard techniques.

GENERAL TIPS

• In general, use a fine 70/10 or 80/11 machine needle and long-staple polyester thread. Sew with a long stitch, about 8 to 10 per inch, since short stitches weaken the fabric with too many needle perforations.

• An even feed, Teflon® or roller foot helps solve stitching problems.

• Press with a low temperature setting on the iron. Use a press cloth to protect the fabric from damage.

• Use a "with nap" pattern layout so all the pattern pieces are aimed in one direction.

• Although a lining is not necessary, it is a nice finishing touch. The garment will slip over other garments more easily, and it will last longer. A silky, washable polyester crepe de chine fabric is most compatible.

• Save all your scraps. They come in handy for accessories such as belts and purses, and make wonderful appliqués.

TIPS FOR MEDIUM WEIGHT SYNTHETIC SUEDE

• A simple vest or skirt is a good first project, but to get the most wardrobe mileage out of the fabric investment, make a blazer or jacket to wear over casual or dressy fashions.

• Simple, boxy garment shapes suit the stiff hand of medium weight synthetic suede very nicely.

• Fit the pattern before you sew by making a test garment in felt or nonwoven interfacing. You can substitute the test garment sections for the tissue pattern for easier layout.

• Depending upon the look you desire, interfacing may or may not be necessary. For example, two layers of synthetic suede may have enough body on their own for a jacket collar. If you prefer to interface, a fusible interfacing usually works well on synthetic suedes.

• Use plain, topstitched or lapped seams, or use a combination of seam techniques within a single garment. Decide which seams you will use and where you will use them before cutting. You can then trim some seam allowances away from the pattern sections in advance, saving on yardage.

• To soften synthetic suede and make it easier to sew, pretreat it. Machine wash it on a gentle cycle with warm water and a mild soap. Tumble dry on a warm setting with terry towels to balance the load and fluff up the suede texture.

• Since synthetic suede is a nonwoven fabric, it has no apparent grain. It does have a directional give, however; the least amount of give is lengthwise and the most is crosswise. There is no true bias grain, but there is a moderate amount of give in the diagonal direction.

• For economical layouts, you can tilt the pattern pieces up to 45 degrees without causing color shading problems (Figure 1).

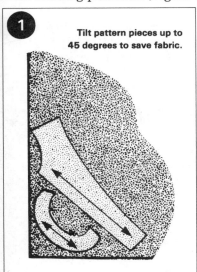

Tilt pattern pieces up to 45 degrees to save fabric.

• Another way to economize on fabric is to piece facings. Butt the cut edges and support them with a layer of lightweight fusible interfacing, then zigzag the edges together (Figure 2).

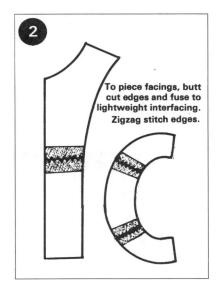

To piece facings, butt cut edges and fuse to lightweight interfacing. Zigzag stitch edges.

• Pins will not leave holes, but use fine, sharp, dress-maker pins.

• Use chalk or a water-soluble marking pen to mark synthetic suede.

• Baste seams together with glue stick to prevent the layers from shifting while you stitch. Sponge the glue away before pressing seams open.

• Baste lapped seams with basting tape or a skinny strip of fusible web before you sew (Figure 3).

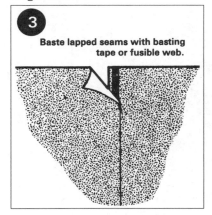

Baste lapped seams with basting tape or fusible web.

• Use a very simple button-hole technique to take advantage of synthetic suede's body and nonraveling quality.

First, stabilize the buttonhole area with an oval of fusible interfacing. Then, sew a rectangle of fine stitches around the buttonhole marking; slash open with a razor blade (Figure 4).

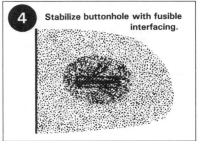

Stabilize buttonhole with fusible interfacing.

• Topstitch hems or sew them by hand. Glued or fused hems will be quite stiff.

TIPS FOR LIGHTWEIGHT SYNTHETIC SUEDE

• When selecting a pattern, think of lightweight synthetic suede as a medium weight woven fabric such as wool crepe or wool flannel.

• Standard sewing techniques work beautifully and no pattern modifications are necessary. Facings and collars can be sewn, turned right side out and pressed without special methods. You can use plain, pressed-open seams.

• Lapped seams are an option for a "real" suede look.

• Seams sewn on a serger are too bulky, but serging can be used as a decorative element for exposed seams and edges.

• Use a serger's knives to trim exposed seams and edges neatly, such as around collars, lapels, cuffs and hems. For a perfect trim, remove the serger needle(s) first.

- Lay out pattern pieces with the greater amount of stretch going around the body if the fabric's stretch is important to the garment's fit or performance.
- If the stretch factor is not important, pattern pieces may be angled in any direction to save yardage since synthetic leather has no nap.
- Needles and pins leave holes, although the holes will disappear somewhat into the textured surface. Take care to stitch and fit correctly the first time.

When possible, substitute weights or masking or quilter's tape for pins. Do not use transparent tape on the right side; it may mar the surface. For quick basting, use paper clips.

- Use an 80/11 ballpoint or universal point needle and long-staple polyester thread.
- If interfacing is needed, use a sew-in type.
- Plain seams work best on stretch synthetic leather. Use a long, wide zigzag stitch so seams will stretch with the fabric. Topstitch or glue the seam allowances to hold them flat and open.
- Instead of using an even feed, roller or Teflon® foot for smoother stitching, apply silicone lubricant to the bottom of a regular presser foot and the throat plate. Another option is sandwiching the fabric layers between sheets of tear-away stabilizer or tissue paper; remove carefully after stitching.

- If skipped stitches persist as a problem, try a larger needle size or apply silicone lubricant to the spool of thread by running the tip of the lubricant bottle down the side of a spool of thread (Figure 5).

5 Lubricate thread for smoother stitching.

Fill the bobbin and thread the needle from this lubricated spool.

✂ TAFFETA

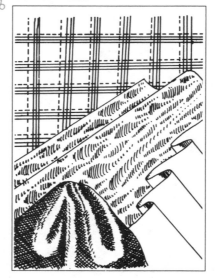

The word taffeta actually refers not to just one fabric but to a group of similar fabrics. All have very fine, plain weaves with a lustrous appearance, crisp hand and the distinctive taffeta rustle.

Add the elegance of taffeta to your wardrobe, showing it off in an elegant evening dress or long skirt, or using it for a wonderful blouse or lounging robe.

TYPES OF TAFFETA

- Taffeta comes in many weights and fibers. While almost any fiber may be used to make taffeta, the most common are polyester, silk and acetate.
- Faille taffeta has fine ribs running crosswise.
- Paper taffeta is lightweight and has a crisp, paperlike finish.
- Tissue taffeta is lightweight and transparent.
- Moiré taffeta is finished by heated rollers to produce a watered surface design.
- Iridescent taffeta, made with two different colors in the warp and filling, appears to change color when viewed from different angles.

SEWING TIPS

- Choose a pattern to suit the taffeta weight. Heavier taffetas suggest sculptured shapes, full sleeves and fitted bodices. Lighter weights suggest full, gathered skirts, flounces and ruffles.
- Silk taffeta generally needs extra support to hold a fashion shape; underline skirts and full sleeves with lightweight net or organza.
- Use a "with nap" layout for uniform color shading of this lustrous fabric.
- Pins and ripped-out stitches tend to leave permanent holes. Pin in the

seam allowances only and take care to stitch seams only once.

• Be sure shears, pins and needles are in top condition. Dulled or damaged points or blades will tear and distort taffeta.

• Because of pressing risks, avoid fusible interfacing. Opt instead for a sew-in interfacing compatible with the weight of the taffeta.

• Test pressing techniques on scraps first, using a light touch and protecting the fabric with a press cloth when pressing on the right side. Use a seam roll or brown paper strips under the seam allowances to prevent imprints.

• In general, do not use steam on taffeta. Some taffetas, particularly those made from acetate fibers, will water-spot. Others may pucker or loose their sheen.

• Since taffeta tends to ravel, finish seams by pinking, over-casting by hand, binding with sheer tricot bias tape or applying a thin coat of seam sealant. Serge raw edges of heavier taffetas.

• A deep 4″ to 5″ hem looks luxurious and adds body to a full, long skirt. Fold the raw hem edge under ¼″ and machine stitch ⅛″ from the fold; sew the hem by hand.

• Since taffeta is such a firm weave, it does not ease well. To handle excess fabric in a shaped hem, fold tiny pleats along the edge as you hem (Figure 1).

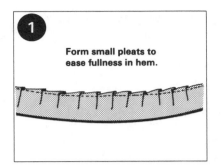

Form small pleats to ease fullness in hem.

✂ TERRY CLOTH

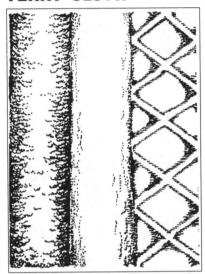

Although soft, absorbent terry cloth has been a staple for beachwear, robes and childrens' clothes for many years, it has changed with advances in the fabric industry. Once terry cloth was woven from 100-percent cotton; now it's often made from a blend of fibers and may be knitted or woven. Colors are brighter and longer-lasting, and the right side may have a velour or sculptured texture instead of the traditional looped construction.

Terry cloth also comes in several weights. Just like bath towels, the heavier weights feel and look deluxe — sure to inspire creative sewing.

SEWING TIPS

• Many terry cloths are finished with a sizing to give body to a loose weave which would otherwise appear limp. Test a stiff terry cloth by rolling a section of the fabric between your fingers to remove the sizing. A heavily sized fabric will lose its shape and body when laundered.

• Preshrink terry cloth. In the process, you will remove any sizing which dulls needles and enables a knitted terry to relax.

• In some terry cloths, there is little or no cotton fiber content. If absorbency is important for the garment you intend to sew, look for terry cloth with a high percentage of cotton.

• Test stretch terry's "memory" by pulling and then releasing a section of the fabric. If it returns to its original size and shape, the finished garment will not stretch out of shape or become baggy.

• Choose a simple pattern style, since terry cloth's surface texture seems to hide design details.

• For stretch terry, you can select a pattern designed for knits.

• Use a "with nap" pattern layout.

• Since the texture seems to swallow pen and chalk marks, use small snips to mark seamlines. Pin-mark pockets and other details by inserting a pin straight down through the pattern and fabric layers (Figure 1); separate the fabric

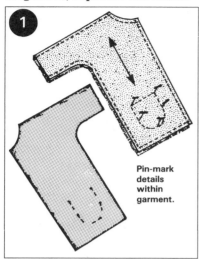

1

Pin-mark details within garment.

layers carefully to avoid dislodging the first pin so you can insert other pins into the fabric to mark.

• Interfacing is rarely required in terry cloth garments, but do reinforce button and buttonhole areas with a layer of sew-in interfacing on the wrong side.

• Seam options include plain seams with zigzagged or serged raw edge finishes, serged seams, mock French and flat-felled seams.

• Another seam technique which works well on terry cloth begins with a plain seam. Trim the seam allowances to ⅜″, press open and zigzag stitch the seam allowances to the garment (Figure 2). Use a wide or three-

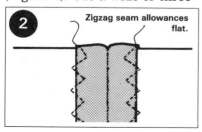

2 Zigzag seam allowances flat.

step zigzag stitch for this, and the stitches will sink into the fabric texture — you will barely see them from the right side.

• To press, cover the ironing board with a terry towel and avoid crushing the right side texture.

• Serge hems on terry cloth garments, or use a double row of zigzagging (Figure 3).

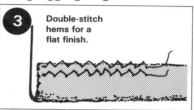

3 Double-stitch hems for a flat finish.

Another option is binding or serging the raw edge and sewing the hem by hand.

✂ VELVET

Gloriously plush velvet elevates even the simplest pants, skirt, dress or coat to luxurious fashion heights, but velvet's practical, too. It's long-lasting and not nearly as fragile as it looks.

If velvet has the reputation of being difficult to sew, it's undeserved. Actually with a bit of care and by following a few guidelines, you'll find sewing velvet can be a true delight.

GENERAL TIPS

• Preshrink washable velvet. Washable velvet actually looks better every time you launder it. If making a tailored garment which will be dry cleaned, steam the velvet thoroughly to preshrink it.

• Choose a pattern with as few seams and details as possible. Velvet can be gathered; in fact, a little gathering at the sleeve cap or the waistline can be beautiful.

• Fit the pattern before you cut. Ripping out seams usually leaves marks behind on velvet.

• Velvet combines well with other fabrics, especially those with contrasting textures. For example, use a velvet collar on a silk or wool garment, or use a velvet yoke on a challis dress. Velvet can also be used as a trim such as binding.

• You don't have to line velvet garments, but a lining makes them easier to wear. You might line just the skirt of a dress or just the sleeves of a shirt.

• In general, use sew-in rather than fusible inter-facings. Fusing tends to flatten the pile, especially on rayon and silk velvets. Some cotton velvets are resilient enough for fusible interfacings; test on scraps first.

• Use lightweight woven wool or satin for facings and undercollar to reduce bulk if the velvet is heavyweight.

• For easier handling, lay out and cut on a single layer of velvet.

• Use a "with nap" pattern layout. Since the pile is perpendicular to the fabric base, you can run the nap up or down without affecting velvet's durability. It can also be cut on the bias grain with little or no shading at the seams.

• Insert as few pins as possible or use weights for layout.

• Mark with chalk or a water-soluble pen on the wrong side of the fabric.

• Use a needleboard when pressing.

• Velvet loves steam. You can press seams beautifully by steaming the fabric, then using your fingers to hold the seam allowances open.

• Keep a nylon pile lint brush handy so you can revive the pile after pressing a seam.

• Make a special velvet press cloth by serging or zigzagging a self-fabric scrap to a heavy-duty press cloth. This cloth allows steam to travel through to the fabric while preventing the fabric from getting wet, and also helps preserve the lush pile.

SEWING TECHNIQUES

• Even if you hardly ever baste when you sew, consider hand basting velvet. Use silk thread which leaves no imprints. Alternate long and short stitches to prevent puckering (Figure 1). Break

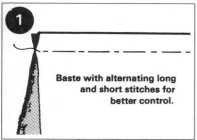

Baste with alternating long and short stitches for better control.

the basting thread about every 10″ to prevent the layers from shifting, or backstitch periodically.

• To pin-baste a seam, place the pins at right angles to the stitching line and use more pins than usual. Remove the pins as you come to them; sewing over pins leaves marks.

• Use a new size 65/9, 70/10 or 80/11 machine needle and about 12 to 14 stitches per inch.

• Stitch in the direction of the pile. This may mean stitching a seam in the opposite direction than you would otherwise.

• Do not backstitch at the beginning and end of a seam, since this can leave marks. Instead, shorten the stitch length to 20 per inch to begin, lengthen the stitch to sew the seam, then shorten the stitch to finish (Figure 2).

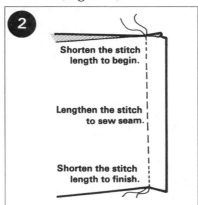

Shorten the stitch length to begin.

Lengthen the stitch to sew seam.

Shorten the stitch length to finish.

• When sewing long seams, such as skirt seams, stop stitching to allow the fabric to relax every 8″ to 10″. Raise the presser foot with the needle in the fabric, let the fabric adjust

---

WASHER WISE

Before prewashing newly-purchased fabrics, I sew the cut ends together, making a tube. This simple technique eliminates twisted yardage and helps keep raw edges from fraying.

B. Rey,
Venice, FL

---

itself, then resume stitching (Figure 3). This method

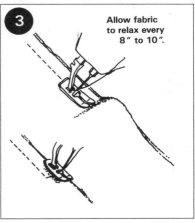

Allow fabric to relax every 8″ to 10″.

eliminates the need for a roller or even feed foot which can leave marks on velvet's pile.

• If you are sewing a soft silk or silk-type velvet, you may have to use a roller or even feed foot to prevent the fabric layers from shifting. Try stitching with a layer of tear-away stabilizer underneath and/or on top of the fabric layers. This requires a great deal of skill, so practicing first is strongly recommended. However, it does work and results in an even seam.

• Since velvet ravels, finish raw edges with serging, over-casting by hand, zigzagging, Hong Kong binding or sheer bias binding.

• Sew darts with the continuous thread method. If you have a sewing machine with a self-winding bobbin, set up the machine by simply winding the bobbin and not cutting the threads.

Otherwise, thread the bobbin as usual but do not thread the needle. Thread the needle backwards (insert the thread from behind the eye) using the bobbin thread.

Tie the bobbin thread to the thread end on the spool. Gently pull the bobbin thread up through the thread guides and wind it around the spool several times (Figure 4). The

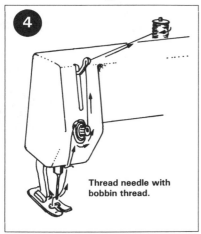

Thread needle with bobbin thread.

bobbin thread and needle thread are now one continuous thread.

Start sewing the dart at the point with very short stitches. Lengthen the stitch after about ½" and sew to the wide end of the dart (Figure 5). Cut

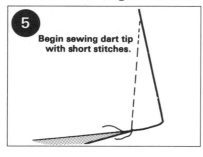

Begin sewing dart tip with short stitches.

the threads at the end of the dart and tie.

• Insert piping in neckline, collar and center front opening seams for crisp, sharp edges.

• Machine-stitched button-holes are not recommended. The presser foot tends to leave marks behind. Hand-sewn buttonholes are one option,

but bound buttonholes using a fabric such as silk or satin for the lips are especially attractive; use seam sealant to prevent the cut edges from fraying as you construct the bound buttonholes.

• A button and loop closure is an excellent choice for velvet garments. Purchased cording makes very stable loops.

• Insert zippers by hand.

• Hemming velvet always presents a challenge. Use this method to bind the raw edge and interface the hem with a soft, lightweight fabric such as silk organza. The hem will not show through as a ridge on the right side.

To start, use pinking shears to cut a bias strip of interfacing twice the width of the hem plus ¾".

With right sides together, pin the interfacing to the cut edge of the hem and stitch a ¼" seam (Figure 6).

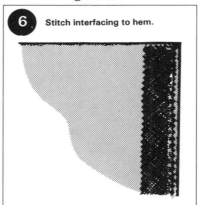

Stitch interfacing to hem.

Fold the interfacing up over the raw edges so the interfacing extends ¼" above the seam (Figure 7). The garment/interfacing seam allowances should be flat. Press lightly.

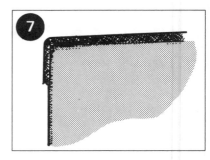

Turn up the hem. The interfacing should extend ½" above the hem allowance (Figure 8).

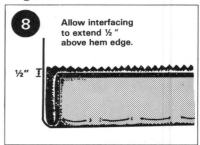

Allow interfacing to extend ½" above hem edge.

½"

Use a loose running stitch to tack the interfacing lightly to the hem fold. Catchstitch the interfacing to the garment and the hem to the interfacing; in both cases, work with the fabric folded back on itself so the catchstitches are "blind" – between the interfacing and the garment and between the hem and the interfacing (Figure 9).

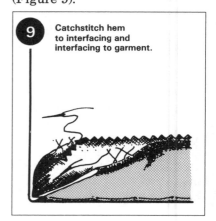

Catchstitch hem to interfacing and interfacing to garment.

VINYL

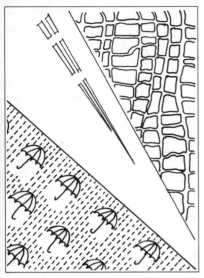

Whether printed to look like leather, frankly fake or brightly colored, vinyl fabrics today are soft and drapable in contrast to the stiff, plasticized types of years past. By sewing your own vinyl fashions, you can duplicate designer looks at a fraction of the price and really let your creativity shine.

Vinyl fabrics are actually two textile layers which are laminated together. The nonwoven vinyl surface may be embossed in almost any type of texture from subtle graining to bold patterning. The soft, knit backing on most vinyls makes them easy to sew and comfortable to wear.

SEWING TIPS

• Choose a pattern with simple lines and minimal easing. Very fitted and shaped garments require extra work, careful handling and plenty of patience.

• Pins and needles leave permanent holes. Use weights or tape for pattern layout.

When pins are necessary for sewing, use fine pins in the seam allowances only.

• Unless there's a surface design to consider, you can angle the pattern pieces jigsaw-puzzle fashion for a very economical layout.

• If working with a vinyl which has significant crosswise stretch, position the pattern pieces so the stretch goes around the body.

• For best results, lay out and cut a single layer of vinyl at a time.

• Mark the backing with chalk or a marking pen. When absolutely necessary to mark on the right side, use transparent tape or masking tape if a test on scraps shows this leaves no permanent mark.

• Baste with glue stick, basting tape or paper clips.

• Use a long stitch to keep needle perforations minimal. Depending upon the weight of the vinyl, use a length of 6 to 10 stitches per inch for seams and a longer stitch for topstitching.

• Select needle size according to the vinyl's weight. Choose a size 80/11 sharp point needle for lightweight vinyls, and up to size 100/16 for heavier varieties. On very heavyweight vinyl, use a wedgepoint needle.

• Vinyl dulls needles, so keep a supply of replacement needles handy.

• Vinyl tends to resist smooth stitching. When possible, sew with the backing side up rather than the slick side.

One technique for smoother sewing is to sprinkle either the machine throat plate or the slick side of the fabric with talcum powder or cornstarch. Or, coat the presser foot and throat plate of the machine with silicone lubricant. A final technique is sandwiching the fabric layers between sheets of tissue paper; tear away the paper afterwards.

• While a roller, even feed or Teflon® presser foot helps to prevent the layers from shifting as you stitch, test first on scraps. In some instances, these feet mar the surface of vinyl.

• Seam options include plain seams with the seam allowances glued or top-stitched open, flat-felled seams and welt seams. Do not use lapped seams, since the knit backing will show at the cut edge of the overlapping side.

• Do not press vinyl with an iron; heat melts vinyl. Finger-press instead.

• Slashed or bound button-holes are easy to make on vinyl garments.

• When making buttonholes by machine, use a long stitch and back the area with a layer of sew-in interfacing.

• Vinyls are waterproof and easy-care. Wipe soiled areas clean with a damp cloth or vinyl cleaner.

• Not all vinyls can be dry cleaned with success. Some become stiff when exposed to the cleaning solvents or separate from the backing. Consult with your dry cleaner to make an informed care decision.

Chapter 3

SAVVY SHORTCUTS

You can sew something beautiful even when your time or patience is limited, for there are many clever and creative ways to make sewing faster and easier today. The shortcut techniques featured in this chapter are dedicated to you – to show how you can make sewing part of your busy life.

Some of the timesaving tips come from efficient ready-to-wear workrooms, while others are actually designer techniques. In many cases, the trick simply is to sew by machine instead of by hand, or to use a special-purpose notion to cut down the number of construction steps.

You may prefer to use sewing shortcuts in some areas of a garment, but not in others. Or, you might sew childrens' clothes the quick way and save the more custom techniques for your own investment wardrobe. One of the best parts about sewing today is choosing from among so many options.

If you're wary of cutting corners, be assured that when you take advantage of contemporary sewing tools, notions and techniques, you can save time without sacrificing quality. Truthfully, you could sew something wonderful to wear using shortcuts every step of the way, and no one would ever guess your secret.

BASTING WITHOUT STITCHES

Today, the word "baste" has a totally new meaning. It no longer has to involve time-consuming stitches; in fact, it can be as quick and simple as unrolling some self-stick tape or spraying a bonding agent. Here's how to use key sewing aids for the most convenient basting ever.

BASTING TAPE

• Water-soluble basting tape is available in 10-yard rolls and in ⅛" or ¼" widths.

• To baste a seam, unroll and finger-press tape to the right side of the fabric, ½" from the cut edge. Remove the protective paper to expose the adhesive (Figure 1).

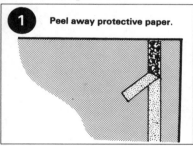
Peel away protective paper.

• Match the cut edges of the adjoining garment section and finger-press. The tape holds the two fabric layers together like basting stitches.

• Stitch a ⅝" seam. If you sew over the tape, don't worry — the tape will not coat the needle.

• After sewing the seam, remove the basting tape by peeling it away from the seam allowance, or submerge the fabric in cold water to dissolve the tape.

• If using tape with leather or another nonwashable fabric, you can leave it in place. It will dissolve when the garment is cleaned.

• Basting tape is very helpful when positioning lapped seams on leather and synthetic suede. Apply the tape to the underneath seam allowance, remove the protective paper and finger-press the overlapping seam edge on top.

• To baste a zipper with tape, apply tape to the outer edges of both seam allowances (Figure 2). Finger-press the

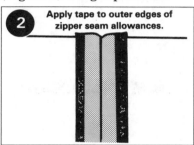
Apply tape to outer edges of zipper seam allowances.

zipper to one seam allowance, lining up the zipper teeth with the seamline. Finger-press the zipper to the other seam allowance.

Topstitch the zipper from the right side. The basting tape will hold the zipper securely in position as you sew.

• Use basting tape to position shoulder pads in garments. The tape will retain its adhesive quality long enough to allow several repositionings of the pads for fitting purposes, and you can leave the tape in place while sewing the pads to the garment.

• Use basting tape to position ribbons, laces and other trims (Figure 3).

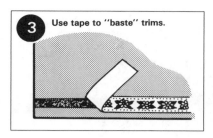
Use tape to "baste" trims.

BASTING SPRAY

• Basting spray, sometimes called pattern spray, is available in 6½-ounce aerosol cans. A temporary bonding agent, it sets dry to the touch, won't spot fabrics and will not make needles sticky.

• Use basting spray to make sew-in interfacings self-stick. Lightly spray the wrong side of the interfacing; gently hand-press the interfacing into position in the garment (Figure 4). Since the spray's

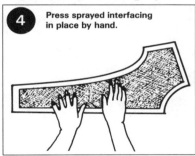
Press sprayed interfacing in place by hand.

bond will break after the first laundering or dry cleaning of the garment, make sure the edges of the interfacing are secured in the seam stitching or with a row of topstitches.

• Spray appliqués to position them on a garment for satin stitching. The basting spray also gives appliqués more body, making them easier to handle.

• Spray tissue patterns lightly, then position them on the fabric for a pinless layout.

Use basting spray especially for slippery fabrics, fabrics that are too thick or bulky to pin into easily, or for fabrics which are easily damaged by pin holes.

✂ BELT LOOPS BY MACHINE

You can make thread carriers for belts the old-fashioned way — by hand — or use a machine shortcut to save considerable time. Take your choice of the serger or zigzag stitch methods below. Use these techniques to create custom "cording" for button and loop closures, too.

SERGER METHOD

Thread the serger with a good color match for the garment, and adjust the machine to sew a narrow, rolled edge.

Lower the presser foot and chain off about 1 yard (Figure 1). Cut and remove from the serger.

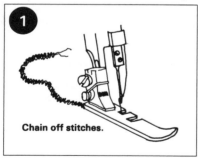

Chain off stitches.

Cut the chain into individual belt loops which are twice the width of the belt plus 2¼". Pin the belt loops to the sides of the bodice front of a dress or jacket, just above the waistline, so the cut ends extend into the side seam allowances (Figure 2).

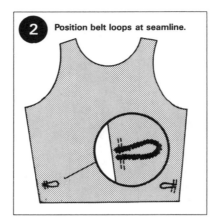

② Position belt loops at seamline.

Stitch them to the bodice front with a short straight stitch, about 20 stitches per inch, ½" from the raw edge. Stitch again close to the first stitching. When you sew the side seams, the loops will be caught in the stitching.

ZIGZAG STITCH METHOD

Cut several strands of thread 1½" longer than the desired finished length of each belt loop. Twist the strands together, and knot them together at each end.

Hold the twisted threads taut and stitch over them, from one end to the other, using a satin stitch (Figure 3).

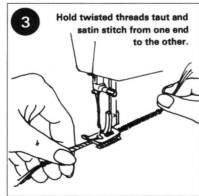

③ Hold twisted threads taut and satin stitch from one end to the other.

Stitch the belt loops to the garment as described for the serger method, above.

✂ BIAS TAPE MADE EASY

Making your own bias tape can be easy, fast and economical. Using the methods below, you can cut more than 30 yards of 1"wide bias from a single yard of 45"-wide fabric. Almost any fabric can be used, and by making your own custom tape, you can match or coordinate bias trims to perfection.

CUTTING BIAS STRIPS

• For best results, cut bias strips on the true bias fabric grain, which lies at a 45-degree angle to the selvage. This grain is very pliant, so it molds smoothly around curves and shaped edges as well as corners and straight lines.

• To find the true bias grain of a fabric, fold the cut crosswise edge to meet the lengthwise selvage edge (Figure 1). Press the fold. The fold is on the true bias grain.

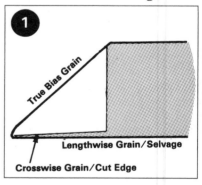

True Bias Grain

Lengthwise Grain/Selvage

Crosswise Grain/Cut Edge

• Use the bias fold as a guide for cutting a small quantity of bias strips. Measure and chalk-mark cutting lines, or use a rotary cutter and transparent ruler.

Cut the bias strips double the finished width desired — cut 2" strips for 1" bias tape.

• To piece the strips together, place one strip at right angles to another with right sides together and the diagonally-cut ends matching (Figure 2).

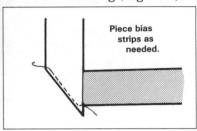

Piece bias strips as needed.

Stitch a ¼″ seam and press open.

Trim away the extending points (Figure 3).

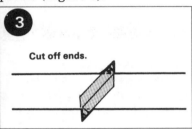

3 Cut off ends.

• To cut a large quantity of bias strips, use the continuous bias strip method. Begin by cutting a perfect square of fabric; the larger the square, the more bias tape it will produce.

Draw a diagonal line between two corners, forming a pair of triangles (Figure 4).

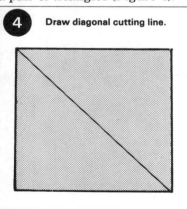

4 Draw diagonal cutting line.

Cut the square on this line. Number the cut edges of the triangles with chalk or a marking pen as shown (Figure 5).

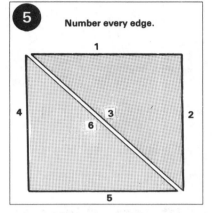

5 Number every edge.

With right sides together, join edges #1 and #5 in a ¼″ seam. Press the seam open (Figure 6).

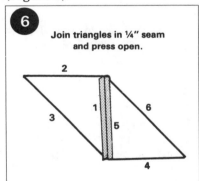

6 Join triangles in ¼″ seam and press open.

Mark the entire fabric with cutting lines for the bias strips, drawing the lines parallel to edges #6 and #3 (Figure 7). If the last strip is

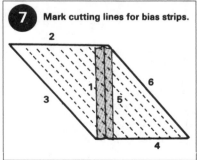

7 Mark cutting lines for bias strips.

an odd width which will not yield a complete strip, trim it away.

Right sides together, offset sides #2 and #4 by one bias strip width and sew the edges together in a ¼″ seam (Figure 8). You will have a slightly

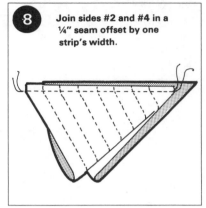

8 Join sides #2 and #4 in a ¼″ seam offset by one strip's width.

twisted tube of fabric. Press the seam open.

To cut the strips, begin at one offset end and cut in a spiral, following the marked cutting lines (Figure 9).

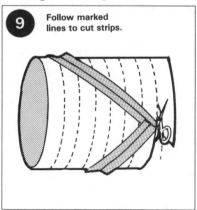

9 Follow marked lines to cut strips.

FOLDING THE BIAS TAPE

• Use metal tapemaker pressing aids to fold under the raw edges of bias strips quickly and neatly. Tapemakers are available in four sizes − ½″, ¾″, 1″ and 2″;

the size of the tapemaker indicates the width of the bias strip after the raw edges are pressed under.

• To use a metal tapemaker, feed the bias strip wrong side up through the wide end and bring it out the narrow tip (Figure 10). Use a pin if necessary to advance the fabric through the channels.

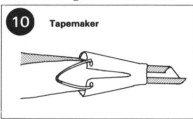

10 Tapemaker

Hold the tapemaker handle in your left hand, and pull it gently as you press the folded tape emerging from the narrow tip (Figure 11).

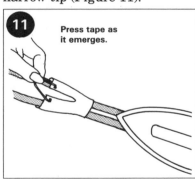

11 Press tape as it emerges.

• Tapemakers create single-fold bias tape. To make double-fold bias tape, fold the single-fold tape in unequal halves along its length (Figure 12);

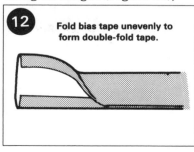

12 Fold bias tape unevenly to form double-fold tape.

press. As you apply the tape to a garment edge, slip the longer side of the tape underneath so you can stitch from the top and catch all layers in a single pass (Figure 13).

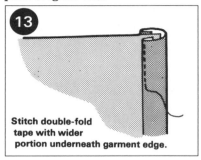

13 Stitch double-fold tape with wider portion underneath garment edge.

• Make bias tape a fusible trim by cutting a strip of paper-backed fusible web slightly narrower than the tape's width. Use a rotary cutter and transparent ruler to cut a quantity of web strips accurately and quickly.

Place the paper-backed web with web side down on the wrong side of the tape; press for three seconds with a hot, dry iron. Allow to cool down. Peel off the paper backing (Figure 14).

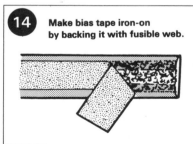

14 Make bias tape iron-on by backing it with fusible web.

Position the tape web side down on the garment to fuse.

• Glue bias tape with permanent fabric adhesive. Apply a fine line of adhesive to the wrong side of the bias tape. Smooth out the adhesive with the applicator tip.

Finger-press the bias tape into position on the garment. Weight the tape with a book for three to five minutes until the bond sets. This constant pressure ensures a proper bond, but avoid applying too much pressure; too much pressure will cause the adhesive to seep through the tape.

• To streamline the application of bias tape to a curved or shaped edge, preshape the tape first by steaming it. Use the pattern piece or the actual garment edge as a pressing guide.

EASY MITERED CORNERS

• When binding an edge with bias tape, finish corners with a neat mitered fold on both faces. To miter a corner, first unfold one edge of the bias tape. Right sides together, match this edge of the tape to the garment edge.

Stitch the tape to the garment by stitching in the ditch of the tape fold; stop sewing ½" (or the width of the seam allowance) from the corner and backstitch (Figure 15). Raise the needle and lift

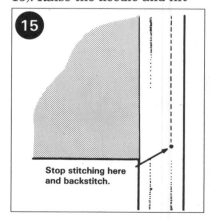

15 Stop stitching here and backstitch.

the presser foot. Pull the garment toward the left of the machine without cutting the threads.

Fold the bias tape toward the right, forming a diagonal fold (Figure 16). Then, fold the tape

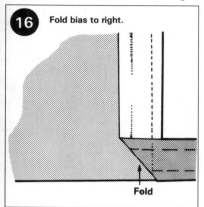

16 Fold bias to right.

Fold

back on itself, toward the left (Figure 17); match the lower edge of the tape to the garment edge.

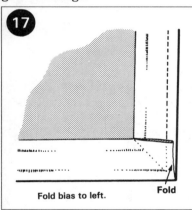

17

Fold bias to left.   Fold

Pivot the garment 90 degrees. Lower the needle where the two seam allowances cross without catching the pleat formed at the corner (Figure 18). Pull the thread loop toward the back, lower the presser foot and backstitch. Resume stitching the seam.

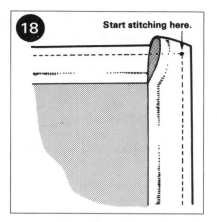

18   Start stitching here.

Press the tape toward the garment edge. Fold the tape over the edge. A mitered fold will automatically form at the corner (Figure 19). Stitch the

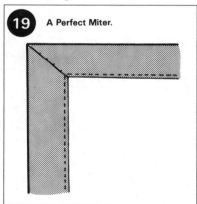

19 A Perfect Miter.

free edge of the tape to the garment. Slipstitch the mitered folds by hand, or slip a small piece of fusible web underneath the fold and press.

BIAS BITS

When making my own bias, I use the free arm of the sewing machine to hold the tube as I cut. The fabric twirls easily as you pull the cut section toward you.

*J. Allen,
New York, NY*

BUTTONS BY MACHINE

Any sew-through button can be attached quickly and easily using a zigzag stitch. You'll find this technique a true timesaver when making shirts, a batch of school clothes for the children or any other time many buttons are required.

• Use a button foot, a special presser foot which has open toes.

• Set the stitch length to "0" or lower the feed dogs.

• Adjust the stitch width to span the holes in the button. Check the stitch width adjustment by turning the hand-wheel slowly to see if the needle swings the correct distance.

• Some machine manuals suggest using the right needle position for sewing on buttons.

• Lay a sewing machine needle over the button and tape needle and button to the garment (Figure 1).

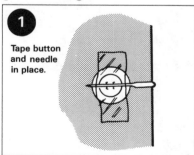

1

Tape button and needle in place.

• Zigzag several times to secure the button, then anchor the stitches by turning the stitch width to "0" and sewing several stitches in the same button hole (Figure 2).

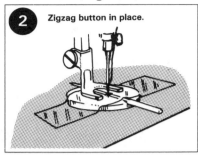

2 Zigzag button in place.

• To finish, make a thread shank, using the slack in the stitches created by the needle taped across the button. Remove the tape and needle. Pull the thread ends beneath the button and wrap them around the slack threads several times (Figure 3). Tie the threads, and clip excess.

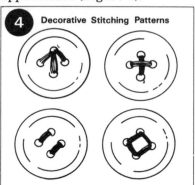

3 Wrap threads around shank and tie off.

To further anchor the knot, dot with seam sealant.

• Add interest to garments by varying the stitching sequence for decorative button applications (Figure 4).

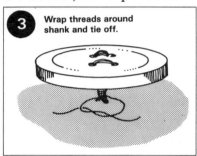

4 Decorative Stitching Patterns

BUTTON LOOPS

With elastic thread and a machine blindstitch, you can create delicate button loops for an attractive closure on a girl's dress (Figure 1) or a lace gown (Figure 2) in a very short time. Use this technique on blouses, dresses and lingerie, too.

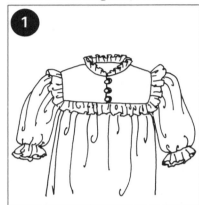

1

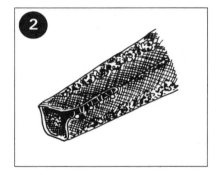

2

For a polished look, European-made elastic thread is preferred to the thinner, American-made elastic thread. Tiny, lustrous ball or half-ball buttons with shanks are the perfect finishing touch.

• Prepare the garment by finishing the neckline, sleeve or other opening with a facing so the raw fabric edges are enclosed. Or, fold back the seam allowance and finish the raw edge.

• Set the machine for blind-stitching, and sew some samples to arrive at the best length and width settings. Each sideways swing of the blindstitch will form a button loop, so adjust the spacing to accommodate the size button you have selected.

• Position the garment edge under the presser foot so the fabric is to the right of the needle. Then, place the elastic thread along the outer edge of the garment (Figure 3).

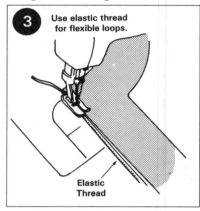

3 Use elastic thread for flexible loops.

Elastic Thread

• Bar tack the end of the elastic to the garment edge (Figure 4). To bar tack, set the

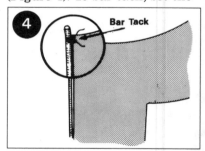

4 Bar Tack

zigzag stitch length to "0" and sew several stitches.

• Blindstitch the elastic, sewing with the straight stitches in the fabric and the periodic zigzag catching the elastic at the garment edge (Figure 5).

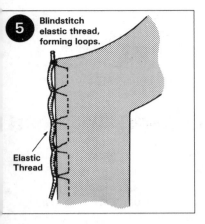

⑤ Blindstitch elastic thread, forming loops.

Elastic Thread

• At the end of the row of loops, leave a long tail of elastic. The elastic tends to stretch as it's being sewn, so work the elastic back through the loops until it's relaxed. Trim off the tail and bar tack the end of the elastic to the garment.

• Sew buttons on the opposite edge of the closure so there is a button for every loop.

BUTTONHOLE HELPERS

If you think buttonholes are too time-consuming, go buttonless no longer. Take a few moments and experiment with the following timesaving tips. With a little practice, you'll know how to make buttonholes quickly and will increase your fashion sewing potential.

• The easiest way to mark evenly-spaced buttonholes is with an expanding gauge. To use it, flex the accordian-style spokes so the points are the

desired distance apart (Figure 1). Mark with chalk or

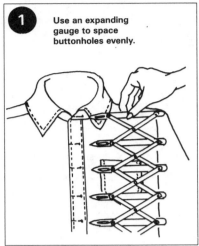

① Use an expanding gauge to space buttonholes evenly.

marking pen through the windows in the spokes, marking the end of horizontal buttonholes or the tips of vertical buttonholes. Use the gauge to mark button placement, too.

• Transparent tape can save you marking time. Mark the buttonhole length on the tape, then apply the tape to the garment. Stitch next to the tape, not through it (Figure 2).

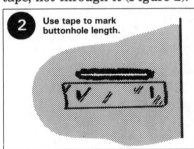

② Use tape to mark buttonhole length.

• For lightweight or silky fabrics, mark buttonhole length and position on a sheet of tear-away stabilizer for easier handling and pucker-free stitching. Pin or baste the stabilizer to the garment to

sew the buttonholes, then tear off the stabilizer when you're finished.

• Stitch in the same direction for each buttonhole. You will not only work more efficiently, but also create buttonholes with a more uniform appearance.

• Keep a small sewing gauge handy to double-check buttonhole length and position as you sew.

• Stitch buttonholes with quality thread. Discount threads can produce uneven stitches.

• Use the same thread in the machine needle and the bobbin for smoother buttonhole stitching.

• Insert a new needle before you begin stitching buttonholes. You'll avoid the snag lines you see around buttonholes on many ready-to-wear garments.

• To cut buttonholes quickly, use a buttonhole cutter.

• To cut buttonholes with a scissors, place a straight pin at each end of the buttonhole. Fold the buttonhole to cut the center, then cut to the pin at each end (Figure 3).

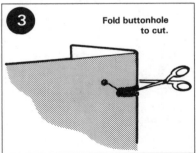

③ Fold buttonhole to cut.

✂ FLIP FACINGS

A flip facing is a combination facing that finishes a neckline and sleeveless armholes in one piece. It not only saves you time, but also makes a smoother finish than if you used separate facings for garments such as sundresses, jumpers, one-shoulder designs and halter tops.

There are two flip facing options. Which one you can use depends primarily on the length of the pattern's shoulder seams.

GENERAL TIPS

• The flip facing must be slightly narrower than the garment across the shoulders; then it will roll to the inside at the armholes. Before cutting the facing, trim ¼″ from the facing pattern armholes, tapering to nothing at the circle matchpoint (Figure 1). If

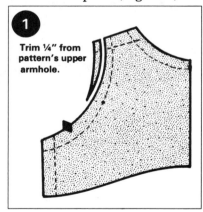

① Trim ¼″ from pattern's upper armhole.

the pattern does not show a circle matchpoint, taper to nothing at a point midway between the shoulder seam and the armhole notches.

• Narrow seam allowances make it much easier to stitch the shoulder area with accuracy. Before sewing, trim the armhole and neckline

seam allowances on the garment and facing sections to ¼″ (Figure 2). Or, if the fabric

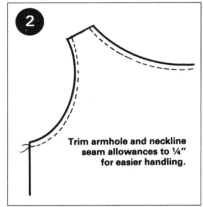

② Trim armhole and neckline seam allowances to ¼″ for easier handling.

is prone to ravel, trim the seam allowances to ⅜″.

• Mark all notches and matchpoints on the armholes and neckline.

• If the pattern does not include a flip facing, draw your own facing pattern using the bodice front and back patterns. Begin with a cutting line several inches below the armhole; taper the cutting line higher at center front and back (Figure 3).

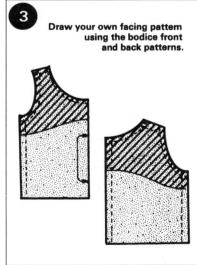

③ Draw your own facing pattern using the bodice front and back patterns.

• In general, the shoulder area on the garment back is wider than on the garment front. This fact will help you keep your bearings as you arrange the sections.

BASIC FLIP FACING

This is the easiest method for sewing an all-in-one facing, however, it can be used only under certain conditions. The pattern must have a center front or back seam, and the shoulders must be at least 4″ wide. Also, the style cannot be too long and full nor the fabric too bulky to turn right side out through the shoulder area. An advantage of this method is you can use it when the garment has a collar or piping trim at neckline and armholes.

To make a basic flip facing:

• Stitch and press open the shoulder seams of the garment.

• Stitch and press open the shoulder seams of the facing. Finish the raw edge along the bottom of the facing.

• Right sides together, stitch the facing and garment together at the neckline and armholes (Figure 4). Clip curves.

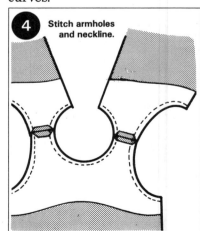

④ Stitch armholes and neckline.

• Underststitch the neckline and armholes to encourage the seams to roll toward the inside of the garment (Figure 5). This

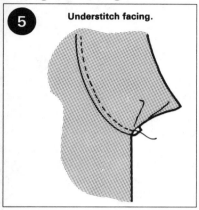

5 Understitch facing.

is easier to do in segments – start at the center of the neckline and understitch toward each end, and start at the shoulder seam of each armhole and stitch toward each end.

• Turn the garment right side out through the shoulder area. Press.

• When stitching the side seams of the garment, continue stitching into the facing (Figure 6).

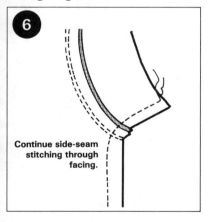

6 Continue side-seam stitching through facing.

NARROW SHOULDERS METHOD

This method takes a little more time, but you can use it when the shoulder seams are quite narrow, such as when sewing small-sized children's garments or halter tops. The shoulder seams of the garment and facing are stitched separately for a fine finish.

To sew this flip facing:

• Stitch the garment side seams.

• Stitch the facing side seams. Finish the raw edge at the bottom of the facing.

• Right sides together, stitch the facing to the garment at armholes and neckline. Stop stitching 2″ from the shoulder seams (Figure 7). Clip and

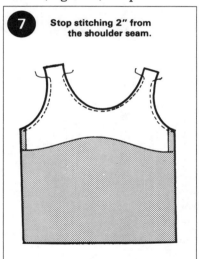

7 Stop stitching 2″ from the shoulder seam.

trim the stitched seams. Turn the garment right side out.

• Right sides together, stitch the garment shoulder seams.

• From the back, reach into the shoulders between the garment and the facing to grasp the stitched garment shoulder seams and the unstitched facing shoulder

seams. Pull the shoulders toward you to expose the unstitched facing shoulder seams. With right sides together, stitch the facing shoulder seams (Figure 8).

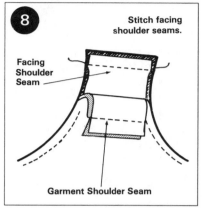

8 Stitch facing shoulder seams.

Facing Shoulder Seam

Garment Shoulder Seam

• Pull the garment front to the back through the shoulder area to stitch the open portions of the neckline and shoulder seams (Figure 9).

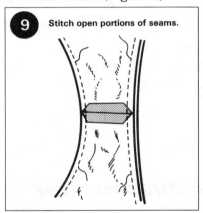

9 Stitch open portions of seams.

• Turn the garment right side out. Understitch, sewing up to the shoulder seams as closely as you can. Press.

✂ JACKET LINING BY MACHINE

There's more than one way to sew a lining into a jacket. There's the custom method, of course, which is sewn almost entirely by hand and is lovely but time-consuming. There are several other, faster methods which combine hand and machine stitching, but by far the quickest trick is lining a jacket entirely by machine. It's the technique used in ready-to-wear jackets, even those with expensive designer labels, so you can feel confident about the quality of workmanship.

Called "bagging" for the "bag" created when the lining is attached to the jacket facing, this method requires no special tools. However, for this speed technique to work correctly, the jacket pattern must have a back neck facing.

It takes a good imagination and the mind of a contortionist the first time you try it. Since the actual steps for stitching the lining to the hems are somewhat difficult to visualize, it's best to follow these instructions carefully your first time through.

PATTERN ADJUSTMENTS

A few minor adjustments to the jacket lining pattern will ensure a perfect fit and allow the lining to hang smoothly inside the sleeve without pulling up the wrist.

• Raise the lining underarm seam (Figure 1). By adding ½″ to ⅝″ at the underarm, the sleeve lining will fit smoothly inside the garment sleeve.

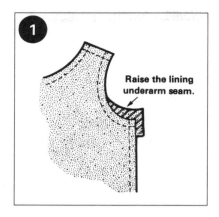

Raise the lining underarm seam.

If the pattern has a side panel, simply reshape the underarm seam in a similar way (Figure 2).

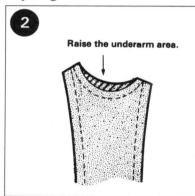

Raise the underarm area.

• Adjust the cut length of the sleeve lining to match the finished length of the garment sleeve.

• Adjust the cut length of jacket front and back lining to match the finished length of the jacket front and back.

JACKET HEM

• Construct the jacket, except for the sleeve and bottom hems.

• Hem the bottom edge of the jacket and each sleeve by basting along the center of the hem allowances; baste by hand or machine through both hem and garment (Figure 3).

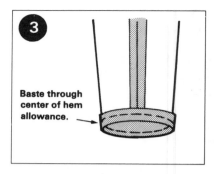

Baste through center of hem allowance.

• At the basting, fold the hem back on itself. Use catchstitches to sew the hem to the garment along the basting line (Figure 4); remove the basting stitches.

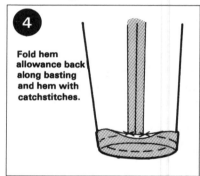

Fold hem allowance back along basting and hem with catchstitches.

LINING CONSTRUCTION

• Sew the lining sleeves, leaving a 12″ opening in one of the underarm seams; begin the opening 1½″ to 2″ below the armhole (Figure 5).

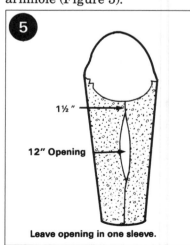

1½″

12″ Opening

Leave opening in one sleeve.

If the jacket pattern has a seam in the center back of the lining and is a short style, leave the opening in this seam instead of in a sleeve for easier stitching.

• Construct the rest of the lining, including setting in the lining sleeves.

LINING INSERTION

• With the bottom edge of the lining aligned with the finished hem edge of the jacket, snip the lining and the facing 3″ from the bottom edges to mark them with a common matchpoint (Figure 6).

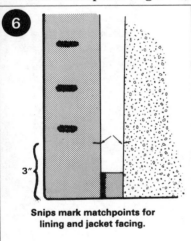

6

3″

Snips mark matchpoints for lining and jacket facing.

Do this on both the right and left sides of the front opening of the jacket.

• Fold ⅝″ seam allowance to the wrong side of the lining from the snip-marks to the bottom edge (Figure 7).

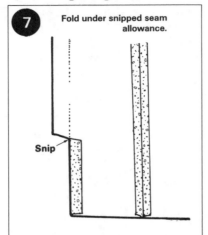

7 Fold under snipped seam allowance.

Snip

• Right sides together, pin and machine-stitch the lining to the jacket facing. Begin at one snip-mark, continue around the front and neck edges, then end at the other snip-mark (Figure 8).

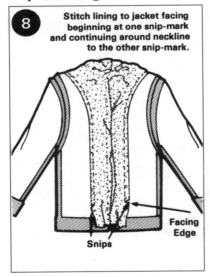

8 Stitch lining to jacket facing beginning at one snip-mark and continuing around neckline to the other snip-mark.

Facing Edge

Snips

• Turn the jacket right side out. Press the facing/lining seam lightly.

• To stitch the lining and sleeve hem together, reach into the sleeve seam opening (or the optional center back seam opening) to pull out the hem edges of one jacket sleeve and the corresponding lining sleeve. Working in a circle and with right sides together, pin and stitch the bottom edge of the lining to the top edge of the sleeve hem allowance in a ¼″ seam (Figure 9). Turn this sleeve right side out.

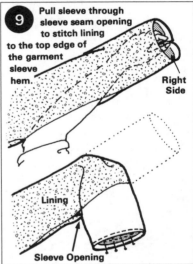

9 Pull sleeve through sleeve seam opening to stitch lining to the top edge of the garment sleeve hem.

Right Side

Lining

Sleeve Opening

Repeat with the other sleeve. This will seem awkward and perhaps impossible at first, but once you've tried it, you'll understand how it works.

• Reach inside the seam opening to pull the jacket and lining bottom hems out through the opening. With right sides together, pin and stitch the raw edges of the jacket hem and lining hem together in a ¼″ seam as for the sleeves, but begin and end the stitching 1½″ to 2″ from the front facings. Turn the jacket right side out.

• Edgestitch to close the opening in the lining sleeve (or center back seam) (Figure 10).

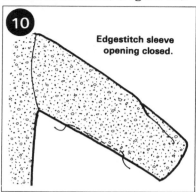

Edgestitch sleeve opening closed.

Be careful not to catch the garment fabric in this stitching.

• At the lower edges of the jacket facing, slipstitch the jacket facing to the hem. Also, slipstitch the loose portion of the lining hem to the jacket hem (Figure 11).

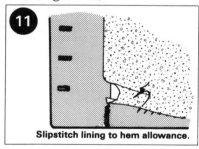

Slipstitch lining to hem allowance.

• To form a jump pleat in the lining hem, smooth the open portion of the lining down into place. A soft fold will form at the bottom edge of the lining. Slipstitch the lining to the front facing (Figure 12).

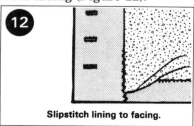

Slipstitch lining to facing.

• Anchor the lining to the jacket so the lining won't stick to blouses and billow out of the jacket when you slip if off. Stitch in the ditch of the underarm seam from the right side through all layers for 1½" below each armhole (Figure 13).

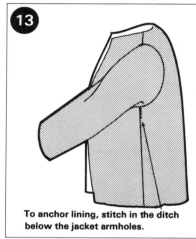

To anchor lining, stitch in the ditch below the jacket armholes.

PRESSING MATTERS

To avoid the hassle of getting up to press while I'm sewing, I place my ironing board at a right angle to the left of my sewing table and lower the height to use comfortably from a sitting position. Now I just swivel my chair around and press, then roll back to the machine – no more wasted time.

B. Patricelli,
Garden City, SC

LINED YOKE

A lined yoke is both a shortcut and a designer technique, proof that saving time does not necessarily mean sacrificing quality workmanship. This method encloses all the raw edges on the front and back yoke seams for garments such as blouses and shirts. It eliminates handwork and extra handling steps, and will surely become one of your favorite sewing techniques.

For a lined yoke:
• Cut a yoke and a yoke facing from the same pattern piece.
• Sandwich the garment front sections between the yoke and yoke facing – layer the yoke right side up, the garment fronts right side down and the yoke facing right side down; stitch the front yoke seams (Figure 1). Trim and

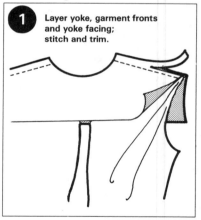

Layer yoke, garment fronts and yoke facing; stitch and trim.

grade the seam allowances. Press the seam allowances toward the yoke and yoke facing.

• Right sides together, pin the garment back to the yoke; keep the yoke facing free (Figure 2).

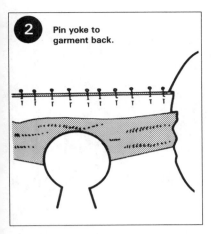

2 Pin yoke to garment back.

• Roll the garment back up to the pinned yoke seam. Roll the garment fronts up to the stitched yoke seams (Figure 3).

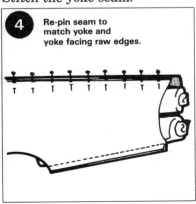

3 Roll garment sections out of the way.

• Wrong sides together, bring the yoke facing to the pinned yoke seam; re-pin the seam to match the yoke facing and yoke raw edges (Figure 4). Stitch the yoke seam.

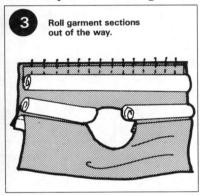

4 Re-pin seam to match yoke and yoke facing raw edges.

• Carefully pull the garment fronts and back through the neckline opening of the yoke to turn the garment right side out (Figure 5).

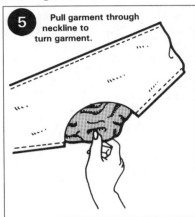

5 Pull garment through neckline to turn garment.

• Press. If desired, edgestitch the yoke seams (Figure 6).

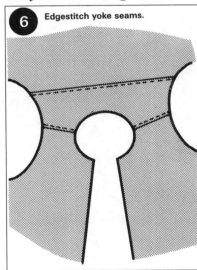

6 Edgestitch yoke seams.

MITERING COMMON CORNERS

Neat, mitered corners separate the amateurs from the pros, but this important detail goes quickly when you know a few secrets. Pressing creases to mark the seamlines and diagonal corner folds makes all the difference when your standards are high but you have one eye on the clock.

HEM CORNERS

• To miter the corner of a hem, begin by folding the fabric on the seamline of the crosswise edge; press. Fold on the seamline of the lengthwise edge; press. Now you have press-marked the key sewing guidelines.

• To sew a miter, fold the corner up toward the right side and align the press-marked seamlines. Press the diagonal corner fold to mark it (Figure 1).

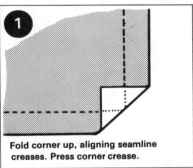

1 Fold corner up, aligning seamline creases. Press corner crease.

• Fold the right sides together to stitch the corner on the press-marked diagonal crease (Figure 2).

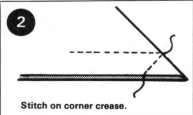

2 Stitch on corner crease.

• Trim the seam allowances to ¼″, and trim across the point. Press the seam open (Figure 3).

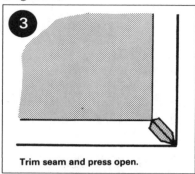

Trim seam and press open.

• Turn the corner right side out to fold the hem to the wrong side; press (Figure 4).

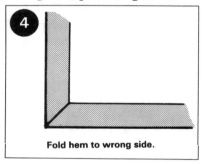

Fold hem to wrong side.

TRIM CORNERS
• For flat, sharp corners when applying flat trim such as ribbon or braid to a finished garment edge, begin by pinning the trim to the finished edge of the garment. Stitch the outer edge of the trim to the corner (Figure 5):

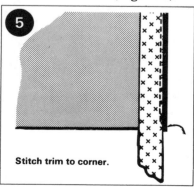

Stitch trim to corner.

pull the threads to the wrong side and tie a knot.
• Fold the trim up on itself so a fold forms at the finished garment edge (Figure 6). Pin the fold.

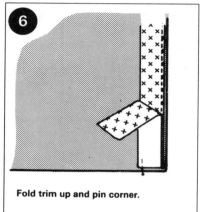

Fold trim up and pin corner.

• Fold the trim down on itself so a fold forms diagonally at the corner (Figure 7). Align the outer

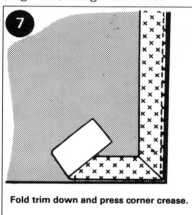

Fold trim down and press corner crease.

edge of the trim with the lower edge of the garment. Press the diagonal crease to mark it.
• Lift up the trim so you can sew a seam on the press-marked diagonal crease (Figure 8). Sew this seam through both layers of trim and the garment. Trim the corner to reduce bulk if necessary.

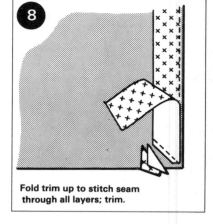

Fold trim up to stitch seam through all layers; trim.

• Fold the trim down to turn the corner. Align the outer edge of the trim with the lower edge of the garment. Starting at the corner, stitch the edge of the trim (Figure 9). Pull the

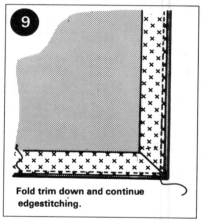

Fold trim down and continue edgestitching.

threads at the corner to the wrong side and tie a knot.
• Stitch the inner edge of the trim to the garment and press.

MOCK SMOCKING

Traditionally worked by hand, smocking is the craft of gathering fabric into tiny pleats in a decorative pattern. It's a classic way to handle fabric fullness on children's clothes, and a beautiful detail to add to your own fashions.

When you lack the time or patience to smock by hand, try mock smocking by machine. This style of smocking is not meant to replace fine handwork, but it does create a special smocking effect in a fraction of the time. Take your choice of two fast-action methods — one features gathering stitches and the other uses elastic thread.

GENERAL TIPS

• Choose a lightweight woven or knitted fabric such as organdy, batiste, lawn or handkerchief linen.

• Use a solid-colored fabric to achieve the most dramatic smocking effect, or choose a print. You will find smocking adds a new, subtle dimension to the character of a printed fabric.

• Before mock smocking, sew a large sample — about 12" square — to see if you like the way the fabric looks smocked.

• You can adapt a hand smocking pattern for machine smocking, or add smocking to a pattern design. Many fashion patterns for blouses, dresses, robes and lingerie lend themselves to this decorative technique. For example, smock the waist or yoke on a dirndl skirt (Figure 1).

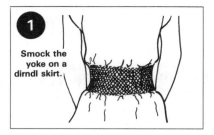

Smock the yoke on a dirndl skirt.

Or, replace the cuff on a sleeve with several rows of machine smocking (Figure 2)

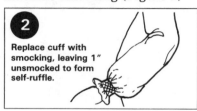

Replace cuff with smocking, leaving 1" unsmocked to form self-ruffle.

— just add length to the sleeve pattern equal to the width of the omitted cuff, plus an inch or so to allow the smocking to form a self-ruffled hem.

• Another approach is to machine-smock a flat panel of fabric, then cut a garment section such as a yoke from the smocked fabric.

• Preshrink the fabric and any trims.

MOCK SMOCKING WITH GATHERS

• The gathered smocking shortcut consists of multiple rows of machine gathering stitches. Pull up the gathering threads for a three-to-one ratio of fabric to finished, smocked size — for example, after smocking, a 24"-wide section of fabric measures 8" wide.

The finishing touch is stitching a narrow (¼"- ¾"-wide) trim such as embroidered braid or ribbon over the gathering stitches, or using decorative machine stitches to conceal the gathering stitches.

• To determine the amount of trim you'll need, experiment with the spacing of gathering rows within the area to be smocked. Test the trim placement by using the tissue pattern piece (Figure 3).

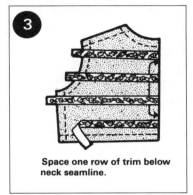

Space one row of trim below neck seamline.

Remember to allow enough trim to extend into the seam allowances, and to double the amount of trim since the pattern is for one-half of the garment.

A good general rule of thumb is space the rows of trim ¾" to 1½" apart. Keep the spacing proportional to the size of the garment; space the rows closer for small children's garments.

• If the garment has a shaped neckline, be sure to space a complete row of trim below the neck seamline. If the garment has a straight neckline, such as in a pinafore, space a complete row of trim about 1" below the cut edge (Figure 4). Finish the edge with decorative serging or a narrow hem, and an attractive self-ruffle will form when the section is smocked.

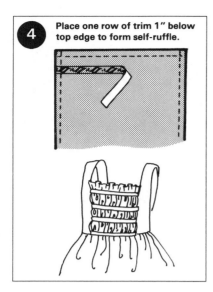

4 Place one row of trim 1" below top edge to form self-ruffle.

• If working with a pattern for hand smocking, the pattern is oversized to allow for smocking. To prepare for machine smocking, cut the pattern from fabric. Unpin the pattern, and staystitch the edges. Mark guidelines for machine gathering on the wrong side with a marking pen (Figure 5). Make sure the

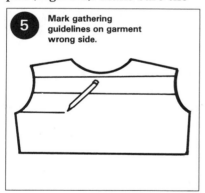

5 Mark gathering guidelines on garment wrong side.

guidelines are marked on the straight fabric grain so the finished smocking will drape evenly.

• If you are adding smocking to a pattern, mark the guidelines for smocking on flat

fabric, draw up the stitches into gathers, and then cut out the pattern.

• To gather, place cord or heavy thread over the guideline marked on the fabric. Zigzag over the cord, using a wide, medium length stitch and making sure the stitches encase the cord rather than pierce it. A cording presser foot with a recessed base makes this step easier. Leave long cord ends.

• Pull the cords to gather the fabric. Distribute the fullness evenly. Leave the seam allowances flat (Figure 6).

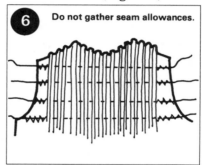

6 Do not gather seam allowances.

• Compare the shirred section with the pattern to check the sizing.

• Edgestitch trim over each row of gathers, stitching each edge in the same direction to prevent puckers (Figure 7).

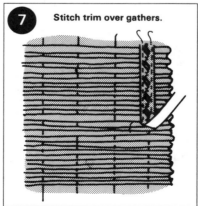

7 Stitch trim over gathers.

Extend the ends of the trim into the seam allowances.

• Or, over each row of gathers, sew a row of decorative machine stitches. It may be necessary to lighten the pressure on the presser foot to keep the gathers from shifting as you stitch.

• Decorative stitches can also be combined with ribbon, or use a twin needle to create a more intricate looking stitch pattern.

MOCK SMOCKING WITH ELASTIC

• This machine version of smocking requires elastic thread in the bobbin. Use a strong elastic thread with good recovery. Quality, European-made spun polyester elastic thread is recommended by many sewing machine manufacturers.

The needle thread, which shows from the garment's right side, can match or contrast with the fabric. Consider using a decorative or variegated thread for added interest.

• Machine-smock fabric before cutting out the garment section. Start with a rectangle the length of the pattern piece. Determine the width needed by a test sample – if a 12"-wide sample draws up to 6", you'll know the rectangle must be twice the width of the pattern piece.

• Use chalk or a marking pen to draw guidelines on the right side of the fabric. Space the guidelines at least ½" apart.

• Hand wind elastic thread onto the bobbin to keep it from tangling. Do not stretch the elastic as you wind it. Insert the bobbin in the machine and thread in the usual manner.

• Select the machine stitch desired.

Use a straight or zigzag stitch to smock the fabric, or experiment with one of the machine's decorative stitches. The honeycomb stitch, often called the smocking stitch, is a natural choice (Figure 8).

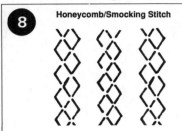

Honeycomb/Smocking Stitch

If selecting a straight stitch, use a medium to long length. If selecting a zigzag stitch, use a 2 mm to 3 mm stitch width and length. If selecting a honeycomb or other decorative stitch, consult the machine manual for suggested stitch width and length.

• Place tear-away stabilizer or adding machine tape under the fabric to keep it flat when smocking, help prevent tension problems and maintain uniform fabric feeding for an even stitch length throughout; stitch slowly.

• Stitch the first row of smocking, then check stitch tension. Adjust the needle thread tension or the bobbin tension as needed so the elastic thread forms a straight line on the wrong side of the fabric.

• Carefully tear stabilizer or tape away from the wrong side of the fabric. Any small particles caught in the stitching will wash out.

• Lay out the pattern pieces on a single layer of fabric, matching the pattern grainline arrow to the fabric grainline. After smocking, the elasticized fabric will mold to the body, so fold out any darts.

Smooth out the fabric to pin the pattern along neck, shoulder and armhole edges; pin remaining pattern edges to the relaxed fabric. The resulting "bubble" in the middle of the pattern pieces (Figure 9) is where the

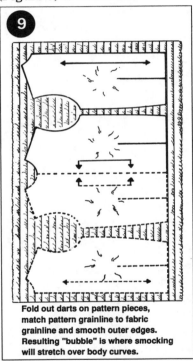

Fold out darts on pattern pieces, match pattern grainline to fabric grainline and smooth outer edges. Resulting "bubble" is where smocking will stretch over body curves.

elasticized smocking will stretch over body curves.

• Trace the outline of the pattern pieces with chalk or marking pen.

Before cutting, zigzag around all marked edges to secure the elastic thread ends. Cut out pattern pieces with 1″ seam allowances.

• Machine-baste garment sections together, using 1″ seam allowances. Try on the garment to check the fit and adjust if necessary; stitch seams permanently. Stitch seams again ⅛″ inside the seamlines to anchor the elastic threads securely.

• Finish raw edges with serging or pinking, trimming off the excess seam allowance. Press seam allowances to one side.

PLACKET IN A POCKET

If you'd rather avoid putting a zipper in a skirt or pair of pants, the placket in a pocket closure is meant for you. Ready-to-wear manufacturers were the first to use this construction technique which not only saves labor, but also material costs. Today, you'll find this quick and easy detail on all types of garments, including those bearing designer labels.

In addition to economy and efficiency, the placket option makes a garment easier to step into than a zippered opening of comparable size. It also allows your weight to fluctuate without the need for garment alterations.

HOW TO SEW A PLACKET IN A POCKET

• It's easy to convert a skirt or pants pattern which has diagonally-set pockets in the front and a zipper at center back (Figure 1). All you have

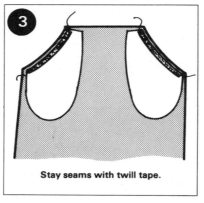

to do is cut the waistband about 10" longer than your waist measurement (Figure 2).

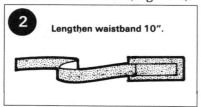

2 Lengthen waistband 10".

The exact slant of the pocket affects the exact amount of extra waistband length you'll need; instead of spending time taking exact waistband measurements, cut the waistband comfortably long and trim it to the correct length later. No adjustments are necessary on the other pattern pieces.

• With right sides together, stitch the pockets to the garment front. To keep the pocket opening from stretching, stay the seam by stitching through twill tape or lightweight selvage (Figure 3).

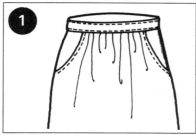

3 Stay seams with twill tape.

• Understitch the pocket seam allowances to keep them from rolling to the right side of the garment (Figure 4).

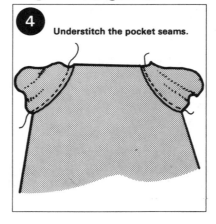

4 Understitch the pocket seams.

• Turn the pockets to the inside and press. If desired, topstitch ½" from the edge of the pocket openings.

• With right sides together, stitch the right side front section to the right pocket. Stitch the left side front section to the left pocket, leaving the seam open after rounding the pocket curve (Figure 5). This seam opening

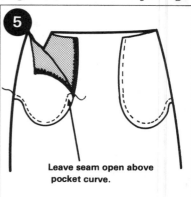

5 Leave seam open above pocket curve.

will become the placket, and should be between 7⅝" and 9⅝" long. Finish the raw edge of each layer at the seam opening by serging, stitching a narrow hem or binding with sheer bias tricot tape.

• Baste the side edges of both pockets to the garment front. Baste the top edges of the right pocket and right side front section to the garment front (Figure 6).

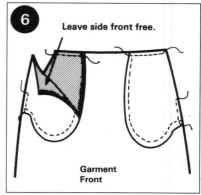

6 Leave side front free.

Garment Front

Baste the top edge of the left pocket to the garment front; leave the top edge of the left side front section free.

• Right sides together, stitch the garment front and back together at the side seams. Clip the front seam allowance at the bottom of each pocket. Press the seam open below the clip; above the clip, press the seam allowances toward the back of the garment (Figure 7).

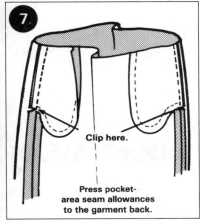

Clip here.

Press pocket-area seam allowances to the garment back.

• Apply the waistband, extending the waistband to the side front section on the left side. Sew hooks and eyes to the overlapping areas of the waistband (Figure 8).

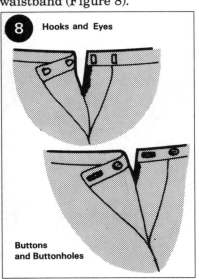

Hooks and Eyes

Buttons and Buttonholes

Or sew a buttonhole at the overlapping and underlapping ends of the waistband; sew one button in line with the side seam and the other button in line with the pocket seam opening.

✂ QUICK-PICKED ZIPPER

A hand-picked zipper suggests couture quality and is one way to identify an expensive garment. However, if hand sewing isn't your forte, be assured your sewing machine can do the job for you. Not only will you save time, but the stitches will be precisely even.

Practice is the key to mastering this technique, but once perfected, you'll have a prestige closure. Just set up the machine for blindstitching and follow these simple steps.

GETTING STARTED

• Buy a zipper that's at least 1" longer than the length specified in the pattern. A zipper with supple, tricot-like tape is preferred.

• With chalk or marking pen, mark the bottom of the zipper opening on the garment seamline.

• Stitch the seam, back-stitching at the mark. Baste the zipper opening closed.

• Set the sewing machine for a 2 mm- to 2.5 mm-wide blindstitch with a stitch length of 2 mm. If your machine's blind hem foot has a narrow toe on the left, use it; if not, opt for the zipper foot.

• Practice the following techniques on fabric scraps using an old zipper until the stitches show uniformly on the right side as tiny, parallel marks. Once you have practiced, apply the zipper to the garment.

APPLYING THE ZIPPER

• Position the closed zipper face down, centering the teeth over the seamline and extending the zipper pull at least 1" beyond the top edge of the garment.

• Using extra-long straight pins such as quilting pins, pin the zipper in place from the wrong side. Insert the pins to enter the zipper tape and fabric 1/4" from the teeth, run under the zipper teeth, and exit 1/4" beyond the other side of the teeth; space pins 1" apart (Figure 1).

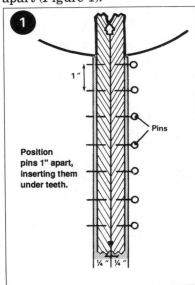

Position pins 1" apart, inserting them under teeth.

Pins

• Fold the seam allowance back to the point where the pins enter the fabric so the zipper is underneath.

• Removing the pins before you stitch over them, blindstitch along the edge of the exposed fold so the straight stitches are positioned on the seam allowance and catch the zipper tape while the zigzag stitches "bite" into the fabric fold (Figure 2).

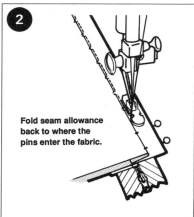

Fold seam allowance back to where the pins enter the fabric.

• Repeat for the other side of the zipper, carefully positioning the stitches directly across from each other. To do this, note where the first zigzag stitch has "bitten" the fold on the first side; set the machine so the first "bite" stitch on the second side is at the same position (Figure 3).

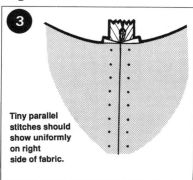

Tiny parallel stitches should show uniformly on right side of fabric.

• Anchor the bottom of the zipper tape to the seam allowance by hand.

• Move the zipper pull to the bottom of the zipper. Stitch the facing or waistband to the garment, catching the top of the zipper in the seam (Figure 4).

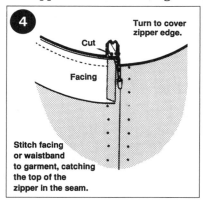

Turn to cover zipper edge.

Cut

Facing

Stitch facing or waistband to garment, catching the top of the zipper in the seam.

• With the zipper open, cut the top of the zipper tape off even with the waistband or facing seam allowance. Finish the waistband or facing.

The waistband or facing stitching should stop the zipper from coming off the track. However, if the zipper does come off-track, simply remove the zipper stop at the zipper bottom and slide the pull back on the track from the bottom. Replace the metal stop, or stitch a bartack across the teeth at the bottom of the zipper.

ZIPPER ZEAL

To be sure of accurate stitching on centered zipper applications, I center a piece of cellophane tape over the right side of the basted seam and stitch along each tape edge. When I remove the tape, I have a perfectly-stitched zipper every time.

M. Casey,
Lakeview, OH

RUFFLER REVELATIONS

The ruffler may be one of the most useful sewing machine accessories you can own. It gathers fabric evenly for ruffles or flounces and makes small pleats or tucks at regular intervals. It can also create a ruffle and stitch it to a garment edge in a single operation.

Once you've mastered the ruffler, you can sew spectacular ruffled skirts, dresses, pinafores, nightgowns, sleeves, dance dresses and costumes to show off your expertise. The options are as infinite as the possible length of your timesaving ruffles.

HOW TO SET UP A RUFFLER

• Rufflers are available to fit most sewing machines. Check your machine's manual or ask a dealer to determine whether your machine requires a high-shank, low-shank or slant-needle version.

• To attach a ruffler to a machine, refer to the diagram below (Figure 1). Remove the

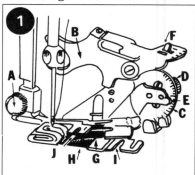

A. Presser Foot Screw
B. Lock Arm
C. Gauge
D. Pointer Screw
E. Pointer
F. Projector
G. Upper Blade
H. Lower Blade
I. Cloth Guide Finger
J. Upper Cloth Guide Slot

presser foot from the machine, then use the presser foot screw (A) and hole in the pressure bar to attach the ruffler. Make sure the ruffler's lock arm (B) is over the needle clamp on the machine.

• The three controls for adjusting a ruffler are the machine's stitch length, the ruffler gauge and the ruffler projector. Get to know the ruffler by setting these three controls in various combinations, then stitch on fabric scraps.

To control the amount of fabric each stitch takes up, adjust the machine stitch length. The shorter the stitch, the fuller the gathers or the closer together the pleats.

Also control the fullness by adjusting the number at which the ruffler gauge (C) is set. To adjust the ruffler gauge, loosen the pointer screw (D). Set the pointer (E) at a number and tighten the screw. The higher the number, the fuller the gathers.

There are four possible settings on the projector (F). Set the projector (Figure 2) at

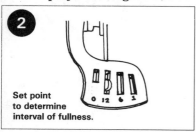

Set point to determine interval of fullness.

"0" to disengage the ruffler if you want to straight stitch while the ruffler is attached to the machine; set at "1" to form gathers; set at "6" to form pleats every 6 stitches; or set at "12" to form pleats every 12 stitches.

TIPS FOR USING A RUFFLER

• To stitch gathers or pleats, slip fabric between the upper (G) and lower (H) blades, then under the cloth guide finger (I) (Figure 3).

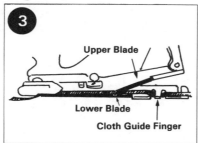

Upper Blade

Lower Blade

Cloth Guide Finger

• On most rufflers the upper and lower blades are blue to help you identify them.

• Pull the fabric away from you when inserting it between the blades. If you pull the fabric toward you, it is possible to break the teeth in the upper blade or snag the fabric.

• To ruffle fabric as you sew it to a garment edge, position the fabric to be ruffled between the two blades and under the cloth guide finger as usual. Position the flat garment edge underneath the two blades and under the cloth finger (Figure 4).

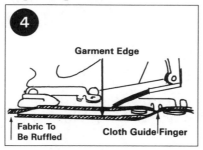

Garment Edge

Fabric To Be Ruffled

Cloth Guide Finger

Gently guide both layers of fabric as you sew so the flat garment edge will not feed more quickly than the fabric being ruffled.

• To encase the ruffle between two layers of fabric (Figure 5), follow the steps

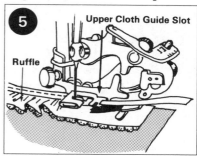

Upper Cloth Guide Slot

Ruffle

above to position the fabric to be ruffled and one flat garment edge. Position the third fabric layer over both blades but under the upper cloth guide slot (J).

• Experiment on a fabric scrap before ruffling or pleating a project, because every fabric gathers differently.

• A crosswise fabric strip will gather up more fully than a lengthwise strip.

• It's easier to pleat or ruffle more fabric than you will need and cut it to size, than to try to figure exact measurements.

FOOT POWER

I've eliminated a roving sewing machine foot pedal by gluing 1″ squares of the hook side of hook and loop fastener under each corner of the control base. The hooks grip the carpet and keep the pedal in place.

N. Luisi,
N. Plainfield, NJ

SALVAGE THAT SELVAGE

Remember when you were admonished never to use selvages in your sewing? It's an old rule that begs to be broken because using selvages can save you time and money.

The selvage, that narrow finished edge on a woven fabric, is a result of the weaving process. The lengthwise (warp) yarns at the edges of the fabric are purposely packed closely to create firm, non-raveling borders. This makes selvages very useful when you need a non-stretch, prefinished edge.

SELVAGE SEWING TIPS

• Use only selvages of good quality. If the selvage is smooth, even and free of puckers, it's a worthy sewing aid. If it's lumpy, irregular or buckled, don't use it.

• Preshrink the fabric, then examine the selvages. If the selvage shrinks so much it draws up the fabric into ripples, avoid using the selvages.

• Use the selvage as a built-in finished seam edge for garment seams cut on the straight fabric grain. Excellent candidates for this purpose include the center back slit opening of straight skirts (Figure 1), the center back

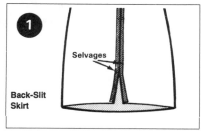

Back-Slit Skirt / **Selvages**

seam of boxy jackets, children's clothes that will see hard wear or be outgrown before they're worn out and loosely-woven fabrics.

• Cut the lining in a straight skirt crosswise and use the selvage as a prefinished hem (Figure 2).

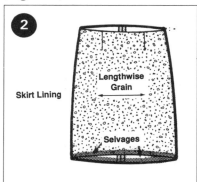

Skirt Lining / **Lengthwise Grain** / **Selvages**

You will need to pre-determine the finished hem length of the skirt before layout, but the rewards of this planning are twofold. First, you eliminate the need to sew the lining hem, and second, the stronger lengthwise lining fabric yarns are positioned around the body; they'll take the strain through the hipline, tummy and thigh areas and add to the life of the lining and skirt.

• Cut straight, pleated skirts such as kilts crosswise, using the selvage as a hem. Omit the hem allowance on the pattern and position the hemline on the selvage during layout. The skirt will press into pleats more easily with this non-bulky hem.

• If the selvage differs noticeably in color or texture from the fabric, you can still use it as a hem shortcut. Just layout the pattern so the hemline falls just above the

selvage. To hem, fold the selvage to the wrong side and stitch by hand or machine. This technique is especially effective to avoid interrupting prints which have border designs that extend to the selvage edge.

• If a garment requires a large quantity of ruffles, cut the ruffles with one edge aligned with the selvage. You'll avoid tedious hemming of yards and yards of fabric.

• Cut waistbands and cuffs with one long edge on the selvage (Figure 3). You'll

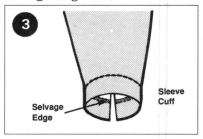

Selvage Edge / **Sleeve Cuff**

eliminate one turned-under raw edge and reduce bulk.

• Use the selvage to make easy belt loops or narrow straps. Determine the desired finished width of the loop or strap and multiply by three. Cut one strip this width, making it long enough to cut all the loops or straps and placing one long edge on the selvage.

Fold the strips in thirds with wrong sides together and the selvage on the outside. From the selvage side, edgestitch close to each fold (Figure 4).

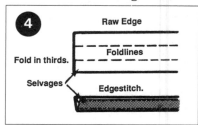

Raw Edge / **Foldlines** / **Fold in thirds.** / **Selvages** / **Edgestitch.**

Cut the strip into individual loops or straps.

• Cut yoke facings with the long, straight edge on the selvage. Use the stitch-in-the-ditch technique to secure the facing edge quickly to the garment (Figure 5).

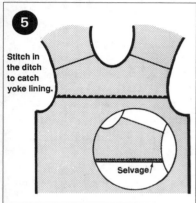

This technique is also useful for front bands on blouses (Figure 6).

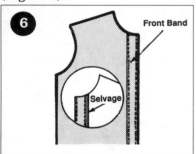

• Cut casing self-facings on simple pants and skirts with the edge on the selvage (Figure 7). By eliminating the

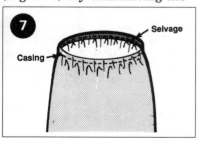

need to turn under the raw edge, you'll save time and reduce bulk.

• Selvages are strong, making them a perfect substitute for twill tape or seam tape to stay a seam. Self-fabric selvages are especially useful when working with a sheer fabric and you need an exact color match to prevent show-through to the right side or for a V-neckline finished with a band (Figure 8).

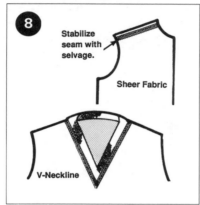

• Save the selvages of lightweight, silky fabrics for use as seam stays on heavier, bulkier fabrics.

✂ SERGER HEIRLOOM SEWING

The lovely, heritage detailing on French handsewn garments can be approximated in less than half the time using a serger and purchased trims. For this shortcut approach, you decorate flat fabric first, then cut out the garment sections.

One of the options is using the decorative stitch capabilities of a conventional machine to add extra detailing to the heirloom serging. When you're finished, you'll have a beautiful garment with workmanship similar to the authentic, old-fashioned kind.

GENERAL TIPS

• By tradition, fine cotton Swiss batiste is the prime heirloom sewing fabric. Polyester/cotton blend batiste or any lightweight, finely-woven fabric such as handkerchief linen or voile also work well.

• Another tradition is sewing with white thread on white fabric, although ecru on ecru, white on pastel or pastel on white are other popular combinations.

• A third tradition is using pure cotton trims. If these are difficult to find, use cotton, polyester or nylon blend laces and embroidered trims. You may mix types of trims within a single garment.

• Types of trims you will find appropriate for heirloom sewing include lace insertion (Figure 1) which has finished, straight edges on both sides for use within the garment

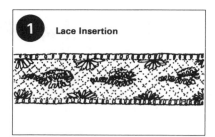

1 Lace Insertion

sections, and lace edging (Figure 2) which has one

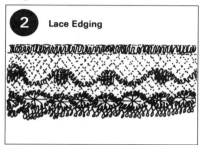

2 Lace Edging

straight and one scalloped edge for decorating hems.

Eyelet trims with delicate embroidery are often added to heirloom-style garments as insertions or edgings. There is also eyelet beading (Figure 3),

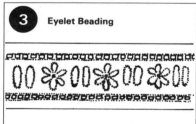

3 Eyelet Beading

which has ladder-like openings through which ribbon can be threaded for a hint of color, and embroidered braid trims with delicate designs (Figure 4).

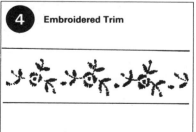

4 Embroidered Trim

• To estimate how much trim you'll need, plan the placement in advance using the pattern pieces. Allow an extra yard of trim for practice serging.

• Preshrink all trims and fabrics.

• Choose a lightweight, machine embroidery thread for a delicate-looking stitch. Rayon thread adds a lustrous sheen to the stitches and is one thread option, but it may break more easily than other threads.

• Choose patterns with yokes, collars, cuffs, straight hemlines, ruffles or pockets to showcase heirloom sewing details (Figure 5).

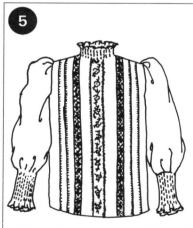

5

• To visualize the heirloom detailing, lay trims and laces over a piece of garment fabric. Decide on the spacing between the rows, the number of rows and how large the finished detailed area will be. Keep the width of the decorative work and the size of the finished garment in proportion.

• Create the decorative fabric first, then cut out the pattern piece. Sew all heirloom details on a rectangular piece of fabric 6″ longer than the pattern piece.

• Begin decorating the fabric in the center and work outward.

• Heirloom decorative designs are usually symmetrical.

• Use a serger rolled hem stitch to attach lace to fabric as well as to make rows of pintucks. Either a 2-thread or 3-thread rolled hem stitch can be used.

• To serge a lace insertion, mark the center of the fabric piece with a pressed crease. Center the lace insertion trim right side up over the crease-mark and pin in place.

Fold the fabric wrong sides together so the fold is at the right-hand edge of the lace insertion trim. With the serger set for the rolled hem stitch, serge the edge of the lace to the fabric fold (Figure 6). Be

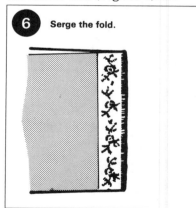

6 Serge the fold.

careful not to cut the lace or the fabric as you serge; disengage the serger knives for added security.

Open the fold and press. Sew the other edge of the lace insertion trim in the same way. Always keep the trim on top so you can see where you are serging.

• Serger pintucking combined with lace trims and decorative stitches creates a special, one-of-a-kind look. To make a pintuck, fold the fabric with wrong sides together, then serge a rolled hem along the fold (Figure 7). Use the

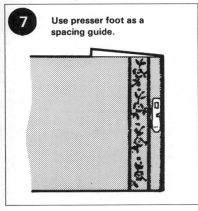

7 Use presser foot as a spacing guide.

width of the serger presser foot as a guide for spacing the rows of pintucks evenly. For wider spacing, press a crease to mark each pintuck.

• If desired, add one or more rows of decorative machine stitches in between the lace insertions and the pintucks (Figure 8).

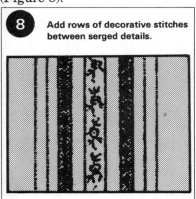

8 Add rows of decorative stitches between serged details.

• After stitching the heirloom details on fabric, cut out the pattern on a single layer of fabric (Figure 9).

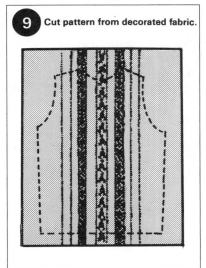

9 Cut pattern from decorated fabric.

Remember to cut a right and left half for each garment section.

PATTERN POINTERS

After I finish a new garment, I make notes on the pattern guidesheet of any tricks, modifications in sewing techniques and alterations used during construction. I also attach a small sample of the garment fabric, so when I go back to use the pattern again I'm reminded of the particulars.

*S. Andriks,
East Hartford, CT*

SERGER SINGLE-LAYER CONSTRUCTION

Sewing a jacket without interfacings, facings or an undercollar is practically unheard of using conventional sewing methods, but it's commonplace when you have a serger. In fact, single-layer garment construction is one of the most creative — and most timewise — ways to use a serger.

Decorative seams are part of single-layer serging and an opportunity for creativity. Experiment with novelty threads that enhance the design lines of the garment and create a one-of-a-kind look.

GENERAL TIPS

• Choose a jacket pattern with a notched, shawl or standing collar as a first single-layer serging project. If the pattern has in-seam or patch pockets, so much the better as they simplify the construction steps even further.

• Decorative seam techniques work best on straight or slightly curved seams which have little or no ease.

• Be sure the pattern fits before you start to serge. After construction, it's too late for garment alterations.

• Select a fabric with enough body to keep its shape without interfacing or facings. Melton, quilted fabric, fleece and sturdy upholstery fabric are excellent choices. Avoid stretchy fabrics which tend to become distorted when single-layer construction techniques are used.

• Both sides of the fabric show in turned-back garment areas such as cuffs, collars and lapels. Make sure both sides of the fabric are presentable before you buy.

SEWING TECHNIQUES

• Cut out the pattern as usual, but omit facings, interfacings and undercollar. Trim hem allowances to ⅝".

• Staystitch curved and bias edges ½" from the cut edge to prevent them from stretching as you serge. The staystitching will be trimmed away by the serger knives as you sew.

• If the edge needs more stabilizing than simple staystitching, serge over two strands of decorative thread when you sew the decorative edge finish.

• To set a serger for decorative stitching, use a novelty thread such as pearl cotton, crochet thread, lightweight yarn or texturized nylon thread in the loopers only; use regular sewing thread in the needle. Loosen the upper tensions. Fine-tune the length and tension settings until the stitch covers the fabric edge like a braid.

• For smooth decorative serging, sew slowly. Also keep some slack in the novelty thread between the spool and the machine.

• To make a lapped seam, combine serging and straight stitching. First, serge the overlapping edge, using decorative thread if desired and trim off ¼" of the ⅝"

seam allowance as you serge. Serge all the overlapping edges at one time.

Then, rethread the serger with regular sewing thread. Serge all the underlapping seam allowances, trimming off ¼" of the ⅝" seam allowance as you serge.

Of course, you will have to plan ahead to decide which side of the seams overlap and which underlap. The sample jacket shown laps the side seams toward the back, the center back seam to the right, the shoulder seams toward the front, and the yoke seams down (Figure 1).

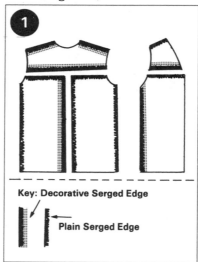

Key: Decorative Serged Edge

Plain Serged Edge

To finish the seam, lap the decorative edge over the corresponding serged edge, matching the seamlines (Figure 2). Topstitch the layers

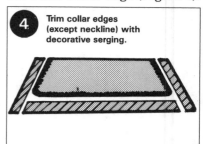

2 Match original seamlines and topstitch.

together on the seamline; use one or two rows of straight stitches.

• Leave 2" of one side seam open at the hem to make it possible to serge the outer edges of the jacket in one step.

• If the pattern has patch pockets, cut out a layer of fusible interfacing for each pocket. Cut the interfacing the finished size of the pocket. Serge across the top edge, trimming off the hem allowance. Serge around the side and bottom edges, trimming off the seam allowance (Figure 3). Topstitch

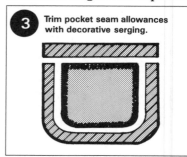

3 Trim pocket seam allowances with decorative serging.

the pocket to the jacket.

• Insert set-in sleeves using standard straight stitching. Finish the sleeve hems with decorative serging.

SINGLE-LAYER NOTCHED COLLAR TECHNIQUE

• For a notched collar, serge the collar ends using decorative thread, then serge the outer collar edge (Figure 4).

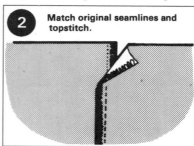

4 Trim collar edges (except neckline) with decorative serging.

• Attach the collar as you serge the decorative edging of the lapels and hemline. To prepare, pin the neck edge of the collar to the jacket, wrong sides together and with notches matching. The wrong side of the fabric will show on the finished lapels and collar.

With the right side of the jacket up, serge the hem, starting at the open side seam (Figure 5). Serge around the

Begin serging here.

jacket in one step – hem, lapel, across the collar, lapel and hem – ending at the open side seam. Remove pins ahead of the serger.

• Tuck the thread chains under the stitching on the wrong side of the side seam opening and secure with a drop of seam sealant.

• Lap the side seam opening and topstitch.

• Press the decorative seam allowance toward the collar. If desired, topstitch through this decorative seam and the collar to hold it flat. The collar rolls over this seam and conceals it.

• Steam the collar and lapels lightly to shape them.

SINGLE-LAYER STANDING COLLAR TECHNIQUE

• Construct the body of the jacket using lapped seams, as described above.

• Pin the collar to the jacket with wrong sides together. Serge the neck seam. Press the seam allowance toward the collar and topstitch (Figure 6).

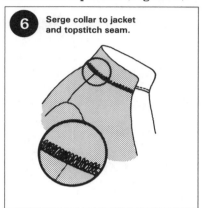

6 Serge collar to jacket and topstitch seam.

• Serge around the jacket edge in one step as for the notched collar above. Start at the side seam opening, continue up the front and around the edge of the standing collar, then serge down the front and around the hem. Secure the thread tails and topstitch the side seam opening as described above.

SERGER AID

Do you have trouble getting your serger to stitch over bulky seams? When approaching the bulky area, apply slight pressure to the front of the presser foot with your left index finger until the bulky area has passed (be careful of the knife). Both the cutting and stitch quality of the serger will be enhanced.

N. Bright,
Medfield, MA

 ## SET-IN SLEEVES WITH BIAS STRIP

There's not a sleeve style as classic nor as versatile as the set-in sleeve. Yet, setting in sleeves smoothly, without puckers, is a common problem.

The key to professional-looking sleeve caps is easing the extra fullness evenly into the armhole. Try this quick technique using a sheer bias-cut fabric strip instead of ease-stitching for faster, smoother set-in sleeves. You can use it on any type of fabric, from synthetic suede to lightweight silks.

• Cut a 1½" x 13" bias strip of sheer or lightweight fabric or use a 13" strip of sheer tricot bias tape.

• Lay the bias strip over the seam allowance on the wrong side of the sleeve cap, between the notches. Stitch with a long stitch (about 8 to 10 per inch), in the seam allowance and next to the seamline (Figure 1).

1 Stitch bias to sleeve cap.

Stretch the strip slightly as you sew between the notches and the shoulder seam mark. Since this area is cut on the bias grain, it eases most smoothly (Figure 2). The area

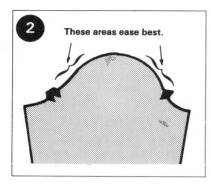

2

These areas ease best.

near the shoulder seam mark is cut on straighter fabric grain and is more difficult to ease.

• The bias strip gently pulls up the fabric, shrinking the extra sleeve cap fabric and shaping it so it fits smoothly into the armhole.

• Sew the sleeve underarm seam. Position the sleeve in the armhole to check the fit.

If the sleeve is too small, clip a few stitches and stretch the bias strip slightly. If the sleeve is too large, pin the sleeve into the armhole and machine-baste; the bias strip will help ease the fullness as you sew.

• Leave the bias strip in the finished sleeve (Figure 3). It

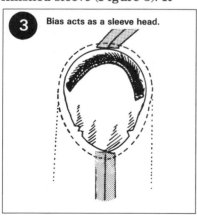

3   Bias acts as a sleeve head.

acts as a sleeve head, cushioning the seam allowances and helping to round the shape of the sleeve cap.

✂ SYNTHETIC SUEDE UNDERCOLLAR

When tailoring a jacket or coat, use synthetic suede for the undercollar. It looks elegant when the collar is turned up, and you can use it on washable or dry-clean-only garments. Best of all, it's an easy technique. You can cut the undercollar to finished size with no seam allowances to turn under, saving time and reducing bulk.

• Use the undercollar pattern piece to cut the synthetic suede collar. Trim the pattern seam allowances, and substitute a fold for the center back seam (Figure 1).

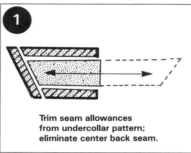

1

Trim seam allowances from undercollar pattern; eliminate center back seam.

Cut the synthetic suede undercollar on the suede crosswise grain, since this is the direction with the greatest amount of give.

• Cut fusible interfacing the same size as the synthetic suede undercollar. Trim off ⅛″ from the interfacing edges and fuse to the wrong side of the undercollar.

• To help stabilize and shape the undercollar, cut and fuse a second layer of fusible interfacing for the stand area (Figure 2).

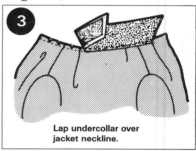

2

Fuse second layer of interfacing here.

Fold the undercollar on the roll line, pin to a dressmaker's ham, and steam it to shape.

• Staystitch the neckline of the jacket ½″ from the raw edge. Clip the curved seam allowance to the staystitching. Lap the wrong side of the undercollar over the right side of the jacket neck seamline. Edgestitch the undercollar (Figure 3).

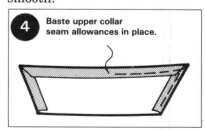

3

Lap undercollar over jacket neckline.

• Turn under the seam allowances on the ends and outer edge of the upper collar; baste (Figure 4). Miter the corners so they are neat and smooth.

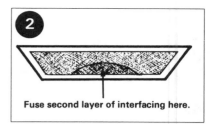

4   Baste upper collar seam allowances in place.

• Stitch the upper collar to the front and back neck facings (Figure 5). Trim, clip and press the seam.

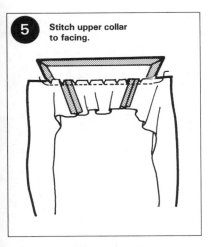

5 Stitch upper collar to facing.

• Pin the facing and upper collar to the jacket front. Stitch the front facing edges and the lapels, but do not stitch the upper collar and undercollar together. Trim, clip and press the seam.

• Loosely baste the facing/upper collar and jacket/undercollar neck seam allowances together.

• Wrong sides together, pin the upper collar to the undercollar (Figure 6). The

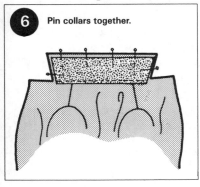

6 Pin collars together.

upper collar edges should extend about ¹⁄₁₆″ beyond the undercollar.

Smooth the collar into finished position to make sure the upper collar completely covers the undercollar and the neck seam. Adjust the upper collar seam allowances if necessary.

• Remove the pins and trim the upper collar seam allowance to ³⁄₁₆″; waiting to trim at this point insures enough upper collar fabric to compensate for the take-up in the turn of the cloth.

• Whipstitch the undercollar to the upper collar by hand.

✂ TAILORING WITH FUSIBLES

The fashion world is constantly changing — and so are tailoring techniques. Years ago, tailoring meant building in shape with crisp hair canvas interfacings and endless small padstitches.

While this labor-intensive approach is still valid if you have the time and patience, the more popular way depends upon fusible interfacings for faster, easier tailoring. It's the way manufacturers and many designers tailor garments, and the results look quite professional. Furthermore, you can use fusible tailoring methods on all types of garments including coats, jackets, womenswear, menswear and children's items.

GENERAL TAILORING TIPS

• In tailored clothing, interface edges, armholes, necklines, front openings and hems (Figure 1). Interfacing adds strength and body as it stabilizes garment edges and areas to prevent stretching.

Also interface details such as collars, cuffs, bands and pockets.

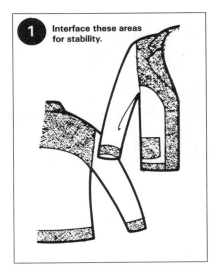

1 Interface these areas for stability.

• The right fusible interfacing for a garment depends on the fabric you are using and the fashion effect desired.

Most tailoring fabrics accept fusible interfacings beautifully, but there are some exceptions. You may want to avoid using fusibles on heat-sensitive fabrics and textured fabrics such as some velvets, seersuckers and velveteens. Test-fuse a sample first to determine the correct interfacing choice.

Contemporary tailored fashions use softer interfacings than the more traditional, crisp types. The fashion fabric should be subtly supported by a flexible, moldable fusible interfacing which does not change the fabric's drape, hand, texture or color. Check the fashion effect when you test-fuse a sample.

• It's a good idea to buy several different fusible interfacings and keep them on hand at home. Use a large fabric scrap to test-fuse at least three different interfacings before you sew.

• For the best fusing results, follow the interfacing manufacturer's directions. The steps have been carefully written to help you have a successful fusing experience, and the directions do vary from one brand to another.

• To add more moisture when fusing interfacing, use a spray bottle to spritz a press cloth with water.

• Use two hands to bear down on the iron when fusing (Figure 2). You must force the

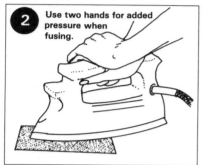

Use two hands for added pressure when fusing.

fusing resins into the structure of the fashion fabric.

• Be patient, and always allow fused pieces to cool down and dry completely before handling them.

• Keep the iron soleplate clean. Use a special cleaning product designed to remove fusible residue so you will not accidentally transfer it to another project.

• A large table press makes fusing interfacings faster and easier. You can fuse interfacing to an entire jacket front in one, ten-second pressing session.

JACKET INTERFACING TECHNIQUES

• If the pattern doesn't include interfacing pattern pieces, or if they aren't shaped like the ones illustrated, cut

your own to get the best possible shape. Draw a cutting line on the pattern tissue to create the interfacing pattern.

• For the best shaping, the longest wear and the least wrinkling, extend the interfacing for the jacket front over the bustline and into the armhole edge (Figure 3). If

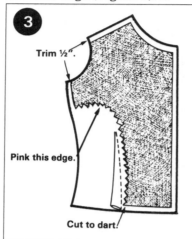

Trim ½".

Pink this edge.

Cut to dart.

there is a front dart, bring the interfacing up to the dart stitching line to cushion the cut edge of the interfacing. If you pink the inner, curved edge of the interfacing, it will blend in better than a sharp, straight-cut edge. Trim away ½" of the seam allowance at the front, neckline and underarm before fusing to reduce bulk – the remaining ⅛" is caught in the stitching for extra stability.

• For the jacket back, you may prefer to use a sew-in interfacing such as firm cotton broadcloth since there are few construction details to help disguise the edge of a fusible interfacing.

If you prefer to use a fusible interfacing, cut the interfacing beginning about 2½" below the

armhole and curving to 4" to 6" below the center back neckline (Figure 4). Trim any

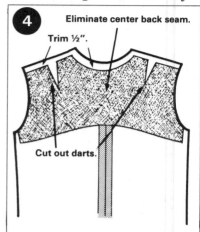

Eliminate center back seam.

Trim ½".

Cut out darts.

darts on the dart stitching lines. Eliminate the center back seam and make it a fold. Trim ½" from the seam allowances at neckline, shoulders and underarms.

• Trim ½" from the undercollar interfacing seam allowances before fusing. For extra shape, cut a second layer of interfacing for the stand area; trim this piece ¼" from the roll line for a smoother collar roll and trim ½" from the neckline seam allowance.

Fuse the stand interfacing after stitching, trimming and pressing the undercollar center back seam (Figure 5).

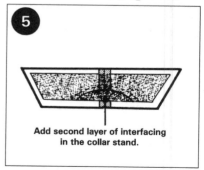

Add second layer of interfacing in the collar stand.

OPTIONAL INTERFACING TECHNIQUES

• For fabrics needing extra body, fuse interfacing to the entire jacket front (Figure 6).

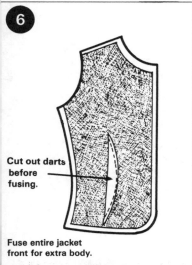

Cut out darts before fusing.

Fuse entire jacket front for extra body.

Cut out darts on the dart stitching lines before fusing.

• For extra crispness at the edges and to help stabilize ravel-prone fabrics, fuse interfacing to the front, front facing, upper collar and undercollar (Figure 7).

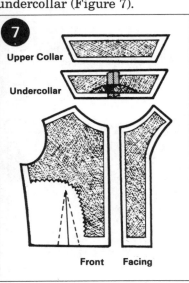

Upper Collar

Undercollar

Front   Facing

• For children's garments and warm-weather jackets which need just a touch of interfacing, fuse interfacing to the lapel area and the facing only (Figure 8).

Front   Facing

• In mens' jackets, fuse interfacing to the entire front. Create a chest piece by fusing a second layer of interfacing to the chest and shoulder area up to the roll line (Figure 9). Fuse a third, graduated layer of interfacing on top.

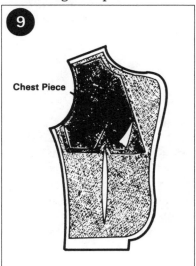

Chest Piece

PATTERN PRESERVATION

When the pattern for my husband's favorite shirt became ragged from repeated use, I purchased lightweight fusible interfacing and pressed it onto the pattern pieces. Now I have a tear-proof pattern that will last for many years.

*C. Hauber,
Phoenix, AZ*

TABLE TRICKS

I keep my checked vinyl tablecloth under my everyday table covering. When I'm ready to cut out a garment, I throw back the top cloth and have a perfect gridded surface for cutting. It beats crawling around on the floor.

*C. Boden,
Noblesville, IN*

VALIANT VALET

Stapling a long piece of the loop side of hook and loop fastener to my closet wall helps me organize the removable shoulder pads I take out of garments before sending them to the dry cleaner. The pads adhere to the strip, remain in pairs and no longer attack panty hose while their garment mates are at the cleaners.

*J. Markham,
Katy, TX*

INTERFACING INSPIRATION

I use the printed plastic instruction sheets that come with interfacings to make a bag for each brand. Simply fold the sheet in half and sew up the sides; tuck the interfacing (and scraps) into the bag. You'll have an organized drawer and no missing instructions.

*M. Harkness,
Delano, MN*

✂ ZIPPER FOOT FACTS

The versatile zipper foot is a handy sewing tool not just for zippers. There are several other ways the zipper foot can work for you.

The zipper foot has a single toe, making it possible to stitch close to any raised edge; the teeth on a zipper are just one type of raised edge you'll encounter as you sew. The single toe also makes it easier to see where you are sewing — a plus in many situations. Here's how to use these zipper foot facts to make sewing easier and faster.

TIPS FOR COVERING CORDING

• The zipper foot is essential for covering cording with fabric to make piping trim.

• To make corded piping, wrap a bias-cut fabric strip around the cording. Position the zipper foot so the toe is to the right side of the needle (or adjust the needle position). The needle should come down in the indentation on the edge of the zipper foot (Figure 1).

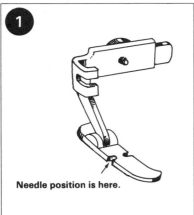

Needle position is here.

Stitch about 1/16″ away from the cording to cover it with bias fabric (Figure 2).

• To insert the corded piping in a garment seam, baste the piping to the right side of one fabric layer first. Baste on the initial piping stitching line positioning the basting 1/16″ from the garment seamline (Figure 3).

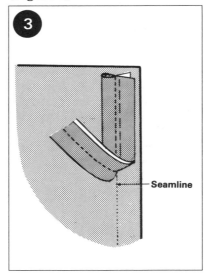

Seamline

To sew the seam, pin the other fabric layer on top of the basted piping. Adjust the zipper foot a fraction of an inch toward the left (or adjust the needle position) so the stitches will be exactly on the seamline (Figure 4).

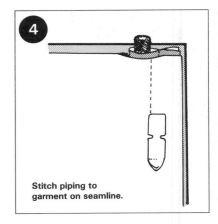

Stitch piping to garment on seamline.

By staggering the stitches, you avoid a build-up of thread in one place. You also pull the bias covering a little more snugly around the cording for a smooth, even piping seam insertion.

TIPS FOR PRECISION STITCHING

• Although stitching in the ditch literally means stitching in the well of a seam, in actual practice it often means stitching next to a seamline with the seam allowances pressed to one side. In this kind of situation, a zipper foot can be especially helpful. Position the zipper foot (or adjust the needle position) to stitch as close to the seam as possible on waistbands (Figure 5), collars and cuffs.

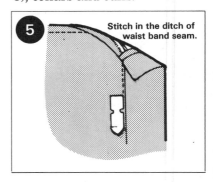

Stitch in the ditch of waist band seam.

• Notched collars require more precise stitching than almost any other detail. A true notched collar has four seamlines converging at each notch (Figure 6) – the upper

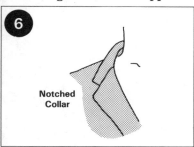

Notched Collar

collar/undercollar, the upper collar/lapel, the undercollar/ garment, and the lapel/ garment front. If you stitch with a zipper foot, you can stitch with greater precision.

Begin at the notch and stitch away from it to prevent creating a bubble at the notch point (Figure 7).

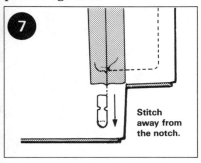

Stitch away from the notch.

• It takes skill to avoid a "step" when sewing the ends of sleeve cuffs. Use a zipper foot, and you can see more easily where to stitch the seams at the ends of the cuff (Figure 8).

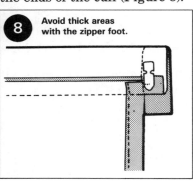

Avoid thick areas with the zipper foot.

• Topstitching isn't difficult, but it can be tricky because the garment varies in thickness, particularly where one seam crosses another.

For easier topstitching, position the zipper foot to the right side of the needle (or adjust the needle position). Align the right side of the foot with the garment edge to topstitch ¼″ from the edge (Figure 9).

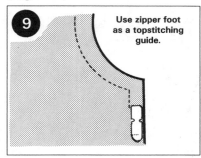

Use zipper foot as a topstitching guide.

• For easier edgestitching, position the zipper foot on the left side of the needle (or adjust the needle position). Align the right edge of the foot with the garment edge to stitch (Figure 10).

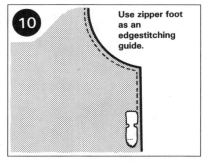

Use zipper foot as an edgestitching guide.

TAPE MEASURE CLOUT

To measure a precise ⅝″ for marking seamlines or top-stitching lines, I use the width of my tape measure — which is exactly ⅝″.

A. Palounek,
Palo Alto, CA

BETTER BASTING

To avoid pulling the wrong thread after inserting a zipper, I baste the zipper opening closed using a contrasting color of thread. After the final stitching, I simply look for the colored thread to pull out the basting.

R. Wack,
Winter Park, FL

ENVIRONMENTAL IMPACT

I make my own "canned air" to clean my serger using an industrial-strength shop vacuum and the crevice tool from my household vacuum. First I use the suction to pick up major lint particles, then reattach the hose to the exhaust side to blow away smaller pieces.

S. Pour,
Mechanicsville, CA

SNAP JUDGEMENT

To accurately place snaps at a closure, I first sew on the ball side of the snap, then rub the ball with chalk and close the garment as it will be when completed. When I gently rub over the snap area, the placement for the other half of the snap is marked by a chalk dot.

T. Anderson,
Ft. Madison, IA

PIN PLUS

I removed the "strawberry" from an old pin cushion and pinned it to the wide end of my ironing board. Now I have a handy place to store needles and pins for quick fixes while I'm pressing.

Mrs. J. Bates,
Clearwater, FL

Chapter 4

FINE DETAILS

Perhaps everyone who sews is really a designer at heart. When your imagination is full of ideas, commercial patterns are just the starting point for creative fashions. Building on the pattern as a base, you can add distinctive touches that stamp a garment as personally yours.

These touches may be elegant designer details, spectacular decorative embellishments or perhaps simply some quiet hand sewing hidden on the inside. You might make new fabric look old or improve the pattern's method for boning a strapless bodice.

The pattern adaptations and fabric enhancements you devise on your own not only add style to your wardrobe, but quality and prestige as well. In a world of mass-produced clothing and cookie-cutter silhouettes, it's satisfying to wear something that's beautifully made and truly one-of-a-kind.

Take pride in fine workmanship and feel free to add your own touch. Most who sew can't help changing the pattern a little here and there anyhow. After all, when you sew, you're entitled to have fashion your way — inside and out.

ANTIQUING FABRICS

Clothing and accessories made entirely or partially from patchwork with a vintage look have a special charm that commands a high price in boutiques. To duplicate this effect at home without cutting up irreplaceable antique quilts, you can artificially age fabrics in a number of ways. You can then cut up the fabrics into garment inserts or patchwork yardage as desired. It takes a little extra time, but there's a great deal of satisfaction in meeting the challenge. It's also an unusual way to achieve an artistic fashion look.

TIPS FOR VINTAGE-LOOK FABRICS

• Use old fabrics. It's not necessary to construct a garment entirely of seasoned fabrics; you can create an antique look by combining one or two old pieces with current fabrics.

While you could purchase aged textiles from antique shops, a more economical approach is to salvage useful areas of used garments. Check garage sales, flea markets and let family and friends know you are interested in old fabrics.

• Purchase new fabrics that look old. This takes a good eye, and you might want to study old quilts to develop your ability to spot fabrics typical of a period. The darker colors used at the turn of the century differ considerably from those of the depression era, for example.

• Tea-dye new fabrics. Just dip fabric into brewed tea until the fabric acquires the proper patina. The stronger the tea and the longer the fabric remains immersed, the darker the mellow glow. However, there is some question about the long-term effect of tea's acids on fabric fibers.

• Over-dye new fabrics. Find cold water fiber reactive dyes in shops that sell weaving supplies, then dye previously colored or printed 100-percent natural fiber textiles.

You can often buy bargain fabrics and make them beautiful with this method. However, use over-dyed fabrics to sew only items which will not be used or washed frequently, as the color may not be hardy.

• Bleach new fabrics. Removing some of the color makes a fabric look older. Soak fabric in diluted bleach or leave it in the sunlight for several days to produce the look desired.

• Abuse new fabrics. You can bake, beat, scrub or rub fabric to make it look old before its time.

• Make the garment, then age the garment. After several washings, you'll experience some shrinkage, a little fading and wear marks at the seams for an heirloom look.

• If making patchwork yardage from vintage-look fabrics, look carefully at the pattern pieces for the fashion garment. Size and shape the patchwork fabric so you don't have to do more work than necessary. It's possible that a very narrow or very wide patchwork section will allow you to position the pattern pieces with less waste than stitching a standard 45″-wide section.

• Save the scraps to create small items such as sachets for gifts.

✂ BIAS SIX-FLARE PLEAT

Add comfort and style to the front of a straight skirt pattern with a graceful six-flare pleat cut on the bias grain. The skirt looks lean and narrow when you're standing, but flares when you walk or sit. Since the pleat increases the bottom width of the skirt, you'll love living with the added ease.

• Modify the skirt front pattern by adding a center front seam with a pleat extension 2″ wide and 15½″ long (Figure 1).

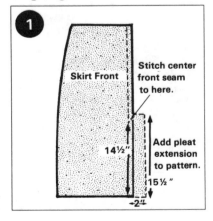

• For the pleat, cut a 22″ fabric square. You may be able to cut this section from scraps leftover from the skirt layout.

• Follow pattern directions to sew the skirt, leaving the center front seam open for 14½" above the hemline in the pleat extension area. Do not sew the hem.

• To form the pleats, fold the square in half diagonally (Figure 2). Mark off a triangle

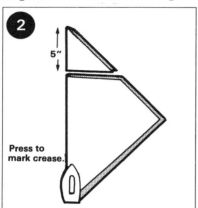

5" down from the top point; trim off the triangle. Press the center fold to mark it.

• To mark the foldlines for the pleats (Figure 3), mark

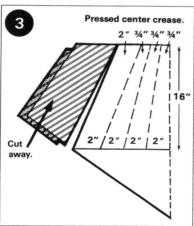

these points on the top edge, measuring out from the center crease: ¾" (pleat fold #1), ¾" (pleat fold #2), ¾" (pleat fold #3), 2" (pleat extension including a ⅝" seam allowance).

Measure 16" down from the top edge and mark these points, measuring from the center crease: 2" (pleat fold #1), 2" (pleat fold #2), 2" (pleat fold #3), 2" (pleat extension facing including a ⅝" seam allowance).

Mark the foldlines on the other side of the crease the same way. Trim off the excess fabric beyond the pleat extensions.

• Fold all the pleats accordian-style toward the center crease, folding them on top of one another. Baste the pleats and press well.

• Trim across the top and bottom of the pleats to make an even, 15½"-long pleat unit (Figure 4).

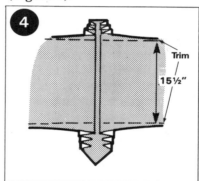

• Right sides together, sew the pleat unit to the skirt pleat extension at the sides. (Figure 5).

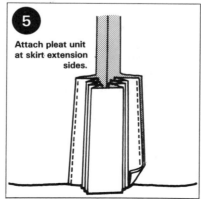

At the top of the pleats, stitch an inverted "V" through all layers for 2" on each side of the center front seam (Figure 6). Hem the skirt.

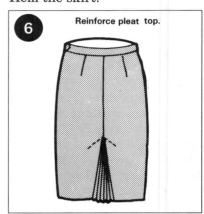

BONING A STRAPLESS BODICE

Whether the garment style is dramatic or demure, a strapless bodice requires special sewing savvy for smooth fit and confident support. From the beginning, strapless designs must be fitted very closely to the figure, which is why the patterns pieces have little or no ease allowed in the bodice area.

In addition, a special stiffener called boning must be sewn into the seams for foundation-style support. Dressmakers used to work with stiff stays made from whalebone, wood or iron to make strapless bodices rigid, but today boning is made of a flexible plastic which is much more comfortable to wear. The easiest type to apply comes encased in a lightweight, bias-cut woven fabric.

As a finishing touch for a boned, strapless bodice, add a waistline stay of firm ribbon or tape. The bodice will be anchored securely to the figure for a full measure of fashionable support.

GENERAL TIPS

• Most patterns for strapless garments include a lining and an underlining; the pattern directs you to sew the boning to the wrong side of the lining.

As an option, you can omit the lining. Sew the boning by hand to the underlining, then finish the bodice edges with a bias-cut facing.

• For underlining, select a strong fabric with the same care requirements as the garment fabric. If you use cotton net, muslin, batiste, silk broadcloth or handkerchief linen as an underlining, the bodice will be more comfortable to wear than if you use a synthetic taffeta or lining fabric.

• Avoid underlining with rayon fabric which may split when saturated with perspiration.

• Cut the underlining on the crosswise grain so the stronger lengthwise grain will encircle the body for maximum support without stretching.

• Strapless designs should fit like a second skin. Most patterns fit so closely they have only about ½" of ease, or extra room beyond the body measurements, so it's especially important to select the right pattern size.

• To test the fit of a strapless bodice, baste the underlined bodice sections together. Pin temporary straps cut from twill tape or selvages to the bodice for easier fitting.

Keep in mind the bodice will look somewhat wrinkled since the boning supports are not yet in position. Fit the bodice by letting out or taking in the seams; reshape the bust area seams for perfect fit.

• Even if not suggested by the pattern, you can add boning to garments with off-the-shoulder necklines or plunging front and/or back necklines for hidden support.

TECHNIQUES FOR APPLYING BONING

• Boning is most effective when placed on the side/front seams nearest the bustline. Boning can also be added at the side seams, the side back seams and between the seams if additional support is needed.

• Don't be afraid to add more boning than called for by a pattern. A strapless bodice that collapses or looks too "soft" will be disconcerting to wear and will look less than professional.

• To cut boning, measure the seam — not including the seam allowances at top and bottom — and add 1" to allow for trimming the boning at each end.

• To trim the boning, slide the fabric casing down and cut ½" off the boning; round off the tip so the boning won't poke through the fabric (Figure 1).

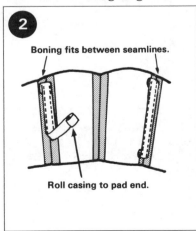

Trim both ends of the boning.

• To apply the boning, roll up the fabric casing to pad the ends of the boning (Figure 2).

Using a zipper foot, stitch the fabric casing to the wrong side of the bodice lining, fitting the boning within the seamlines at the top and bottom of the bodice.

• The boning has a slightly bowed shape; position the boning so it curves toward the body.

• If fitting a bodice with a dropped waistline, try on the bodice and sit down. If the boning buckles, it's probably too long; you may want to shorten the boning so it ends at the waistline.

• For a special garment that must look absolutely smooth, sew boning into a foundation-style underpinning built into the garment, rather than into the garment itself. To cut the underpinning, use the bodice pattern pieces after adapting the bodice front pattern piece by adding the following extra bust dart.

Trace the bodice front pattern, and add a horizontal bust dart at center front for closer fit (Figure 3). To add the

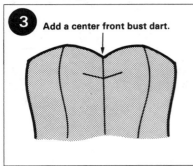

3 Add a center front bust dart.

dart, draw a line from the bust point to the center front seam; cut the pattern from the center front seam and stop cutting 1″ before you reach the bust point. Spread the pattern 1″ on this slashed line to form the dart. Tape paper underneath the dart.

When you spread the pattern to add a center front bust dart, the pattern forms a small pleat at the side/front seam allowance. Add the amount removed by this pleat to the top of the seam to restore the seam to its original length (Figure 4).

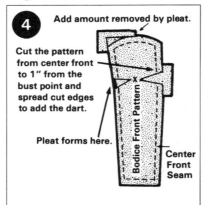

4 Add amount removed by pleat.

Cut the pattern from center front to 1″ from the bust point and spread cut edges to add the dart.

Pleat forms here.

Bodice Front Pattern

Center Front Seam

Sew the bodice underpinning together, add boning, and test the fit by trying it on. After assembling the garment bodice, baste the underpinning to the wrong side of the bodice at top and bottom edges. Handle the layers as one during the remainder of the construction.

• To save time, instead of constructing an underpinning, you can purchase a long-line bra and sew it into the garment.

• Patterns rarely include instructions for sewing a waistline stay, but it's important to have one in a strapless garment. The stay takes the strain off the zipper or other closure, improves garment fit, and helps support the bodice from the waist up. Fit the stay slightly more snugly than the waistline of the garment.

Use twill tape or ½″ grosgrain ribbon to make the stay. Cut it 2″ longer than the waistline of the garment. Center the stay at the center front of the waist seam of the garment (or the waistline of a dropped-waist garment). Holding the stay taut, pin it to all the vertical seams and darts; tack the stay to the seam and dart allowances (Figure 5).

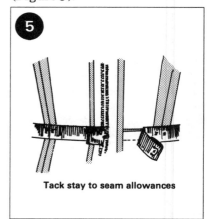

5

Tack stay to seam allowances

With the zipper or other closure closed, fold under the ends of the stay ½″ twice so they meet. Sew the folds, then sew one or two sets of hooks and eyes to close the stay.

DOWEL DUTY
Use 12″-long dowel rods in various diameters as seam rolls for pressing loops, straps, narrow sashes and other hard-to-reach areas. Simply insert the dowel into the open end of the sewn tube to press seam allowances flat before turning — no more burned fingers trying to manipulate these tiny areas.

*K. Anderson,
Brooklyn Center, MN*

BUTTON ART

When you sew creatively, buttons and buttonholes become more than just closures. They become designer details which show fine workmanship and add great fashion appeal. They're also a way to put your personal stamp on the garments you sew or to decorate a plain garment in an artistic but practical and wearable manner. The next time you're ready to make a buttoned closure, use your sewing skills to make it something special.

TIPS FOR CREATIVE BUTTON CLOSURES

• Use a decorative thread to sew on buttons. Make the stitches decorative by using contrasting thread, metallic thread, embroidery floss or pearl cotton.

• Layer sew-through buttons to make a unique, composite button. As you sew, stack a small button on top of a larger button (Figure 1). Or, add a small bead to the stitches as you sew on the button.

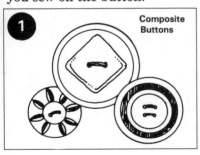

Composite Buttons

• For an eclectic look or to show off a collection of beautiful vintage buttons, use buttons of similar size but different shapes or colors (Figure 2).

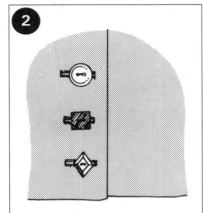

• Space buttons in groups of two, three or more instead of spacing them evenly on a front closure.

• Make bound buttonholes in a contrasting fabric. Use a coordinating solid color of the same fabric type to cut the buttonhole lips, or cut a plaid or stripe on the bias grain (Figure 3).

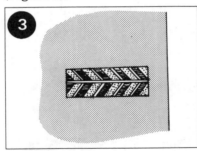

• Cover your own buttons. Use purchased button forms and cut the button covering from a circle of creative fabric. You might cut the circle so a fabric's print motif is centered on the finished button, sew pintucks in the fabric, or add machine embroidered or hand cross-stitched designs to the fabric before covering the button (Figure 4).

• Add an embroidered motif to a machine-made buttonhole (Figure 5). Work a hand button-

hole over the machine-made buttonhole with silk twist, embroidery floss or pearl cotton, then use twist, floss or cotton to embroider the motif. If you embroider a flower, the button then becomes the center of the flower.

• Dress up a closure with an appliqué (Figure 6). Plan the

Appliquéd Closure

appliqué to span the closure, padding the appliqué with lightweight quilt batting for a three-dimensional look if desired. Sew the buttonhole through all layers of the appliqué.

• Add purely decorative button details to garments. Arrange white shirt buttons as a border for a jacket, vest or skirt (Figure 7), or sew on a collage of assorted buttons.

You can combine decorative buttons with beads, rickrack and embroidery, or fold ribbon and sew a button next to each fold (Figure 8).

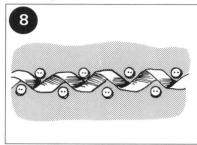

• Use buttons to tuft quilted garments. For an extra show of color, sew each button over a small bow (Figure 9).

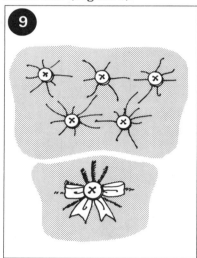

TECHNIQUES FOR CORDED CLOSURES

• Instead of a buttonhole, make a rouleaux loop and use double buttons. For a simple tab, take 8″ of purchased bias-covered cording or round braid. Fold it into a figure eight with the raw edges meeting under the point where the loops cross, and whipstitch the raw

edges together. Slipstitch one loop to the garment (Figure 10). Leave the other loop hanging free.

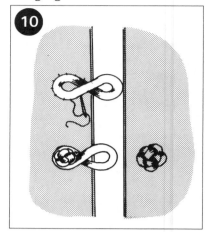

Sew one button over the loop which is attached to the garment. Sew the other button on the opposite side of the closure to insert into the free-hanging loop to close the garment.

• Cover cording with fabric to make custom rouleaux for decorative frog and ball button closures. About 12″ of rouleaux is needed for each button or a frog with four loops. The heavier the cording, the larger the button.

To cover cording, cut a bias fabric strip wide enough to encircle the cording plus 1″ for seam allowances; cut the cording twice the length of the fabric strip.

Wrap the right side of the fabric around the cord, starting at the midpoint of the cord. Using a zipper foot, stitch across the cording to the raw edges, pivot and taper the stitches close to the cording (Figure 11). Turn right side

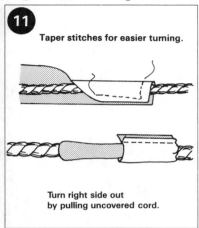

11

Taper stitches for easier turning.

Turn right side out by pulling uncovered cord.

out by pulling the uncovered cording. The tapered stitches make it easier to start sliding the fabric tube back over the uncovered cording.

• To make a ball button with rouleaux, tie interlocking loops for a Chinese knot (Figure 12). Conceal the raw

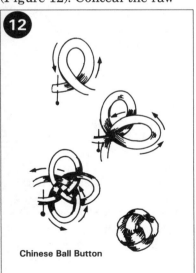

12

Chinese Ball Button

ends of the rouleaux inside the knot and stitch to the button.

• To make a four-loop frog with rouleaux, hide the end under the loop crossings (Figure 13). Whipstitch the

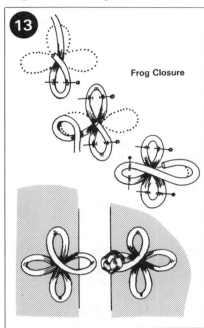

13

Frog Closure

loop crossings securely; whipstitch three loops to the garment, allowing the fourth to hang free to accept the button.

• To make more elaborate frogs, draw the design on tear-away stabilizer. Baste the rouleaux to the stabilizer, whipstitch the loop crossings together, and tear away the stabilizer before sewing the frog to the garment.

CORNER CAPERS

To prevent stitched corners from fraying on collars and cuffs, I apply a drop of seam sealant to the trimmed seams before turning.

A. Downing,
Fresno, CA

✂ CHANEL-INSPIRED TRIMS

An elegant, Chanel-style cardigan jacket deserves its status as a fashion classic. It creates a slenderizing silhouette when worn with a skirt or pants, and it can be worn from one season to the next. The investment in time and materials to create this perennial favorite is modest. However, to duplicate the look faithfully, you'll want to use coordinating braid trims.

These can be difficult to find, but you don't have to settle for plain jackets or trims that are not quite right. Sew, serge, knit or crochet your own custom trims to create a jacket Coco Chanel herself would have admired. Since wool yarn comes in so many varieties and colors, it's the perfect raw material for making elegant, Chanel-inspired embellishments.

TWISTED CORD

• Twisted cord takes only minutes to make since you just

twist several lengths of yarn together. Use the resulting trim not only as a braid, but also for belts or drawstrings.

• To make twisted cord braid, cut several strands of yarn the desired finished length plus a little extra for finishing the ends. Be creative, mixing yarn colors, textures and weights for designer-style elegance.

Tie the strand ends together on a hook, drawer handle or door knob (Figure 1). Pull the

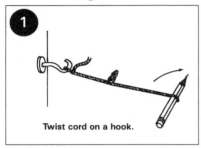

Twist cord on a hook.

strands taut and start twisting the loose end. If using more than two strands, tie the loose ends to a pencil or knitting needle before twisting them.

Twist until the cord begins to kink. Fold the cord in half and allow it to twist. Wrap the cord ends with a single strand of yarn to secure them; dab with seam sealant and allow to dry.

BRAIDED TRIM

• Braided trim is made just like a school girl's braids. Cut lengths of yarn 1½ times the desired finished length of the braided trim. Clip the ends together in a hair barrette and pin to an upholstered chair or a cutting board. Braid the yarn, keeping tension even so the width is the same throughout (Figure 2).

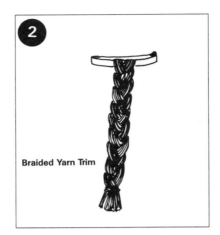

Braided Yarn Trim

• To cut shorter lengths of braided trim to trim pockets or sleeves without the trim's unraveling, mark the trim where you want to cut it. Wrap a single strand of yarn or all-purpose thread on each side of the mark. Dab the wrapped areas with seam sealant and let dry. Cut the braid into sections at the mark.

• A variation of braided trim can be made with a serger set on the longest stitch length. Using a two-thread or three-thread stitch and lightweight yarn or another decorative thread in the upper looper, serge over soutache braid, yarn or narrow trim. Braid several of these serged strands together (Figure 3).

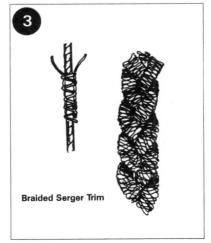

Braided Serger Trim

COUCHED YARN

• Apply a knitting worsted or heavier weight yarn directly to a jacket by couching it with a zigzag stitch (Figure 4).

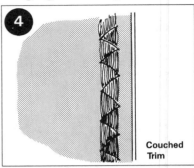

Couched Trim

Choose a textured yarn that will help to hide the machine stitches.

• To prepare the jacket for couching, mark the trim placement with long basting stitches or air-soluble marking pen. In general, this trim is applied after the jacket is faced but before it is lined. Trim pockets before sewing them to the jacket.

• To couch the yarn on the jacket use a medium-wide, long zigzag stitch. A straight stitch or blindstitch could also be used, but these stitches demand more accuracy as you sew and the thread may be more conspicuous.

• To help hide the machine stitches, thread the machine needle with thread matched to the yarn, and the bobbin with thread matched to the fabric.

• Do not stretch the yarn as you couch it to the jacket.

• Couch several rows of yarn side by side for a deluxe, wide, braid-style trim.

KNITTED CORD & BINDING

• Using double-pointed knitting needles in a size appropriate for the yarn, you can knit a tubular trim in the Chanel mode.

• In general, use knitting worsted and needles in the size 6 to 9 range. Smaller needles will knit tighter cords, while larger needles will knit looser cords.

• To knit tubular trim, cast on three or more stitches. The more stitches cast on, the wider the cord.

Knit one row. Slide the stitches to the other end of the needle so you can begin knitting from the opposite side (Figure 5).

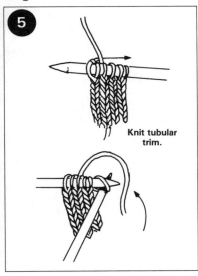

Knit tubular trim.

Knit the second row, pulling the yarn taut as you take the first stitch so the knitting forms into a tubular cord. The tube will form more obviously as the knitting continues.

Continue to knit, slide the stitches and knit the rows to create the trim length required.

• Sew the knitted cord to the jacket by hand. Use all-purpose sewing thread, hiding running stitches under the tube.

• To make binding, knit as described above, but do not pull the tube into a full round as you start to knit each new row.

CROCHETED TRIM

• Even the most basic crochet stitches yield gorgeous trims when you blend two or three colors of textured yarns.

• Use a crochet hook in the size F to J range – whichever size produces the desired look and hand with multiple strands of yarn.

• To crochet braid-style trim, loosely chainstitch the length desired.

Work one single crochet in the second chain from the hook. Then work one single crochet in each chain to the end (Figure 6). Fasten off.

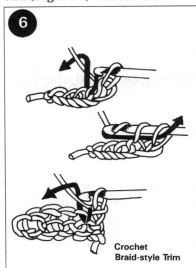

Crochet Braid-style Trim

• For a wider trim, work one half-double crochet starting in the third chain from the hook, or a double crochet starting in the fourth chain from the hook. Or, increase the number of yarn strands or the size of the hook.

• For a narrower trim, chain or double crochet evenly and use as is. Or, decrease the number of yarn strands or the size of the hook.

• To apply the trim, steam-press it if necessary to prevent it from curling. Sew to the jacket by hand, using all-purpose thread and hiding the stitches underneath the trim.

MASTER PATTERN POINT

When tracing a master pattern, I use waxed paper. I simply tear off the length I need. If I need a wider panel, I use the warm, dry heat of the iron to fuse sheets together. My master pattern remains intact and I can have an inexpensive copy in several sizes.

B. Faske,
Brenham, TX

TOWEL TOOLS

I fastened an Irish linen tea towel to the wall next to my sewing machine. It's a convenient place to keep needles and safety pins when not in use, and it acts as a bulletin board for samples, miscellaneous notes and my current project pattern instruction sheet.

L. Stark,
Eugene, OR

DECORATIVE STITCHES

Take full advantage of the decorative stitches on your sewing machine by using them in creative ways on the fashions you sew. Decorative stitches can be bold and dramatic or subtle and elegant, depending on the thread color and texture, the stitch pattern and its scale, and the character of the background fabric.

Spend an hour or so with your machine to discover the many possibilities. Begin with a few spools of machine embroidery thread, which is finer and more lustrous than all-purpose sewing thread, and make a sampler of all the machine's decorative stitches. Select an awning or ticking stripe fabric so you can use the individual stripes to help you place and guide the stitches. Sew a different stitch pattern on each stripe; vary the stitch length and width every inch or so to explore the various effects each stitch pattern can create. When the sampler's completed, hang it near your machine. You then have a handy guide for selecting appropriate treatments for future sewing projects.

GENERAL TIPS

• Put your machine in top condition by cleaning and oiling it. Also, insert a new needle.

• To prevent many of the stitch problems sometimes experienced with decorative stitch patterns, use an embroidery or satin stitch presser foot on your machine. This foot has a groove on the bottom to prevent thread pile-ups and an open toe for better visibility as you sew.

• Loosen the needle thread tension slightly so the stitches interlock on the fabric wrong side.

• Since the bobbin thread should not show on the right side of the fabric, in theory it doesn't matter which thread color you use in the bobbin. In practice, it's a good idea to match the bobbin thread to the background fabric.

• Wind several bobbins before sewing a decorative stitch, and you'll avoid having to interrupt your work to rewind a bobbin.

• For smooth decorative stitches that won't pucker or tunnel the fabric, support the fabric with a backing as you stitch. Use tear-away stabilizer, or use strips of adding machine tape. Remove the backing after stitching.

• Always perfect the stitch on scraps first, then sew it on the garment.

CREATIVE TECHNIQUES

• Use decorative stitches to apply trims such as ribbon, bias tape or rickrack to a garment. Use a single row of stitches on narrow trims and multiple rows on wide trims.

• Combine rows of several decorative stitches to design borders and ribbon-like trims. Use one color of thread and vary the stitch patterns, create a blended look by using shades of the same color thread or mix and match thread colors for a rainbow effect. Also consider using white thread on white fabric for an elegant effect.

For a symmetrical border, begin with the center row of stitches, then add rows alternately on one side and the other (Figure 1). To create

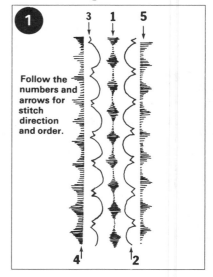

Follow the numbers and arrows for stitch direction and order.

a symmetrical effect when the stitch itself is asymmetrical, stitch one side in one direction; turn the work and stitch the other side in the opposite direction. The two rows of stitches will form mirror images of each other. Or, if your machine has a mirror imaging capability, take advantage of it for symmetrical stitches.

• Substitute a decorative stitch for the satin stitch when making appliqués. Or, outline an appliqué in satin stitches, then use decorative stitches for embellishment.

• Substitute a decorative stitch for straight topstitching on collars, cuffs, sleeves or hems. Use one or more rows of decorative stitches.

- Use a decorative stitch for inserting or applying lace trim (Figure 2). Add a second row of

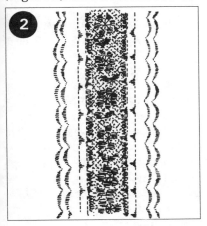

decorative stitches alongside to echo the application treatment.

- Create custom fabric for details such as collars, yokes, cuffs and pockets by stitching row after row of decorative stitches onto flat fabric. Lay out and cut the pattern pieces after decorating the fabric.

- Add decorative stitches to plaid, striped or printed fabrics to create a unique, custom fabric with a three-dimensional quality.

- Machine-quilt with decorative stitches instead of a plain, straight stitch.

- Use decorative stitches to create individual motifs for spot decoration such as a crest on a blazer pocket.

- Instead of using satin stitches for monograms, use decorative stitch patterns in block letters (Figure 3).

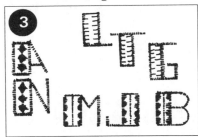

- Create custom trim by embroidering bias tape with a decorative stitch. Apply it to the garment with a straight stitch or a decorative stitch.

- Sew over cord or yarn with a decorative stitch.

- Finish garment edges such as collars, sleeves, necklines or pocket tops with a decorative stitch. Select a stitch that covers the edge, such as a scallop stitch, and layer the pieces with wrong sides together. Stitch the edge, then trim excess seam allowance close to the stitches (Figure 4).

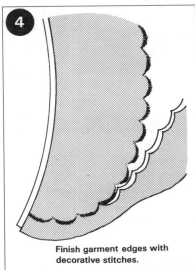

Finish garment edges with decorative stitches.

- Use decorative stitches to cover machine gathers when mock smocking.

DOUBLE NEEDLE STITCHING

Add designer detailing to the garments you sew by stitching special decorative effects with a double needle. Sometimes called a twin needle, it's made with two needles on one needle shaft and can be used on almost any machine.

A double needle makes two perfectly parallel rows of straight stitches on the right side of the fabric. On the wrong side, the single bobbin thread looks like a zigzag stitch.

While you can use a double needle for practical tasks such as sewing hems or pants creases, with a little practice and some imagination, you can use this special needle for creative fun. Pintucks and surface textures are two of the many possibilities covered by the tips and techniques below.

GENERAL TIPS

- The most common double needle size is 2.0/80. This type of labeling means there is a 2 mm space or about ⅛" between the two needles, and the needle size is European 80 or equivalent to an American 11 or 12.

- Various double needle sizes are available, with the sizing differing somewhat from one brand to another. See a sewing machine dealer for exact needle sizes available for your machine.

- To stitch with a double needle, use an all-purpose foot with wide needle opening on your machine. A clear foot with open toes offers the best visibility.

• To thread the machine for double needle stitching, insert the double needle with the flat side of the shaft toward the back.

Use two spools to thread each needle separately. If your machine does not provide two spool pins, wind a bobbin and place it on top of the spool of thread — both on the same spool pin. If your machine has a horizontal spool pin, check the machine manual for the correct double-threading steps.

As you thread each needle, be sure to keep the threads separated at the tension discs, threading one on each side of the thin metal plate in the disc. Some machines have two thread guides just above the needle; others do not. If yours has two, thread the left thread through the left guide and the right thread through the right guide. If yours has one, bring one thread through the guide and leave the other thread out of the guide to prevent the threads tangling.

• Make sure the needle is at the center position.

• Adjust the needle thread tension normally or slightly tighten it.

• Set the stitch width at "0". Adjust the stitch length to suit the fabric weight; the heavier the fabric, the longer the stitch should be.

• To become aware of the potential of double needle stitching, make a sampler on a smooth, medium weight fabric such as muslin or broadcloth. Then, make a sampler on thin, lightweight fabric such as batiste.

On each fabric, begin with straight stitches. Then, try simple zigzag stitches, blindstitches, overedge stitches and serpentine or three-step zigzag stitches; note, however, the stitch width settings are limited to half the widest possible stitch when you sew with a double needle. A too-wide stitch can cause the needle to break. After setting the stitch width, turn the hand wheel slowly to be sure the double needle clears the presser foot.

• To turn a corner with a double needle, stitch almost to the point and leave the tips of the needles in the fabric. Raise the presser foot. Pivot the work 45 degrees, take one stitch, leave the tips of the needles in the fabric, and raise the presser foot to pivot the work another 45 degrees (Figure 1).

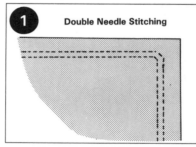

1 Double Needle Stitching

PINTUCK TECHNIQUES

• Pintucks can be used to decorate garment hems and front closings as well as details such as collars, cuffs, pockets, yokes and bands.

• A double needle tends to pull up the fabric into a ridge. To emphasize this effect for decorative surface treatments on lightweight fabrics, increase the needle thread

tension slightly. This will create a narrow, raised channel.

If you'd rather not create this surface texture, loosen the needle thread tension until the fabric lays smoothly.

• To create true pintucks on all but the lightest weight fabrics, use a special pintuck presser foot which has grooves on the underside. These grooves help raise the fabric into a ridge and help guide the fabric for parallel rows of double stitches. Place the row of double stitches just stitched next to the foot to space the pintucks evenly.

• Each pintuck foot requires a particular size of double needle:

PINTUCK FOOT SIZE	DOUBLE NEEDLE WIDTH (mm)
3-groove	4.0
5-groove	3.0
7-groove	2.0
9-groove	1.8

• The most often-used pintuck feet are the 7-groove and the 9-groove sizes.

• To be sure you have selected the correct double needle for a pintuck foot, turn the foot bottom side up and see if the double needle points fit the spacing of the grooves.

• For successful pintucking, choose a foot with many grooves for lightweight fabrics and one with few grooves for heavier fabrics. For example, the 3-groove pintuck foot is suitable for velour or denim, while the 5-, 7- and 9-groove feet are most often used on fine crepe, chiffon, batiste or lawn.

• On some machines, it is possible to incorporate a fine cord into the pintuck. Check the machine manual for information on how to cord a pintuck.

•A good first project is lattice pintucks on a blouse yoke (Figure 2). Begin by

cutting an ample rectangle of fabric large enough to make the pintucks plus cut the yoke on the bias. Cluster pintucks in groups on the lengthwise grain, then stitch similar pintucks on the crosswise grain; cut the yoke pattern from this decorated fabric (Figure 3).

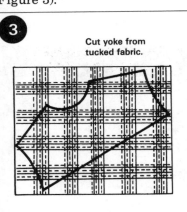

Cut yoke from tucked fabric.

• Create a custom fabric for wearable art by pintucking strips of fabric. Cut into squares and sew together with alternating squares cut from plain fabric (Figure 4).

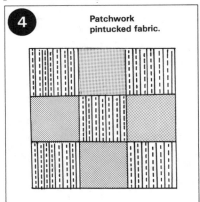

4

Patchwork pintucked fabric.

SUPER STUFF

To avoid frustration when stuffing small detail areas of appliquéd wearable art garments, use long tweezers. Just a pinch of stuffing can be put in exactly the right place to make a smooth and lump-free project.

M. Cary,
Fulton, NY

HEM HELPER

To machine-stitch an evenly-deep hem in children's garments is a challenge because the fabric covers the seam allowance markings on the throat plate of the machine. To solve this dilemma, place a large rubber band over the free arm of the machine at the desired distance, butt the folded hem edge against it, and you have the perfect seam guide for almost any hem width.

B. Sarnowski,
LaFarge, WI

FRINGING FABRIC

Making a self-fringe hem on a loosely-woven fabric adds a distinctive touch to shawls, scarves, tunics and straight-cut skirts. Before you start, make sure the fabric will form a fringe easily — if you can remove a yarn by pulling it across the grainline at the cut edge without the yarn breaking, the fabric will probably form a lovely fringe.

ZIGZAG METHOD FOR FRINGING

• Cut the fabric carefully so the fringe edge is on the straight fabric grain.

• Mark the desired depth of the fringe with a marking pen, making sure the marked line follows a yarn exactly.

• Set the machine for a tiny zigzag stitch. Stitch on the marked line (Figure 1). The zigzag stitches will anchor the fringe.

1

Stitch a tiny zigzag to act as an anchor for the fringe.

↕ Depth of Fringe

• Using the point of a pin or tapestry needle, lift the yarns and pull them away one at a time (Figure 2). Stop removing yarns when you reach the zigzagged line.

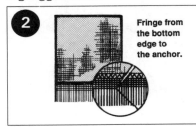

2

Fringe from the bottom edge to the anchor.

• For a thicker fringe, cut a self-fabric strip 1" deeper than the fringe. Fringe this strip, finish the raw edge and stitch in place behind the first fringe.

SERGER METHOD FOR FRINGING

• After marking the fringe depth as described above, use a serger flatlock stitch to anchor the fringe.

Fold the fabric to the wrong side on the marked line. Flatlock along the fold, being careful not to cut the fold. The flatlock stitches should be halfway over the folded fabric edge (Figure 3). Move the

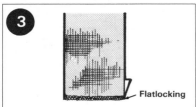

Flatlocking

upper knife out of the way if possible, or remove it entirely for mistake-free flatlocking on a fold.

• Unfold the fabric and pull carefully from the cut edge to flatten the fold. Remove the yarns one by one up to the flatlocking (Figure 4).

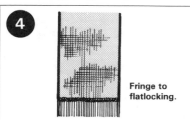

Fringe to flatlocking.

FAST FRINGE

To simplify the task of fringing a scarf edge, pin the fabric to a work area (cork-top table, pillow, chair arm, etc.) and brush each edge with a metal-bristled wig brush. The brush removes one or two threads at a time and keeps the fringe neat and tangle-free.

William E. Kurtz,
Oklahoma City, OK

HANDY HELPER

I use my presser foot as a "third hand" to help hold garments for handwork. Hemming, basting or tacking linings goes much quicker by having this additional help — just lower the foot onto the area you need to hold in place.

E. Prevenos,
Kingwood, TX

QUICK PICKUP

I made a handy "thread grabber" from an 8″-long strip of the hook portion of hook and loop fastener. Simply sew the ends together to form a circle. To use, fit it around the palm of your hand, and as you sew it will "grab" the thread ends you cut off, saving a mess on the floor. I clean my "grabber" when I'm finished with each project.

Editor's note: Be careful when using this tool on fabrics that snag easily.

C. Stevens,
Decatur, IL

✂ HAND SEWING TECHNIQUES

If hand sewing seems almost like a forgotten art today, it may be because modern machines and techniques have made it possible to accomplish almost the same thing in other, faster ways. However, you will find sewing by hand a valuable way to shape, mark, baste, finish and embellish garments.

Because they are so rare, fine hand stitches add value to the fashions you create. They satisfy purists and impress connoisseurs who appreciate couture-style workmanship. You might want to sew by hand when you're in the mood to sew something very special or you feel the need to relax. Or, you might want to sew by hand extensively as part of your personal style; this custom touch might become one of your professional trademarks.

In spite of the cachet handwork enjoys, sewing by hand is actually a skill you could call easy, but one that requires practice to achieve perfection. All you need are two basic tools — a thimble and a needle — and you're ready to sew.

TIPS ON HAND SEWING TOOLS & SUPPLIES

• The best thimbles are made of traditional materials such as steel, brass, sterling silver or gold with deeply-cut depressions called "knurls" in the top. There are also leather thimbles, and some who sew prefer them.

• A thimble should fit the middle finger of the sewing hand very snugly. The closed top should rest just beyond the fingertip; otherwise, it will feel clumsy to use.

• A tailor's thimble has an open top which allows ventilation.

• If you have trouble using a thimble, try a smaller thimble or a shorter needle.

• The finest needles are made of polished steel. They're sized from 1 to 12; the higher the number, the smaller the size and the shorter the needle.

• There are several different types of needles (Figure 1).

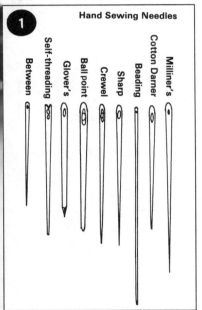

Hand Sewing Needles

Between, Self-threading, Glover's, Ballpoint, Crewel, Sharp, Beading, Cotton Darner, Milliner's

Milliner's, cotton darners and beading needles are long needles with sharp points. The easy-to-thread cotton darner has a larger eye than the milliner's needle; unfortunately, darners are difficult to find in small sizes. A beading needle is slender, with a small eye, so it can pass through the tiny hole in beads and sequins.

Sharp, crewel or embroidery, ballpoint, glover's and self-threading needles are all medium length. Sharps have small, egg-shaped eyes while embroidery needles have long eyes; both have sharp points. Self-threading or calyx-eye needles have a slot for easy threading. Ballpoint needles have rounded points and small eyes. Glover's needles have special cutting points to penetrate leather and suede easily without causing tearing.

Betweens are the shortest needles. Traditionally used by tailors, betweens have small eyes and sharp points.

• To select the best needle for hand sewing, consider the type of stitch you will make, the fabric and the thread. In general, select the smallest needle that will slip through the fabric easily without bending or breaking.

Use short needles to make short, fine stitches; use long needles to make long, large stitches. The thinner and more delicate the fabric, the smaller and finer the needle should be. Select a large-eyed needle when using thick or heavy thread.

• Many threads are described by a number system which indicates thread size as well as the number of plies twisted together to make the thread. The higher the thread number, the finer the thread. For example, size 60/2 indicates a fine thread made from two plies; size 40/3 indicates a coarse thread made from three plies.

• Many 100-percent polyester threads are not marked by size. In general, they are size 50.

• Some silk thread manufacturers label thread size by letter. Size A is a fine silk thread suitable for most hand sewing. Size D is a much heavier thread or buttonhole twist for decorative stitching, sewing on buttons and making hand-worked buttonholes.

• For basting, a cotton thread with a glazed finish works well. It won't knot or twist so you can use a generous length without problems. It's also easy to place and remove.

• For most hand sewing, any good quality thread can be used. However, the finer the thread, the less conspicuous your stitches will be.

• If sewing on a lightweight silk fabric, you can unravel a thread near the selvage and use it for hand sewing.

GENERAL TIPS

• Relax and make yourself comfortable. Keep your hands relaxed and slightly curved. Think positively, too. You are a talented artist, and the more you practice, the better you will become.

• Before sewing delicate fabrics, smooth rough hands by rubbing them with one teaspoon sugar and one teaspoon salad oil; rinse thoroughly.

• Sew smoothly with an even rhythm.

• Avoid pulling stitches too tightly or placing them too closely together.

• To strengthen thread and prevent it from twisting and snarling, coat it by pulling it through a cake of beeswax.

• When sewing dense weaves or other difficult-to-sew fabrics, lubricate the needle point by inserting it into a bar of soap. Or, coat it with needle lubricant.

• Use a double strand of thread for sewing on buttons. Wax the thread and twist it into a single strand before beginning – roll the thread between the palms of your hands, then wind the rolled section around your left thumb (Figure 2). Continue until all the thread is twisted.

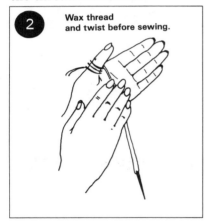

Wax thread and twist before sewing.

• Most hand sewing is done with a single strand of thread. Cut a length of thread at an angle. Make it about 20″ to 22″ long; if you are basting, cut the thread about 30″ long.

• One of the most common mistakes is sewing with thread that is too long. This is awkward because it affects the arm/hand rhythm and also causes the thread to snarl, twist and break.

• To thread a needle, hold the thread with the thumb and forefinger of the right hand,

about ¼″ from the end. If necessary, sharpen the thread end with a little saliva and twist the end between the left thumb and forefinger.

Insert the thread end into the needle's eye. Catch the end of the thread, pull it through and knot it.

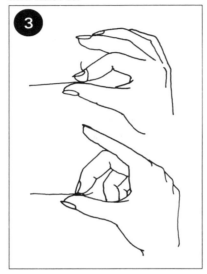

• To knot the thread, wrap the thread end around the end of your right index finger (Figure 3). Slide the right thumb to the end of the forefinger, rolling the thread forward. When the thread rolls off the fingertip, use the thumbnail against the middle finger to slide the knot to the end of the thread. At the same time, hold the remainder of the thread taut in your left hand.

• Knots, both at the beginning and the end of a line of stitches, should be concealed between two layers of fabric. Whenever possible, do this by beginning and ending on the underside of a seam or hem allowance.

• To avoid inadvertently pulling the knot through the fabric, begin sewing with a small backstitch.

• When the bulk of a knot would be undesirable under a button, snap, hook, eye or end of a buttonhole, begin and end with two backstitches, one on top of another.

• To sew, pick up the needle with your right thumb and forefinger so the needle point is to the left and the eye is to the right (Figure 4). Hold the

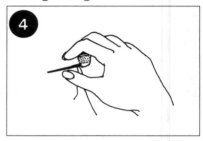

needle firmly, close to the needle point. Keep the thimble against the eye end of the needle. Any part of the thimble can be used, however the sides and bottom rim are preferred to the top of the thimble.

Hold the fabric firmly between the left thumb and forefinger. To make a stitch, insert the needle into the fabric, pointing the needle toward the middle of the left thumbnail. Lift the right thumb, and using the thimble, push the needle through almost to the eye. Catch the needle tip between the thumb and forefinger of the right hand, and pull the thread toward your right shoulder (on occasion, it might be better to pull the thread toward your left shoulder).

• To knot the thread at the end of a line of hand stitches, take a backstitch, leaving a small thread loop (Figure 5).

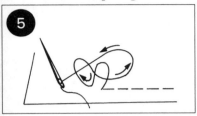

Insert the needle into the loop, then turn the needle around and run it back through the second loop. Pull the thread taut to form a knot.

To hide the thread end, insert the needle into the fabric as close to the knot as possible. Take a short stitch through all fabric layers. Pull the thread sharply, popping the knot between the fabric layers.

• If you find it difficult to thread a needle, hold the needle eye against a contrasting background.

• To save time, thread several needles before beginning a project.

• In general, sew from right to left or from top to bottom. One exception is catchstitches which are worked left to right.

• To avoid wrinkling and crushing the fabric, work at a table. Allow the bulk of the fabric to rest on the table while you hold the area to be sewn in your left hand (Figure 6). Rest your arms on the table

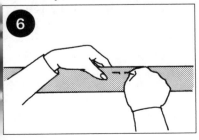

to relieve tension, increase accuracy and improve speed.

• If you sew while watching television or visiting with friends, allow the bulk of the fabric to rest in your lap. Rest your arms on the arms of the chair, holding the edge you're sewing in your left hand. Do not attempt to hold the work in mid-air.

TYPES OF HAND STITCHES

• Basting stitches (Figure 7),

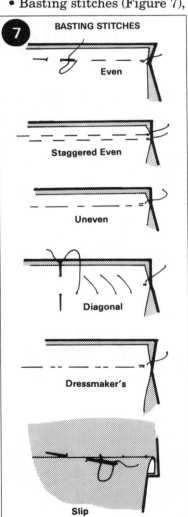

among the simplest and most essential hand stitches, hold fabric layers together temporarily. In custom sewing, basting stitches are also used to mark stitching lines and grainlines.

Even basting stitches are running stitches about ¼" long which look the same on both sides of the fabric. These stitches are used to baste intricate or closely-fitted seams for fitting or stitching, to prevent fabric layers from shifting during topstitching and to maintain a desired shape while pressing.

A staggered, double row of even basting stitches holds two fabric layers with extra security.

Uneven basting combines a ½"-to 1"-long stitch on the right side with a short ¼"-long stitch on the wrong side. It's used for the construction or fitting of straight or slightly-curved seams.

Diagonal basting consists of long, diagonal stitches on the right side and short, parallel stitches on the wrong side. It's often used along the edges of tailored garments prior to pressing.

Dressmaker's basting, some-times called thread tracing or tailor basting, is used most often to mark grainlines and placement lines. It's made by alternating one long stitch with two short stitches.

Slip basting is used to join intricate seams or when plaids, stripes or prints must be matched precisely. To sew, work from the right side of the garment, making short ¼"-long stitches in the folded edge of the top fabric layer; insert the needle in the bottom fabric layer so it's exactly opposite the thread to make a ladder of stitches. To prevent the layers from shifting, you cannot weave the needle from one layer to the next; you must make the stitches parallel.

• In general, start and end a row of basting stitches with a backstitch. To remove basting, clip the thread every 4″ to 6″ first; pulling a too-long thread can mar the fabric.

• To baste pleats, lapped seams, bias seams, long seams, underlinings or make thread markings, keep the work flat on the table. Use the left forefinger to push the fabric onto the needle while the right hand pushes the needle into the fabric layers or fabric fold.

• For professional results, remove basting stitches before pressing or use silk thread which leaves no imprint.

• A variety of hand stitches can be used for hems (Figure 8); most of these stitches have other uses, too.

The blindstitch is sometimes called a tailor's hem, and you'll see it used frequently on top quality garments. Worked "blind" between the garment and the hem allowance to build in a little slack, the stitches should be slightly loose so they will be almost invisible from the right side of the garment.

To sew blindstitches "blind", fold the hem allowance back on itself and take a tiny stitch in the garment; take a small stitch in the hem allowance about ½″ away. Alternate stitches between the garment and the hem allowance, making small "Vs".

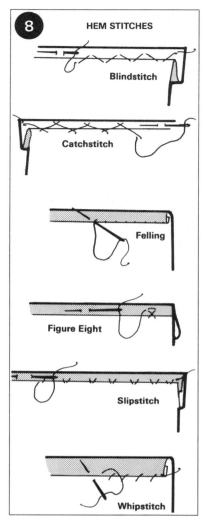

8 HEM STITCHES

Blindstitch

Catchstitch

Felling

Figure Eight

Slipstitch

Whipstitch

The catchstitch, sometimes called the herringbone stitch and made like large cross stitches, has more elasticity than a blindstitch. Besides hems, catchstitches are useful for tacking facings, securing lining pleats, tacking inter-facing edges and applying labels. Catchstitched hems can be worked "blind" between the garment and the hem allow-ance, and they work well on almost any fabric but especially on heavy fabrics and knits. On lined garments,

catchstitched hems are worked over the hem edge in the standard manner rather than "blind." An exception to the usual right-to-left rule, catch-stitches are sewn from left to right.

The felling stitch, a tailoring technique, is sometimes called vertical hemming. This short, neat stitch can be used not only for hems, but also for closing seams from the right side, and securing bands, collars and bindings. When properly sewn, the thread floats between the fabric layers, looks like a machine stitch on the right side and is barely visible from the wrong side.

To make felling stitches, secure the thread in the hem allowance or fabric fold. Hold the needle parallel to the folded edge and pick up a tiny stitch in the garment opposite the thread. Slip the needle point under the fold and pick up the edge about ¼″ to the right; pull the thread through. Space felling stitches $\frac{1}{16}$″ to ½″ apart.

The figure-eight stitch is used for invisible hems in fabrics such as knits and crepes, and makes a very secure hem. Since each stitch is independent of the stitches on either side, you can space them ¾″ to 1″ apart. To sew, secure the thread in the hem allowance. Take a small stitch in the hem, then take another stitch in the hem on top of the first one. Take a stitch directly opposite, in the garment, then return to the hem to take a third stitch on top of the first two. Allow some slack in the thread between stitches.

The slipstitch can be used only when the hem allowance has a folded-under raw edge, as the stitches "slip" through this fold. Also use slipstitching to attach pockets and apply linings.

To sew slipstitches, secure the thread in the hem allowance. Take a tiny stitch in the garment, then take a ½" stitch in the fold of the hem. Alternate stitches between the garment and hem to make small "v's".

In addition to hems, the whipstitch or slanted hemming stitch can be used for closing seams from the right side of the garment and securing cuffs, collars, bands and bindings. To sew, secure the thread in the hem allowance or fabric fold. Pick up a tiny stitch in the garment about ¼" to the right, then pick up the edge of the hem or fold and pull the thread through. Repeat, picking up two stitches each time before pulling the thread. Space the stitches ⅛" to ¼" apart.

• Some utility stitches for hand sewing have special purposes, while others are multipurpose (Figure 9).

The backstitch was the primary stitch used for garment construction before the widespread use of the sewing machine. It's a strong and elastic hand stitch, and you can use it to sew seams, insert zippers or repair seams. The pick stitch or prick stitch and the half stitch are all backstitch variations.

To sew backstitches, secure the thread and take a small stitch by inserting the needle to the right of the thread. For

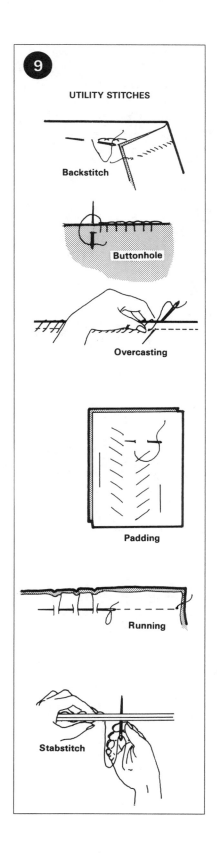

9

UTILITY STITCHES

Backstitch

Buttonhole

Overcasting

Padding

Running

Stabstitch

a full backstitch, insert the needle at the end of the previous stitch. Keep all the stitches even.

For a half stitch, insert the needle midway between stitches. For a pick stitch or prick stitch, insert the needle slightly to the right of the thread, covering a tiny bit of the fabric.

The combination stitch is stronger than a running stitch, but not as strong as a backstitch. It consists of a backstitch spaced between several running stitches.

The buttonhole stitch is used to make hand-sewn buttonholes. It's also used to attach hooks and eyes, and make thread loops. To sew, insert the needle into the wrong side of the fabric ¹⁄₁₆" to ⅛" from the edge. Loop the thread behind the needle eye and under the needle point. Pull the needle through to form a purl stitch along the fabric edge.

Overcasting is used to finish raw edges of seam and hems; a couture standard, it forms the flattest and least conspicuous finish. To sew, use a fine, between type of needle. Work from left to right and space the stitches ⅛" to ¼" apart. Use your left hand to hold the fabric and the thread as you form the next overcast stitch and pull the thread through the fabric. Do not weave several stitches onto the needle before pulling the thread. If desired, overcast stitches can also be worked from right to left. Or, if the fabric frays easily, make overcast stitches first from left to right and then from right to left to simulate a fine zigzag stitch; this technique has been dubbed "cross your hand".

The padding stitch is vital for hand tailoring, as it's used to shape lapels and collars. It's made like the diagonal basting stitch, but the stitches are smaller. To padstitch, work from top to bottom, then work the next row upward from bottom to top using the same length of thread. Work the stitches in chevrons or in parallel patterns.

The running stitch is a multipurpose basic, useful for basting, gathering, sewing French seams by hand, making tucks and sewing seams that are not subject to stress. It can also be used as a substitute for the slipstitch when applying pockets and linings. To sew, weave the needle in and out of the fabric to take several small, even stitches on the needle; pull the thread through and repeat.

A stabstitch is worked up and down through fabric which is too bulky or dense to allow ordinary backstitches or running stitches, to sew zippers and to attach shoulder pads. To sew, insert the needle vertically into the fabric layers. Pull the thread through, then insert the needle to the right of the thread to form a backstitch or to the left of the thread to form a running stitch. Pull the thread taut between stitches to insert a zipper securely, otherwise keep the stitches loose to avoid creating dents in the fabric.

• Tailor's tacks are used to transfer pattern markings to fabric, especially when other marking methods leave stains or are otherwise unsuitable. To sew, use a double thread and do not knot it. Sew through the pattern piece and both fabric layers with a long, loopy basting stitch. Clip the loops between each stitch and remove the pattern. Separate the fabric layers about ½″ and clip the threads in between (Figure 10).

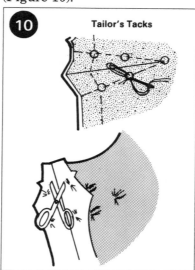

10 Tailor's Tacks

TAILOR TACK TRICKS

When making tailor tacks through the pattern tissue, use the tip of your needle to make a short slit in the tissue, then make the tack. When you remove the pattern piece, the tack threads will slide through the slit without ripping your pattern.

L. Pecora,
Massapequa Park, NY

✂ HAND-PICKED ZIPPER

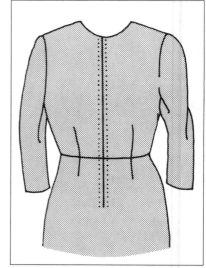

Inserting a hand-picked zipper is one of the easiest and most elegant ways to add a designer touch. This sewing technique looks best on garments made of quality fabrics. It's especially practical if a fabric is marred by machine stitching or has a surface texture which looks better without a row of straight stitches spoiling the effect. Such fabrics include satin, velvet, lace, fine silks and wools, and fabrics which are permanently pleated, embroidered, beaded, metallic or sequined.

Sometimes, however, a hand-picked zipper looks out of place. Don't try to elevate the status of a casual garment or an inexpensive fabric by hand picking the zipper. When this technique is used appropriately, it's lovely; when it's used inappropriately, it signals amateur work.

• A centered zipper application is traditionally used when hand picking, even when the zipper is positioned at a side seam.

• Select a lightweight zipper with a small pull tab. Press the zipper lightly to remove any creases or ripples in the zipper tape.

• Serge, overcast or bind the raw edges of seam allowances in the zipper area to prevent raveling.

• Mark the seamlines in the zipper area and press the seam allowances to the wrong side. Be careful not to stretch the edges as you press.

If the seam is shaped, as it would be for a zipper at the hipline, press the seam allowances over a dressmaker's ham. This is your last opportunity to shape this area; once the zipper is set, you cannot press the fabric thoroughly.

• If the zipper opening is not on the straight fabric grain, stay each side of the opening with lightweight hem tape or selvage to prevent rippling. Sew the stay to the seamline by hand so the stitches don't show on the right side.

• Open the zipper. Working from the wrong side of the garment, pin the zipper in place with the edges of the zipper teeth aligned with the pressed folds of the seam allowances. Place the pins perpendicular to the opening for easier basting.

If the zipper opening will be finished with a band such as a waistband, position the top zipper stop ⅛" below the seamline at the top of the opening if working on light-weight fabrics and ¼" below if working on medium or heavy-weight fabrics. If the zipper opening will be finished with a facing, position the top zipper stop ¼" to ⅜" below the seamline to allow room for a hook and eye plus turn-of-cloth at the facing seam.

• Baste the zipper in place with short, even stitches (Figure 1).

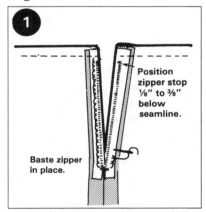

Position zipper stop ⅛" to ⅜" below seamline.

Baste zipper in place.

Close the zipper and check the alignment of any crossing seams, the top edges and any fabric designs which must be matched. Check also that the two fabric edges meet at the center of the zipper.

Try on the garment. Check to be sure the zipper lies smoothly.

• Use a single strand of fine polyester/cotton sewing thread or fine silk thread to sew the zipper. Prepare the thread by pulling it over a cake of beeswax.

• Working from the right side of the garment, use a prick stitch – a variation of the backstitch – to sew the zipper (Figure 2). On

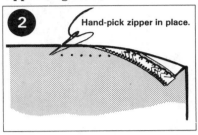

Hand-pick zipper in place.

lightweight fabrics, space the stitches about 1/16" from the zipper teeth and about ⅛" apart. On heavier fabrics, space the stitches about ¼" from the zipper teeth. The stitches should be very inconspicuous from the right side of the garment.

• After you've sewn one side of the zipper, close it to be sure it operates smoothly. Open the zipper, then sew the other side.

• To hide the zipper pull tab, stop sewing about 1" below the top. From this point to the top of the zipper, do not sew through the garment; sew the zipper tape to the garment seam allowances only.

On the right side of the garment, make prick stitches in the unsewn area so it matches the rest of the zipper application, even though the stitches are "false." The pocket formed between the garment and the seam allowances hides the pull tab when the zipper is closed.

• For a stronger zipper application on closely fitted garments, use a zipper foot to sew the zipper tape to the seam allowances by machine. Stitch next to the prick stitches.

IN-SEAM BUTTONHOLES

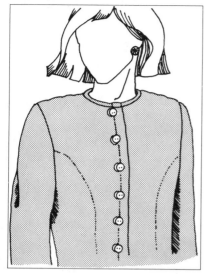

An attractive detail used by couture designers, in-seam buttonholes can be added to almost any pattern. This design feature is functional, too; you can use this technique to avoid making buttonholes on tricky fabrics such as bulky tweeds, knits or double-faced fabrics. Garments using this technique are lined or faced to finish the wrong side attractively.

FRONT FLAG

When making elastic-waist slacks or skirts, I sew a colored square of fabric at the center front casing. This makes it easy to tell the front from the back when dressing.

V. Brotherson,
Council Bluffs, IA

• In-seam buttonholes are usually placed in the seam joining a band to the garment, a collar seam or a yoke seam (Figure 1).

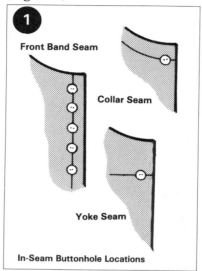

Front Band Seam

Collar Seam

Yoke Seam

In-Seam Buttonhole Locations

• If the pattern doesn't have a seamline in the desired position, draw a new seamline on the pattern. For a front closing, draw the new seamline on the center front line. Mark the buttonhole locations on the new seamline, and mark the grainline arrow on both sections. Cut the pattern apart on the new seamline, then add a ⅝" seam allowance to each edge (Figure 2).

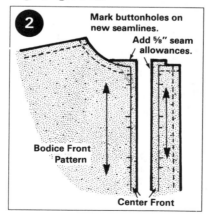

Mark buttonholes on new seamlines.

Add ⅝" seam allowances.

Bodice Front Pattern

Center Front

Repeat the same steps to add a matching seamline on the facing or lining pattern.

• As a reinforcement, fuse ⅜"-wide strips of fusible interfacing to the seam allowance of each garment and facing or lining edge that will have in-seam buttonholes (Figure 3). Align the edge of

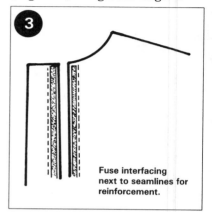

Fuse interfacing next to seamlines for reinforcement.

the interfacing with the seamline.

• With right sides together, stitch the seam, backstitching carefully at the beginning and end of each buttonhole. Press the seam open.

• Apply the facing or lining to finish the wrong side, backstitching at the buttonhole seam openings as above.

• To finish the buttonholes, slipstitch the garment and lining or facing folds together at the buttonhole openings.

LEATHER ACCENTS

In response to changing fashion currents, real leather has become as soft, supple and easy to handle as ordinary fabric. This makes it very appealing for creative sewing.

Consider adding couture style to your wardrobe by trimming garments with leather, suede or reptile skins. Or, enhance the rich colors and distinct textures of leather with decorative techniques such as quilting, patchwork and stenciling to make your leather accents truly fine details.

GENERAL TIPS

• To sew leather, use quality long-staple polyester or cotton/polyester thread.

• Use a sharp sewing machine needle size 80/11 or 90/14. A wedge-point needle is not recommended because it makes large holes in supple skins.

• Use a long stitch, about 6 to 8 per inch. Do not back-stitch, as this weakens leather; tie thread ends instead.

• For smoother sewing, use a roller, Teflon®, even feed or walking presser foot on the machine.

• Use lapped, serged or double-stitched seam techniques.

• Needles and pins leave holes. Use weights, paper clips, hair clips or tape instead of pins.

• Cut leather with a rotary cutter or sharp shears.

• For hand sewing, use a glover's needle which has a chiseled point.

LEATHER TRIM TIPS

• Combine leather trims with garment fabrics of a compatible weight such as heavy linens, denims, wool gabardines, fake furs, tweeds and bulky knits.

• Patterns with straight-edged sections or softly-curved details are most suitable for leather accents.

• You might trim a wool coat with leather piping, cut the sleeves from leather for a sweater knit pullover, make jacket pockets and yoke from leather, or cut hip yokes for skirts and pants from leather. Tabs, pocket bands, welts, appliqués, epaulets, upper collars, cuffs and waistbands are more examples of fashion details that look elegant cut from leather.

• Balance leather details with the total look of the garment. A good rule of thumb is to use no more than half a square foot of leather to trim any single section of a garment.

• You may be able to cut collars or small detail pieces from economical scraps of leather. Cut them off-grain, if necessary; off-grain cuts are not recommended when cutting major garment sections from leather, but the grain will not be noticeable on small detail pieces.

LEATHER QUILTING TECHNIQUES

• Besides adding fashion appeal and a three-dimensional look, quilting leather insulates it. This is a plus if you're cutting garment sections such as sleeves from leather.

• Quilt leather before cutting out pattern pieces.

• For quilting, use a thin garment leather. When combined with batting and a backing, it should feed easily and evenly through the sewing machine.

• To prepare leather for quilting, mark quilting lines on the right side of the leather with chalk or soap. Use traditional crossed diagonal lines, draw parallel lines for channel quilting, or try an experimental format such as zigzagged sawtooth lines.

• Space the quilting lines no more than 4″ apart.

• For filler, use 4-ounce to 6-ounce unbonded polyester batting or ½″ polyurethane foam; for a backing, use a durable lining or broadcloth. Sandwich the filler between the leather (right side up) and the backing (right side down).

• Or, for flatter quilting, use bonded batting without a backing; place the batting bonded side down and the leather right side up on top to quilt. Because you have not used a backing, plan to finish the garment section later with a lining.

• Begin quilting by stitching the line in the center of the piece. Then, stitch alternately on each side of the center to prevent the fabric layers from slipping to one side and to minimize puckering (Figure 1).

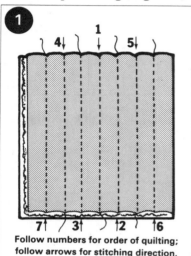

Follow numbers for order of quilting; follow arrows for stitching direction.

• When cutting pattern pieces from quilted leather, allow 1″ seam allowances as a fitting margin. Leather seams can be taken in, but they can not be let out without the needle perforations showing.

LEATHER PATCHWORK TECHNIQUES

• Leather colors and textures combine beautifully for patchwork, and this is a good way to use assorted leather scraps. However, avoid using thick or heavy leathers for patchwork; combine leathers which are similar in thickness.

• Complete the patchwork, then cut out the pattern from the pieced leather.

• Stabilize soft leathers before cutting by fusing a light- to medium weight nonwoven interfacing to the wrong side. Place the leather right side down on a fluffy towel and press for 2 to 3 seconds with a dry iron to fuse; test-fuse on a leather scrap first, as not all leathers can be fused successfully.

• Any pieced design can be used for leather patchwork. Omit seam allowances when cutting the individual patches, butt the edges, and zigzag them together. If desired, use a decorative thread such as buttonhole twist, fine machine embroidery thread or metallic thread.

• Strip piecing, an efficient method, works especially well with leather. To strip piece, cut the leather into strips. Butt the edges to sew the strips together, cut the combination strips apart, align in a decorative design, and sew the next section of seams (Figure 2).

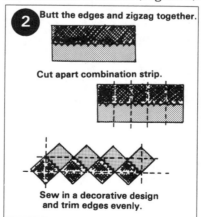

Butt the edges and zigzag together.

Cut apart combination strip.

Sew in a decorative design and trim edges evenly.

• Line leather patchwork by applying lightweight, soft leather to the back with rubber cement.

LEATHER STENCILING TECHNIQUES

• Art expertise is not a prerequisite for stenciling leather. You can purchase pre-cut stencils in craft and fabric stores, although it's easy to create an original design and cut your own stencil.

• Read label information carefully on all paints. Conventional stencil paints are acrylic and should not be dry cleaned. Use these paints on washable leathers only. To stencil leather for dry-clean-only garments, use only fabric dyes or paints labeled accordingly.

• Test paints or dyes on leather scraps to check for colorfastness and durability.

• Pre-mixed stencil colors cost more but are convenient. For custom colors, purchase basic colors and take the time to mix your own. Keep in mind that most paints dry darker than they appear wet.

• Be sure to stir paints thoroughly.

• Fabric dyes can be mixed to a thick, stencil paint consistency.

• Permanent ink markers can substitute for stencil paints, especially for small or dainty designs. Although color coverage is not as dense nor as even, ink markers wear, wash and dry clean well.

• Stenciling works best on leather that has a sueded, embossed, rough or porous texture.

• Tape the stencil to the leather so the stencil fits as closely to the leather surface as possible. Place pins vertically to hold the stencil "bridges" to prevent the paint from bleeding underneath; use pins sparingly, as they may leave marks.

• For even coverage, use a blunt stencil brush to apply paint or dye.

Dip the tip of the brush into the paint to pick up a small amount of paint; dab the brush on paper towels or rags to remove excess.

• For multicolor stenciling, mask selected portions of the stencil with tape to apply the first color if separate stencils for each color are not provided. Allow the paint to dry thoroughly. Remove the tape and mask other portions of the stencil to apply additional colors.

MORE CREATIVE LEATHER TECHNIQUES

• Rubber stamp designs on leather, using the stencil guidelines given above.

• Cut leather into strips, then weave, plait or knit them into unique custom "fabrics".

• Since the cut edges of leather do not ravel, leather appliqué is simple. Cut the appliqué without seam allowances and stitch in place.

• Adapt cutwork designs for leather. Cut out the open areas, then zigzag the leather openwork to a background fabric. Or, apply cutwork unbacked for a peek-a-boo effect.

✂ NEEDLEWORK EMBELLISHMENTS

Make otherwise ordinary garments look unique by decorating them with prepared vintage or contemporary needlework. Simply cut the needlework portion from handkerchiefs, napkins, guest towels, table runners or tablecloths and use this decorated fabric as an integral part of the garment you're making. Or, use the needlework as appliqués for garments.

Look for needlework pieces in attics, antique stores, gift shops and linen outlets. Use unpaired pillowcases or the pristine portions of stained table linens and worn tea towels as accents.

GENERAL TIPS

• Look for needlework pieces with appealing designs. Pieces should also be durable enough to survive garment wear and tear, worked on a firm background fabric of uniform color and

sized appropriately for cutting appliqués or garment details such as collars, cuffs, yokes and pockets. If selecting a vintage piece, consider whether or not it will require restoration before you recycle it.

• Launder or dry clean the needlework to preshrink it according to the care method you will use for the finished garment.

• To whiten pieces yellowed by age, squeeze-wash them gently in a mild solution of water and sodium perborate (available at a pharmacy). Do not wring the pieces. Let them dry flat, smoothing out as many wrinkles as possible. When the item is dry or nearly dry, press it on the wrong side. Cushion the pressing surface with a towel to avoid flattening the needlework.

• To add body and make the needlework easier to handle, treat it with spray starch before pressing.

• Underline delicate needlework with nylon net, tulle, organdy or organza.

• To use the needlework for garment sections such as collars or cuffs, apply a lightweight sew-in interfacing, or use organdy or organza for support. Fusible interfacings are not recommended to back needlework.

SEWING TECHNIQUES

• Use a small needlework motif as a patch pocket to accent a simple garment (Figure 1).

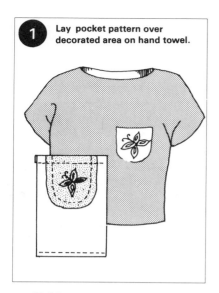

1 Lay pocket pattern over decorated area on hand towel.

• Fold a larger needlework piece to cut a garment collar or yoke (Figure 2).

2 Lay yoke pattern over decorative border on guest towel.

• Cut a square handkerchief or napkin diagonally to create a collar for a V-neckline (Figure 3). Insert the collar in the seam as you stitch the neckline facing in place.

3 Cut square handkerchief diagonally to create a collar.

• Use both borders of a table runner to cut a front and back yoke (Figure 4).

4 Lay yoke patterns over decorative borders on ends of table runner.

APPLIQUÉ TECHNIQUES

• Appliqué is especially suitable for lingerie items such as teddies, camisoles, slips, robes, pajamas and nightgowns. Other ideas include pinafores, aprons, and clothing for infants and children.

• To appliqué, cut around the needlework, leaving a ¼″ margin. Use fabric glue to baste the appliqué on the right side of the garment and position tear-away stabilizer on the wrong side.

Straight stitch the appliqué to the garment ¼″ from the raw edges. Trim the excess seam allowance close to the stitches, then satin stitch over the straight stitches covering the appliqué's raw edges. Remove the stabilizer.

• As an optional appliqué method, turn under the raw edges ¼″, baste the appliqué on the garment and edgestitch in place.

• For a lace-trimmed appliqué, cut and glue-baste the needlework to the garment; glue-baste tear-away stabilizer on the wrong side. Frame the appliqué by lapping lace trim over the raw edge of the needlework, mitering the lace trim corners if necessary (Figure 5). Stitch both edges of

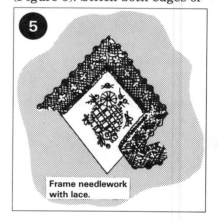

5 Frame needlework with lace.

the trim through all layers. If desired, carefully cut away the garment fabric close to the innermost row of stitches behind the appliqué to create a shadow effect.

NO-ROLL WAISTBAND

Men's waistbands are constructed in two sections with a center back seam. This seam is stitched after the waistband sections have been applied — when the back crotch seam is stitched.

For a quality menswear waistband, use the following technique. Select a special, stiff waistband interfacing designed especially for waistbands so the finished detail will have a crisp, flattering appearance.

• Purchase the waistband interfacing according to the desired finished width of the waistband — 1", 1¼", 1½" or 2". The long edges of the waistband interfacing are prefinished and should not be trimmed.

• If necessary, modify the waistband pattern pieces to make them 1½" wider than the waistband interfacing. Cut the waistband sections to the original length and transfer any pattern markings to the cut fabric sections.

• Cut a left waistband interfacing equal to the length of the left waistband pattern minus the center front overlap and center back seam allowance (Figure 1).

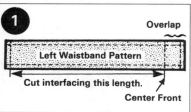

• Cut a right waistband interfacing equal to the length of the right waistband pattern minus the center front and center back seam allowances (Figure 2).

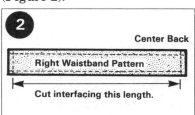

• To prevent the stiff yarns of the interfacing from poking through the garment fabric, bind the short ends of both interfacing sections with lightweight fabric such as broadcloth or tricot bias tape.

• Cut a bias strip of pocket lining fabric as a facing for each waistband section. Cut the bias strip the length of each waistband section and 2¼" wider than the waistband interfacing. Press under 1" on one long edge of each facing section.

• Complete the details on the pants back and front sections, then sew them together at the side seams. Right sides together, pin the waistband sections to the pants. Stitch in a ⅝" seam. Do not press the seam allowances.

• With the waistband wrong side up, pin the interfacing to the pants seam allowances, positioning the interfacing edge just above the seamline (Figure 3). Topstitch the lower edge of the interfacing to the seam allowances.

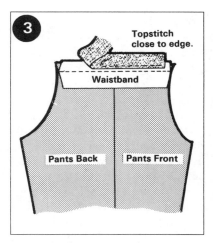

• Grade the seam allowances. Press the waistband up.

• Wrong sides together, pin the unfolded, raw edge of the facing to the raw edge of the waistband. Stitch in a ⅝" seam.

Turn the facing right side out over the top of the waistband and press (Figure 4).

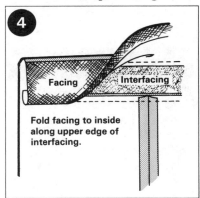

Finish the waistband and complete the pants according to pattern instructions.

✂ PANTS PERFECT

Attention to fine workmanship will help you sew pants that fit beautifully and look terrific. While figure measurements and pattern alterations are important, at least 30 percent of pants fit is achieved during the actual sewing. There are steps you can take to guarantee straight legs, smooth side seams, knees that don't look baggy, a sharp crease straight down the center of the pants legs and above all, wearing comfort.

In addition to these quality hallmarks, you may want to line the pants. Although patterns rarely include a lining, it's easy to devise one on your own. You'll find a lining is a good sewing investment, as lined pants wear longer, retain their shape better and are more comfortable than unlined styles.

SEWING TIPS FOR IMPROVING PANTS FIT

• Pants with a center back zipper generally looks more flattering and fit better than those with a fly front zipper.

• The center back seam in pants is a fitting seam. The greater the difference between your hip and waist measurements, the more bias the center back seam should be. If your waist and hip measurements are similar, straighten the center back seam for better fit.

• Back darts should be parallel to the center back seam. If you alter the center back seam on the pattern, also change the angle of the darts.

• Fabric choice affects pants fit. You can use the same pattern with two different fabrics and notice fit differences. It's a good idea to cut out pants patterns with 1″ seam allowances to allow for fine-tuned fitting.

• Maintaining the fabric grainline is paramount for good fit in pants. Be sure to preshrink the fabric and straighten the grain before layout.

• Mark three new grainlines on the front and back pants pattern pieces before layout (Figure 1).

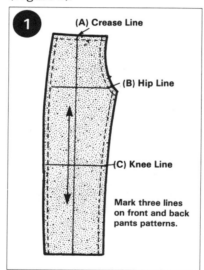

1 (A) Crease Line

(B) Hip Line

(C) Knee Line

Mark three lines on front and back pants patterns.

Draw a crease line (A) down the center of the pant leg. Locate the center halfway between the seamlines at the bottom of the pant leg and draw it parallel to the printed grainline arrow.

Draw a hipline grainline (B) at right angles to crease line (A) from side seam to crotch seam at the fullest part of your hip. To find the fullest part of your hip, measure from your waist to the fullest part at the side; measure the pattern in

the same way to mark grainline (B) below the waistline.

Also locate and draw a knee grainline (C) to mark the position of the center of your knee.

• Mark all construction symbols including the three new grainlines on cut pants pieces. Mark grainlines clearly by using silk thread and uneven basting stitches. You can press over silk thread without leaving imprints in the fabric.

• If you are using a fabric made from natural fibers, shape the front pants legs from knee to hem by steaming them. The finished pants will not ride up in front and break below the knee. This technique makes the front pant leg slightly narrower from knee to hem and tightens the fibers in that area. You will be amazed at how straight your pants will hang and how they will stay that way thanks to this trick of the trade.

To steam-shape, pin the pants front to the ironing board across the knee. Using a press cloth, apply plenty of steam to the knee area and below. Hold the knee line with your left hand as you stretch the leg to make it ⅜″ longer from knee to hem (Figure 2).

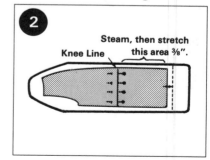

2 Steam, then stretch this area ⅜″.

Knee Line

You may have to repeat the steaming and stretching several times to make the area a full ⅜″ longer.

Since this makes the pants front longer than the pants back, trim ⅜″ off the bottom edge of both front pants sections.

• To prevent the perennial problem of baggy knees, begin with a little figure analysis. Look at your legs and notice how they curve in at the knee; the goal of the following technique is to make the pants conform to this body curve as much as possible without sacrificing comfort.

Before sewing the leg seams, mark new stitching lines in the knee area. Begin marking at the knee ⅛″ inside the side seams and inseams, tapering to the original seamlines 2″ above and below the knee line (Figure 3). Although both leg

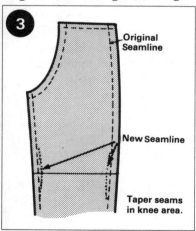

3

Original
Seamline

New Seamline

Taper seams
in knee area.

seams curve inward slightly, the finished pants will appear straight.

After stitching the leg seams, you will find the seam allowances in the knee pocket area will not lay flat. To remedy, clip one seam

allowance at an angle just above the knee line and the other just below (Figure 4).

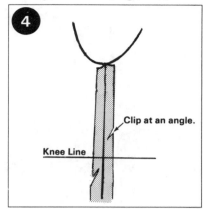

4

Clip at an angle.

Knee Line

• If your figure has a little dip or hollow between the fullest part of the hip and the top of the thigh, minimize it by including a 1″ x 7″ strip of woven interfacing in the seam. (It will help fill out the figure hollow, resulting in a very smooth side seam.) Center the strip over the back side seam allowance at the point where your figure hollow occurs.

• Press hipline side seams and darts over a dressmaker's ham to shape the pants to your figure.

• To sew the crotch seam, slip one pants leg into the other right sides together. Stitch from back to front, stretching the crotch curve area slightly as you sew. To stabilize the crotch area, which is on the bias grain, center a piece of ⅛″- to ¼″-wide twill tape over the seamline as you sew. Stitch the curved area of the crotch a second time ⅛″ away from the first stitching; do not catch the stay tape in this second row of stitching.

Trim the crotch curve to ¼″ and overcast the raw edges. This portion of the crotch seam should always stand up for the most comfortable fit.

• To crease pants, fold the legs along the basting-marked crease line and press lightly. Try on the pants to check the crease.

To set the crease, dampen a press cloth with a solution of ½ water and ½ white vinegar. Place the dampened press cloth on the crease line, steam and use a wooden clapper in a rocking motion to capture the steam and permanently set the crease. Press the front crease from the hipline to the hem. Press the back crease from the bottom of the crotch curve to the hem.

HOW TO LINE PANTS

• Trouser-style pants patterns are most appropriate for adding a lining. Jeans-style patterns should not be lined because a lining will interfere with the slimmer silhouette and close fit.

• Use the major pants pattern pieces to cut the lining. Pin or tape any yoke pattern to the adjoining pattern piece, lapping the seamlines. Do the same for

CLEVER CASINGS

When I make a garment with a waistline casing, I use a small piece of fusible web to hold down the seam allowances inside the casing. The elastic insertion goes more smoothly when you're not fighting loose seam allowances.

Mrs. W. Neff,
Muscoda, WI

any slant front pockets and trim off any fly front extension (Figure 5).

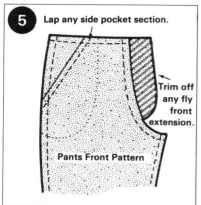

5 Lap any side pocket section.

Trim off any fly front extension.

Pants Front Pattern

• Sew the pants lining together, leaving the seam which has the closure open 1" below the bottom of the closure. At the waistline, convert any darts to soft pleats; if the pants have soft pleats at the waist, fold the lining pleats in the opposite direction from the pants pleats to reduce bulk.

• In the closure area, press seam allowances under ⅝", then fold them under again ¼" to ⅜" and press. Edgestitch the fold.

• With wrong sides together, baste the lining and pants together at the waistline. Attach the waistband.

• Mark the lining hem 1" shorter than the pants hem to protect the edge of the lining from abrasion and to prevent it from getting caught on the heel of your shoe. Hem the lining and pants separately.

✂ PASSEMENTERIE TRIM

The graceful scrolls of passementerie trim are sure to satisfy any craving for stunning decoration. A classic couture technique requiring some skill and patience, passementerie is defined as loops and swirls of lustrous, narrow black braid stitched onto white or red background fabric.

Today, however, the fashion thinking is much more liberal and there are many color options. Some combinations used by designers include black braid on gray fabric, white on white, red on black and metallic gold on cream. Since suitable braids come in many colors including soft pastels and vibrant brights, you can be as creative as like.

GENERAL TIPS

• Passementerie is usually applied as a border design. On a blouse, the collar, cuffs and front placket band are natural areas for this trim treatment.

On a jacket, loop traceries of braid along the hem, up one side of the front opening, around the neckline and down the other side of the front opening in a continuous stroke; add a complementary border to each sleeve.

Decorate the front panel of a gored skirt, then continue the swirls of trim around the side and back hemlines. Or, ornament a high-rise waistband with a dramatic design.

• Accessories such as belts, hats, purses and gloves are also suitable for passementerie accents.

• Soutache braid is the classic trim used for passementerie. This narrow braid looks like two cords with a channel through the center; guide the stitches in this channel to sew the braid to the garment.

• Other flexible braids from $\frac{1}{16}$" to ¼" wide can also be used. Since the trim must be pliant enough to curve smoothly, ribbons and middy braid are not recommended.

• Add other trims to enhance a passementerie design. For example, stitch small buttons, rickrack flowers, ribbon roses or tassels near the base of individual loops. Add frog or button-and-loop closures to complement the swirling passementerie trim, and insert lustrous twisted cording in the seams or bind the edges with foldover braid. Also consider passementerie buttons, either authentic ones which are covered with fine braid or plastic buttons which are molded to look like the real thing.

• The crisper the background fabric, the easier it is to stitch passementerie trim smoothly. Suitable fabrics include linen, velveteen, satin, taffeta, wool flannel, finely-textured tweed, ottoman and heavyweight faille. If working with a lightweight blouse or dress fabric, temporarily stiffen the fabric with spray starch for easier handling.

• If you plan extensive passementerie, use a fabric with plenty of body to support the stitching and the trim.

To add body, back fabric with lightweight interfacing or underline it.

• Some commercial patterns include transfers for passementerie motifs, or you can create your own design. Typical passementerie designs feature loops in graduated spirals or identical figure eights (Figure 1).

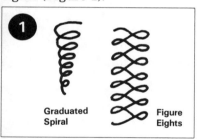

Graduated Spiral   Figure Eights

Some patterns alternate small and large loops or cluster the loops (Figure 2).

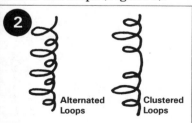

Alternated Loops   Clustered Loops

A line of straight braid positioned between the loops and the finished garment edges helps anchor airy designs. Round corners slightly rather than squaring for easier stitching (Figure 3).

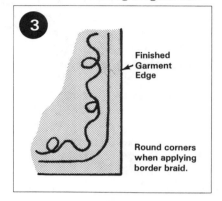

Finished Garment Edge

Round corners when applying border braid.

• Size the loops and scale the entire design for the silhouette. For example, the loops on a full-length skirt should be larger and more plentiful than those on the cuffs of a blouse.

• Keep in mind that large loops are easier to sew than small ones.

• To finish the braid ends, plan the design with a continuous length of braid beginning and ending in a seam.

• Draw your design on the pattern pieces, overlapping seam allowances to match the design at the seams (Figure 4).

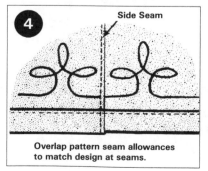

Side Seam

Overlap pattern seam allowances to match design at seams.

• To transfer the patterning to the cut garment sections, clearly mark the design on the right side of the fabric. If the fabric is semi-transparent, lay the garment section right side up over the design and trace with chalk, pencil or soluble marker.

If the fabric is opaque, mark the design on the wrong side of the garment section with dressmaker's carbon paper and a tracing wheel, then thread-trace the design so it shows on the right side.

SEWING TECHNIQUES

• Apply braid to the individual garment sections before joining them, or leave side and underarm seams open so the garment is still flat.

• To apply braid by machine, lay the braid over the marked line and stitch through the center of the braid. An embroidery or satin stitch presser foot with a recessed groove on the underside helps accommodate the braid's thickness.

Work slowly, easing the braid around curves so it lies flat.

• To apply the braid by hand, baste the braid in place by hand first if desired. Avoid pinning, which can cause the braid to buckle and shift. Save glue stick for another time — it doesn't hold the braid securely enough.

Sew with small backstitches through the center of the braid. Release the basting stitches as you sew.

• To finish any braid ends not caught in a seam, seal the raw ends with seam sealant; fold under the raw ends ¼". Butt the folds and stitch through all layers (Figure 5).

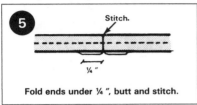

Fold ends under ¼", butt and stitch.

• Or, finish the braid ends with this couture technique if the fabric weave cooperates. Separate the yarns of the background fabric and pull the cut braid ends through to the wrong side; secure the ends with several small hand stitches.

TABLE TALK

To make a cutting table for my sewing room, I purchased a 32"-wide unfinished door and covered it with self-adhesive decorative paper. The "table" rests on two filing cabinets and is perfect for cutting fabrics even 60" wide.

*L. Smith,
Benicia, CA*

✂ PATCH POCKET WITH INVISIBLE STITCHING

Patch pockets with no visible stitches on the right side look very polished. You can duplicate this designer-style invisible stitching technique when applying pockets to wool garments. Wool is easy to press and shape – a definite plus when using this method.

Until you've perfected invisible stitching, reserve this method for a single-pocket garment. In theory, you could invisibly stitch any number of pockets, but in reality it takes practice to sew perfectly-matched pockets. Choose a garment with only one mid- to large-sized pocket until you master the skill.

• Choose a pocket pattern with rounded corners or modify a square pocket pattern at the bottom corners.

• Make a cardboard template ⅜" smaller than the finished size of the pocket. Mark notches at the bottom center, on the curves at the corners and above the curves (Figure 1).

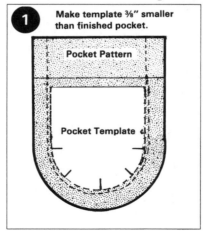

Make template ⅜" smaller than finished pocket.

Pocket Pattern

Pocket Template

• Trace around the template to mark the pocket position on the right side of the garment, marking the notches.

• Use the template to mark the notches with small snips on the raw edges of the pocket section.

Fold over the hem at the top of the pocket. Sew the hem with the seam allowances at the side extended (Figure 2).

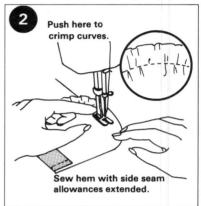

Push here to crimp curves.

Sew hem with side seam allowances extended.

Machine stitch around the pocket ¼" from the edge using the ease-plus technique to crimp the curves. Place your right index finger on the machine just behind the presser foot and push firmly so the fabric piles up and crimps as you stitch.

• Right sides together, place the pocket on the garment so the cut edge of the pocket lines up with marked pocket position on the garment (Figure 3).

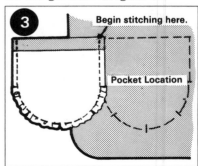

Begin stitching here.

Pocket Location

Begin stitching at the corner of the pocket, ⅜" from the edge. Stitch around the pocket, matching the notches as you go. When you get to the center of the pocket, the notches must match perfectly; if they don't, remove the stitches back to the last notches that match and stitch again. Continue stitching the pocket in place.

• Press the pocket. The pocket should roll smoothly over the stitched line, concealing any irregularities in the seam.

• Reinforce the upper pocket corners by hand from the wrong side of the garment by making several small cross stitches through the garment, the seam allowances and the hem.

PLEATS & TUCKS

You can add impressive pleats and tucks to a garment by pleating or tucking the fabric before you lay out and cut the pattern. This strategy allows you to skip complicated pattern alterations and makes it simpler to visualize the placement and decorative effect of the pleats or tucks. The following tips and techniques will help you individualize your custom creations with cleverly-spaced folds of fabric.

INVERTED PLEAT FOR A SLEEVE

• Cut a fabric rectangle twice the widest part of the sleeve pattern plus 8" and the length of the sleeve pattern.

• Lay the sleeve pattern on the flat fabric, leaving a 2" margin of fabric on the left. Mark the sleeve cap center with a snip as shown (Figure 1).

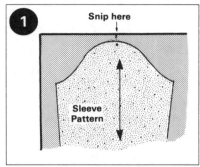

Snip here

Sleeve Pattern

• Remove the pattern, fold the top and bottom fabric edges together and mark the bottom fabric edge with a matching snip. Make snips 2" on each side of the center snip at the top and bottom edges (Figure 2).

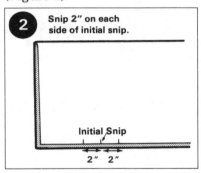

Snip 2" on each side of initial snip.

Initial Snip

2"   2"

• Unfold the fabric and pin it right side up at the center snips to the ironing board. Fold the outer snips to meet the center snips, forming an inverted pleat (Figure 3). Pin and press. Baste the pleat at top and bottom.

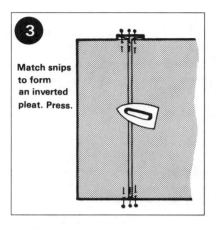

Match snips to form an inverted pleat. Press.

• Repeat the steps above to baste a matching pleat in from the other side of the fabric rectangle. Fold the fabric wrong sides together, match the pleats, and cut the sleeves (Figure 4).

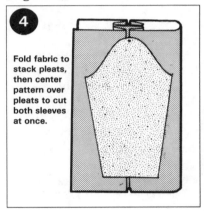

Fold fabric to stack pleats, then center pattern over pleats to cut both sleeves at once.

ADD DIRECTIONAL PLEATS

• To enhance a garment using a series of pleats pressed to one side, first determine the size and spacing of the pleats.

Keep in mind that the larger the pleats, the fewer there should be. A greater number of narrow pleats can create a broader illusion than fewer, deeper pleats.

Also, if you want the stitching on the pleats to show, space the pleats widely. To hide the stitching, create pleats that are wider than the spaces between them.

• Cut a fabric rectangle the length of the pattern piece and wide enough to allow for the number and depth of the pleats you have planned. Lay the pattern piece on the fabric and snip to mark the first pleat fold. Beginning at this snip-mark, pleat the fabric according to your plan. Fold the fabric to make matching snips at top and bottom as described above.

• After stitching and pressing the pleats, lay the pattern on the prepleated fabric to cut out the single garment section.

• For allover diagonal pleats or tucks, prepare the fabric by making shallow, evenly-spaced pleats from selvage to selvage. Lay the pattern piece on the bias grain to cut the garment section (Figure 5). You'll get

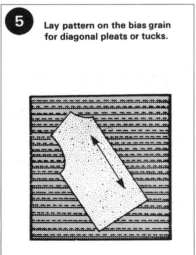

5 Lay pattern on the bias grain for diagonal pleats or tucks.

the bias-cut look, but without the rippling that occurs when you stitch pleats or tucks on the bias grain.

• For easy pleats and tucks, use a striped or plaid fabric. Use the woven or printed design as folding and stitching guidelines. You can often fold the pleats or tucks to emphasize one color bar, creating a custom designed fabric (Figure 6).

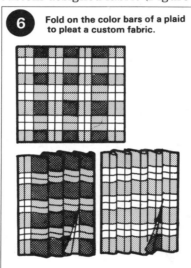

6 Fold on the color bars of a plaid to pleat a custom fabric.

DIMENSIONAL TUCKS

• Tucks or narrow, stitched-down pleats can be sewn on almost any light- to medium weight fabric. When you stitch the tucks in one direction then another, you twist the folds for a creative, textured surface.

• To sew, stitch a series of evenly-spaced tucks on the straight fabric grain; press the tucks to one side (Figure 7).

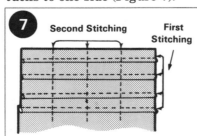

7 Second Stitching   First Stitching

Stitch across the pleats in the direction in which they were pressed, then stitch across the pleats in the opposite direction to twist the tucks (Figure 8).

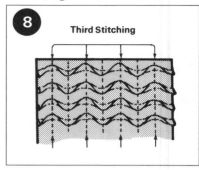

8 Third Stitching

STONE SURE

When attaching rhinestones, I press the prongs over the jewels with a thimble. I have no more sore fingers and the sparkles stay on more securely.

H. Lammi,
Astoria, OR

CUTTING CUES

When a pattern piece is labeled "cut four", I photocopy the piece or trace it onto transparent paper and copy all the markings. This simple step keeps me from forgetting to cut the extra two.

H. Wright,
Houston TX

STRAIGHT SHOT

Make a new ironing board cover from checked or striped fabric so you can use the lines for straightening projects, cutting bias, etc.

B. Wickham,
Carmichael, CA

QUILT A JACKET

A custom-quilted jacket is a classic form of wearable art you can wear for years, knowing it will always look distinctive as it turns heads and inspires admiration. This versatile item graces designer collections from one year to the next. Be imaginative when choosing a fabric since the quilting technique works with a wide variety of textiles.

For example, designers have used polished cottons, challis, brocades, large-scale floral prints, animal prints and sheer wools.

In addition, while fabrics such as chiffon, sheer metallics and taffetas would probably never be used in an ordinary jacket, they work beautifully when quilted and are a delightful surprise for the eye and the hand.

GENERAL TIPS

• Choose a light- to medium-weight fabric, avoiding any heavy, stiff or bulky fabric. Remember you will be quilting the fabric to a filler and a backing.

• Choose a lightweight silky lining fabric for the backing to make the jacket easy to slip on and off. Preshrink all fabrics.

• For the quilting stitches, choose a thread that blends with the fabric or select a thread which contrasts, depending upon the effect you desire. An effective way to suggest evening opulence is to quilt an ordinary black fabric with glittering metallic thread.

• Choose a simple pattern design. Intricate detailing will detract from the interest you create with quilting stitches. Consider a pattern with only three main pieces (front, back, sleeve) or two main pieces with cut-on kimono or dolman sleeves.

• Select a thin polyester batting or fleece for the filler. Quilt batting has more loft for a softer, puffier effect, but fleece's thinner, flatter effect is more flattering to the figure.

• Experiment on scraps to determine the best quilting design and to perfect your machine quilting technique.

• The more quilting and the closer together the rows of quilting stitches, the firmer the fabric will become.

• Draw quilting lines with chalk or soluble marker on the right side of the fabric if necessary.

SEWING TECHNIQUES

• Cut the jacket, backing and filler slightly larger than the pattern pieces. Allow an extra ¼" to 1" on each edge, depending upon how extensively you plan to quilt and the loft of the filler; the more quilting and loftier the filler, the more the layers will "shrink" in size as the quilting stitches take up fabric.

• Stack the layers beginning with the backing right side down, then the filler, then the fabric right side up. Pin the layers together around the edges and throughout the interior. Staystitch around the edges to anchor the layers, removing pins as you sew (Figure 1).

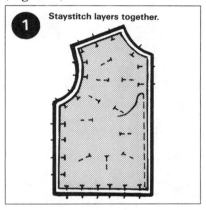

1 Staystitch layers together.

• There are many options for quilting the layers together in a beautiful design. A classic choice is to outline print motifs (Figure 2).

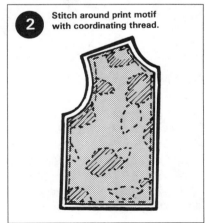

2 Stitch around print motif with coordinating thread.

An interesting alternative is to quilt across print motifs in a contrasting series of lines, such as quilting parallel rows across a floral print (Figure 3).

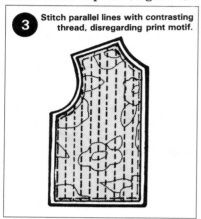

3 Stitch parallel lines with contrasting thread, disregarding print motif.

To stitch even rows, attach a quilting guide to the presser foot (Figure 4).

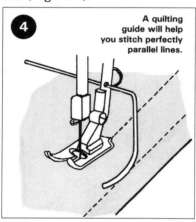

4 A quilting guide will help you stitch perfectly parallel lines.

Another option is to quilt teardrop shapes on a plaid fabric, thus softening the angular effect of the plaid with rounded lines. To stitch this type of free-form quilting, begin with large, flowing teardrops sewn at different angles from all the edges (Figure 5). Remove pins as

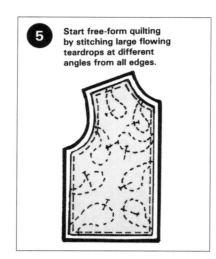

5 Start free-form quilting by stitching large flowing teardrops at different angles from all edges.

necessary, rotating the fabric smoothly as you sew. Then, echo the large teardrops by sewing parallel to the original stitching, using the presser foot toe as a stitching guide (Figure 6).

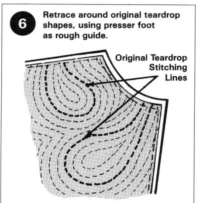

6 Retrace around original teardrop shapes, using presser foot as rough guide.

Original Teardrop Stitching Lines

You can also stitch geometric designs in this manner. Begin with a large, straight-lined motif (Figure 7). Fill in with

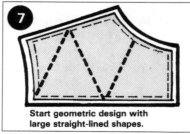

7 Start geometric design with large straight-lined shapes.

other geometric motifs (Figure 8).

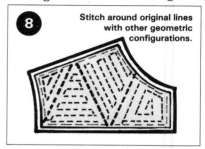

8 Stitch around original lines with other geometric configurations.

Especially creative is a combination of outlined motifs and straight lines of stitches (Figure 9). If you use a printed

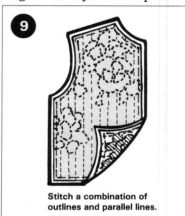

9 Stitch a combination of outlines and parallel lines.

backing fabric and a solid outer fabric, you can quilt around the motifs on the backing fabric to create a decorative design on the outer fabric.

• After quilting the individual garment sections, lay the tissue pattern on each section and trim the edges to size if necessary.

• To make the quilted jacket reversible, bind the trimmed raw edges of seams with self-fabric bias strips or another decorative seam treatment.

Chapter 5

JUST ASK

Sometimes you don't realize there's a gap in your sewing knowledge until you're in the middle of a project and you can't figure out what to do next. Other times you may forge ahead only to end up with a flop instead of a masterpiece.

Don't be discouraged. When something stumps you or goes wrong, just ask. Everybody, whether new to sewing or quite experienced, feels perplexed once in a while. If it's happened to you, chances are it's happened to somebody else, too.

Fortunately, you can turn to sewing experts who are happy to share their knowledge and help you over the hurdles. On the following pages, you'll find answers to the most-asked sewing questions plus dozens of helpful tips for handling assorted sewing slip-ups. There's sound advice for everything from serger snafus to fitting faux pas. You'll find out how to fix garment lumps, bumps, puckers, wrinkles and curls. You'll see there's more than one way to hem a shirt or fit a bustline. You'll find there's a solution for every sewing problem.

One of the reasons sewing keeps your interest for a lifetime is there's always more to learn, and experience is an excellent teacher. Just don't let the obstacles stop you.

BIAS STRIP SEAMS

Do you know a trick for joining bias strips easily and accurately, without getting uneven widths at the seamlines?

If you haven't found success with the classic method for joining the slanted ends of bias strips, try this easy technique:

• After cutting the bias strips, cut the short ends of each strip at a right angle to the long edges (Figure 1).

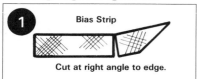

1 Bias Strip
Cut at right angle to edge.

• With right sides together, overlap the ends of two bias strips to form a right angle. Draw a diagonal stitching line from the upper left corner of the top strip to the lower right corner of the bottom strip (Figure 2).

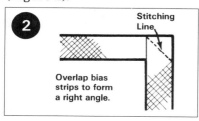

2 Stitching Line
Overlap bias strips to form a right angle.

• Stitch on the line. Trim away the upper right corner ¼" from the stitching (Figure 3).

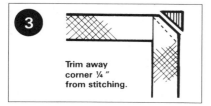

3 Trim away corner ¼" from stitching.

• Press the seam open. Repeat with any remaining bias strips. With a little practice, you probably won't need to draw the stitching guideline.

COLLAR CURL CORRECTION

I'm an experienced seamstress, but I can't seem to conquer the lapel and collar on blazers I sew for myself and my husband. They always curl up and won't lie flat against the shoulder and chest area. Can you give me some advice?

This is a common tailoring problem. The following steps should resolve your dilemma:

• Before cutting out the pattern, compare the upper collar and undercollar pieces by matching the pattern notches and dots; also compare the jacket front and front facing pieces. Be sure each of these pattern pairs allows extra fabric for turn of cloth — the upper collar should be at least ⅛" larger than the undercollar, and the front facing should be at least ⅛" larger than the jacket front.

The exact amount allowed for turn of cloth varies according to the thickness or bulkiness of the fabric and is a matter of judgement. As a guide, for medium weight fabrics the difference between the pattern pieces should be about ¼"; for heavy coatings, it should be as much as ⅜".

If your pattern doesn't comply with these guidelines, add to the outer edges of the upper collar and facing (Figure 1).

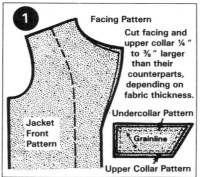

1 Facing Pattern
Cut facing and upper collar ¼" to ⅜" larger than their counterparts, depending on fabric thickness.
Jacket Front Pattern
Undercollar Pattern
Grainline
Upper Collar Pattern

• When you're ready to sew the facing to the jacket front and the upper collar to the undercollar, pin a tuck called a tailor's blister to control the extra fabric (Figure 2).

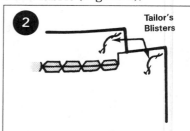

2 Tailor's Blisters

• After stitching the collar and front facing, press the seams open using a contoured pressing board to get into the curved and pointed areas. Then, clip the seam allowance at the end of the lapel roll line marked by twill tape applied earlier (Figure 3).

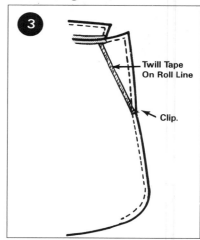

3 Twill Tape On Roll Line
Clip.

Below the clip, trim the jacket seam allowance to ¼" and the facing seam allowance to ⅛". Above the clip, trim the facing and upper collar seam allowances to ¼", and those of the jacket and undercollar to ⅛" (Figure 4). If you've used

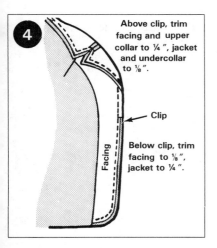

Above clip, trim facing and upper collar to ¼", jacket and undercollar to ⅛".

Clip

Facing

Below clip, trim facing to ⅛", jacket to ¼".

fusible interfacings, you can trim the layers a little more, because the fusing stabilizes the edges and prevents the fabric from raveling. To remember which seam allowance should be wider, note the wider layer in a graded seam is the one next to the side of the garment which shows.

• After trimming and grading, turn the garment right side out and press the finished edge. From the collar notch to the end of the roll line where you made the clip, roll the edge of the collar to the underside and the edge of the lapel toward the garment right side. Roll the remaining front edge — below the clip — toward the facing (Figure 5).

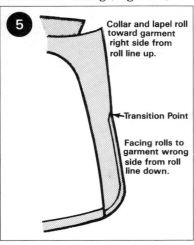

Collar and lapel roll toward garment right side from roll line up.

Transition Point

Facing rolls to garment wrong side from roll line down.

Steam-press, using a tailor's clapper to force the steam into the fabric layers and create a smooth, flat, thin edge. Allow to dry and cool down completely before moving.

• Baste through all layers close to the pressed edges using silk thread. Leave the basting intact until the jacket is completed.

If the above steps do not solve your problem completely, take the following additional steps:

• Try on the partially-completed jacket. Adjust the collar, lapels and facings so they're flat and smooth against the shoulders and chest. Ask someone to help you pin the facing to the jacket along the roll line and continue around the neckline to pin the collar roll line (Figure 6).

Pin facing to jacket at roll line and neckline.

• Remove the jacket and baste the roll lines as pinned. Use silk thread so you can lightly steam the basted roll lines without leaving imprints. Allow the steamed areas to dry and cool down.

• On the inside, sew the neckline seams together as they lie with a long running stitch (Figure 7). Don't worry

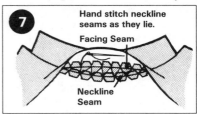

Hand stitch neckline seams as they lie.

Facing Seam

Neckline Seam

if the seamlines don't match; they may need to be mis-aligned to allow for turn of cloth. If you force the seams to match, the collar points will curl and the back neckline seam will show underneath the collar.

• Lift the front facing and use a loose catchstitch to secure it to the jacket interfacing at the roll line as basted. So these stitches don't show from the right side, catch only a thread of the facing and take a larger stitch in the interfacing as you sew.

• Finally, be sure the lining fits properly. If the lining is too tight, it can pull on the lapels and cause them to curl.

VIEW FINDER

To save time locating specific pieces in multi-view patterns, refold individual components so the piece number is facing outward. At a glance you'll be able to tell which pieces are needed for a specific view without having to unfold a mound of tissue.

H. Fry,
Philadelphia, PA

COLLAR STAY SOLUTION

How do you insert collar stays on men's dress shirts?

Sew pockets on the undercollar for the stays with this technique:

• Fold the collar pattern at the point so the center front edge meets the lower edge. Press a crease to mark the pocket stay line (Figure 1).

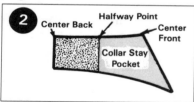

• After cutting, mark the pocket stay line on the wrong side of the undercollar.

• From shirt fabric, cut two stay pockets the shape of the front half of the collar pattern (Figure 2).

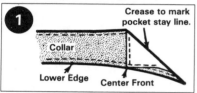

• On the undercollar, make a ½" buttonhole on the pocket stay line 1½" from each collar point (Figure 3). Back each

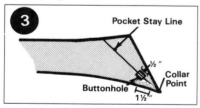

buttonhole area with a small piece of fusible interfacing for stability; cut buttonholes open.

• Wrong sides together, stitch the collar stay pocket sections to the undercollar. To form the pockets, stitch ¼" from the pocket stay line, on each side (Figure 4).

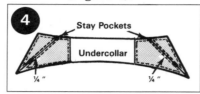

• After completing the collar, insert the stays through the buttonholes on the undercollar. Remove the stays to launder the shirt.

CREASE REMOVAL

How can I remove a stubborn center crease from a cotton blend fabric?

The crease may actually be a fade line, and if so, nothing will remove it. Before you admit defeat, dampen the fabric with undiluted white vinegar, cover with brown paper strips and press until dry.

CROSSING SEAMS PRECISELY

Do you know a foolproof method for matching crossed seams perfectly, besides stitching them over and over again until they meet?

Many people pin the two previously-sewn seams together and then sew over the pin. This may work on some lightweight fabrics, but sewing over pins is always risky. In addition, as the fabric weight increases, the seams can shift as the needle "jumps" over the pin. Also, this forms larger stitches which weakens the seam and makes it prone to popping under stress.

To eliminate these problems, place pins parallel to the seam 1" from the raw edge (Figure 1).

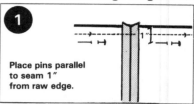

This pin positioning allows the presser foot to pass without encountering the pins, yet the pins anchor the fabric layers to prevent shifting.

Another technique, often used by quilters when assembling quilt blocks, can be used for seam allowances which are pressed to one side rather than pressed open. Alternate the direction you press the seam allowances to stagger the seam allowances and provide a natural brace for stitching the connecting seam precisely (Figure 2).

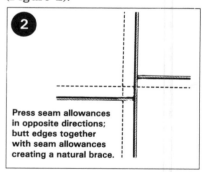

CUT-ON SHOULDER FIT

How do you alter the pattern shoulder width on blouse, dress and jacket styles with cut-on sleeves?

To fit the shoulder width on this type of garment, first "separate" the sleeve from the bodice. Draw line A parallel to the grainline, extending it from the shoulder (about

4″ from the neckline) to just below the underarm curve. Draw line B at right angles to the grainline so it meets the lower end of line A. Cut the pattern apart on these lines. (Figure 1).

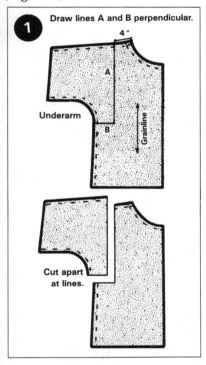

1 Draw lines A and B perpendicular.

4″

A

Underarm

B

Grainline

Cut apart at lines.

To increase the shoulder width for broad shoulders, spread the pattern at the shoulder seam the necessary amount. Tape tissue paper underneath, then blend the cutting and stitching lines at the underarm and shoulder seams (Figure 2). Make a

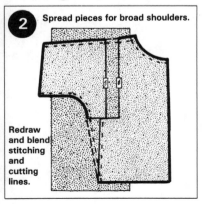

2 Spread pieces for broad shoulders.

Redraw and blend stitching and cutting lines.

matching adjustment on the front and back pattern pieces. Check the new sleeve length and adjust if necessary.

To reduce the shoulder width for narrow shoulders, overlap the pattern pieces the amount needed. Tape tissue paper underneath, then blend the cutting and stitching lines at the underarm and shoulder seams (Figure 3). Make a

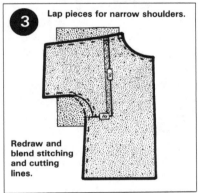

3 Lap pieces for narrow shoulders.

Redraw and blend stitching and cutting lines.

matching adjustment on the front and back patterns. Check the new sleeve length and adjust if necessary.

DARTS FOR PLUS BUST CUPS

How do you alter and reposition darts for a bust cup sized C or larger?

When closely-fitted bodices are in fashion, dart fit becomes a timely issue. Patterns are sized for a B bust cup, so you will need to adjust the pattern to fit a C, D or DD cup size. First, reposition the dart so it points to the fullest part of your bust. Then, increase the dart.

You can choose between two methods to reposition the dart. For either method, begin as follows:

• Determine your bust point measurements by measuring from the center of your shoulder to your bust point, and then from bust point to bust point (Figure 1).

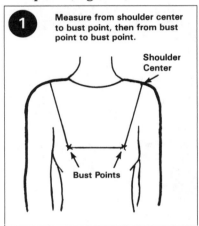

1 Measure from shoulder center to bust point, then from bust point to bust point.

Shoulder Center

Bust Points

Mark the intersection of these two measurements on the bodice front pattern (Figure 2).

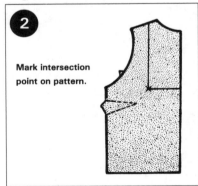

2

Mark intersection point on pattern.

Then, draw new dart stitching lines to angle the original dart toward the new bust point (Figure 3); stop the

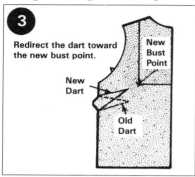

3 Redirect the dart toward the new bust point.

New Bust Point

New Dart

Old Dart

new lines 1″ away from the new bust point. Or, draw a box around the dart, cut out the box, and slide the box up or down as needed (Figure 4);

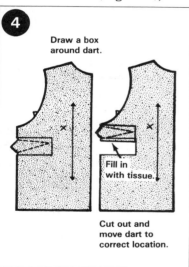

4 Draw a box around dart.

Fill in with tissue.

Cut out and move dart to correct location.

tape tissue paper underneath to fill in any gaps and redraw the side seam.

After you have moved the dart into a better position for your figure, enlarge it:

• To mark the adjustment lines (Figure 5), draw the

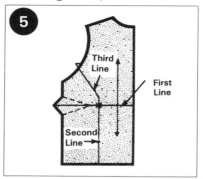

5 Third Line

First Line

Second Line

first line through the center of the dart, through the bust point, to center front. Draw the second line from the bust point to the waistline and parallel to the grainline. Draw the third line from the bust point to the armhole notch.

• Cut the pattern from the waistline through the bust point to the armhole notch, being careful not to cut all the way through, then cut on the dart center line up to, but not through, the bust point.

Spread the tissue ½″ for a C cup; fill in the resulting gaps with tissue, keeping the edges of the vertical cut parallel (Figure 6). For a D cup,

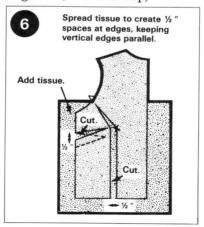

6 Spread tissue to create ½″ spaces at edges, keeping vertical edges parallel.

Add tissue.

Cut.

½″

Cut.

½″

spread the tissue ¾″; for a DD cup, spread the tissue 1¼″.

• Draw the new dart (Figure 7).

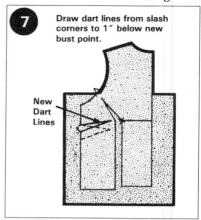

7 Draw dart lines from slash corners to 1″ below new bust point.

New Dart Lines

• Finally, cut the tissue from the center front to the bust point and lower the resulting piece so the bottom edge is even with the side area of the pattern; adjust any front facing pattern to match (Figure 8).

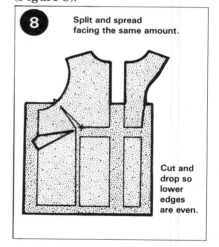

8 Split and spread facing the same amount.

Cut and drop so lower edges are even.

DARTS NEEDED

How can I add darts to dartless designs to accommodate a large bust?

The add-and-fit method is among the easiest:

• First, try on a blouse that has no bust darts. Then, stand in front of a full-length mirror and note diagonal wrinkles that extend downward from the bust point to the underarm seam (Figure 1).

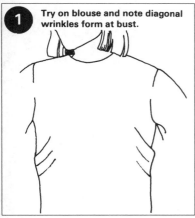

1 Try on blouse and note diagonal wrinkles form at bust.

• Pin these wrinkles into bust darts until the original, diagonal wrinkles disappear or are reduced enough for the blouse to drape smoothly below the bust (Figure 2).

2 Pin darts until blouse hangs smoothly.

Disregard the effect on the blouse back — examine only the garment drape in front. The point of the dart should be from 1″ to 3″ from your bust point, depending upon the fullness of your bust.

• Remove the blouse. Draw an adjustment line on the front bodice pattern to correspond to the pinned dart location on the blouse; mark your bust point on this line (Figure 3).

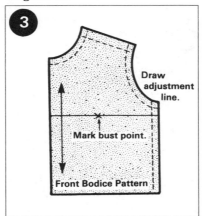

3 Draw adjustment line.

Mark bust point.

Front Bodice Pattern

• Cut the pattern on this line and spread the edges apart by an amount equal to the total amount pinned out in each dart at the blouse underarm seam; add tissue underneath and draw the dart so it ends 1″ to 3″ from your bust point (Figure 4).

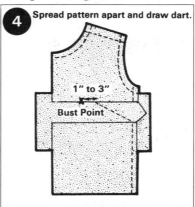

4 Spread pattern apart and draw dart.

1″ to 3″

Bust Point

• Tape tissue underneath and draw the new dart. Correct the cutting and stitching lines at the underarm seam.

DARTS TOO OBVIOUS

Although I'm careful when pressing darts so they don't form imprints on the right side of the fabric, sometimes they're still too obvious by my standards. What can I do to correct this problem?

A dart may be obvious because of the bulk of two fabric layers pressed in one direction, creating three layers of fabric in one spot. To remedy the problem, cut a 1″- to 1½″-wide bias strip of self-fabric slightly longer than the dart. Center it under the dart so it will be caught in the stitching (Figure 1).

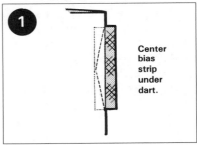

1 Center bias strip under dart.

Press the dart in one direction and the strip in the other so similar layers of fabric are on both sides of the stitching line (Figure 2). Trim the bias strip edges to simulate the dart shape.

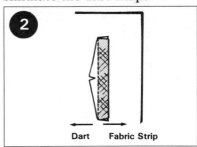

2 Dart   Fabric Strip

DIAGONAL DESIGNS

Why is it so difficult to find patterns for fabrics with diagonal prints? Pattern after pattern states "unsuitable for diagonals."

To choose a pattern for a diagonal fabric, sometimes you just have to bite the bullet and use your own judgement. Use the following guidelines to make a wise choice:

• Simple styles with few seamlines are always best, since it takes real planning to match diagonal fabrics when cutting and sewing. Basic cardigan shapes are a suitable jacket choice, for example.

• Avoid lots of shaped seams. Look for straight rather than curved seamlines, and choose straight-cut, fitted or gathered skirts rather than bias or flared skirts.

• One-piece jacket sleeves are better than two-piece sleeves.

• Avoid tailored notched collars with lapels because the diagonal fabric design will run in different directions on the collar points.

• Straightforward, classic pants and trouser patterns should work out well.

EASE-PLUS SECRETS

I've heard the differential feed feature on a serger resembles the ease-plus technique on a conventional sewing machine. What is ease-plus?

Ease-plus, also called crimping, makes a fabric edge slightly shorter as you stitch. You can use it to ease a larger layer of fabric to fit a smaller layer, such as when setting in a sleeve. You can also use the ease-plus technique to control the fullness in curved hems. Ease-plus is not a substitute for gathering, but rather a quick way to ease a small amount of fabric smoothly.

To sew with the ease-plus technique, hold your finger behind the presser foot and apply pressure to prevent the fabric from coming out the back as fast as it is being fed from in front of the foot (Figure 1). The fabric will "shrink" slightly.

To ease-plus, feed the fabric into the machine more quickly than it's being released out the back.

The stitch length and amount of pressure to apply depend upon the fabric weight. The heavier the fabric, the more pressure and the longer the stitch needed to allow more fabric to be drawn into each stitch.

If you accidentally ease too much, simply pull the fabric to smooth it out; pop a thread if necessary. To ease more fabric, pull up a thread or repeat the ease-plus stitching.

FACING SLICK TRICK

When I'm finishing a neckline with a facing and there's a center back zipper closure, the facing always looks bulky at the top of the zipper. How can I prevent this?

Here's how to handle the facing at the center back for smooth results. Before inserting the zipper:

• Prepare the facing by stitching the shoulder seams and finishing the lower edge. Then, turn under the facing seam allowances 1″ at the center opening (Figure 1).

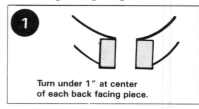

Turn under 1″ at center of each back facing piece.

• Pin the facing to the garment neckline, folding the back neck opening ⅝″ over the facing seam allowances to stitch the neckline seam (Figure 2).

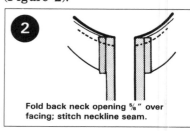

Fold back neck opening ⅝″ over facing; stitch neckline seam.

• Grade and clip the neckline/facing seam. Understitch the neckline/facing seam, stopping at the raw edge of the facing seam allowance on each side of the center back opening (Figure 3).

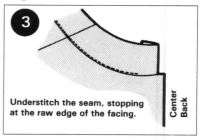

Understitch the seam, stopping at the raw edge of the facing.

Center Back

• Using a ⅝″ seam allowance in the center back opening, insert the zipper using a centered application. Fold back the facing seam allowances to insert the zipper (Figure 4).

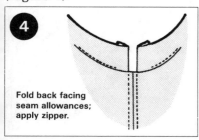

Fold back facing seam allowances; apply zipper.

• On the wrong side, fold down the ends of the zipper tape and press. Fold the facing to the inside, press and slipstitch the facing edges to the zipper tape (Figure 5).

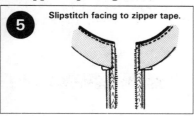

Slipstitch facing to zipper tape.

FLY FRONT TWIST

No matter how hard I press, I always get wrinkles in fly front zipper plackets. How can I prevent the fabric from twisting?

Twisting occurs because the center front of the fly was not cut on the straight fabric grain. To prevent the wrinkles, make a simple pattern alteration before you cut:

• First, extend the grainline arrow on the front pattern up to the waistline.

• Measure to see if the center front at the top and bottom of the fly area are the same distance away from the grainline arrow (Figure 1).

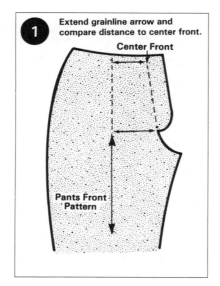

Extend grainline arrow and compare distance to center front.

Center Front

Pants Front Pattern

• If these two measurements are not equal, slash the pattern on the center front mark from the waist to the dot marking at the bottom of the fly front opening; spread the slashed edges to make the center front line parallel to the extended grainline arrow (Figure 2). Tape tissue underneath to bridge the gap.

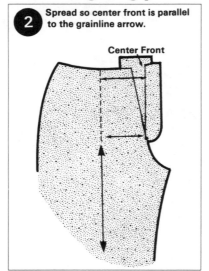

Spread so center front is parallel to the grainline arrow.

Center Front

• Measure the amount you have added to the waistline by this adjustment. It usually is in the ¼″ to ½″ range. Remove this amount at the side seam, darts or ease it into the waistband.

HAND-ROLLED HEM HELP

How do I handle the corners of a hand-rolled hem on scarves?

On a hand-rolled hem, the hem allowances overlap at the corners, and it takes a little practice to hem corners smoothly. For best results:

• Hem one edge to the corner. Then pivot the scarf so the next edge to be hemmed is held horizontally in your left hand with the wrong side toward you (Figure 1).

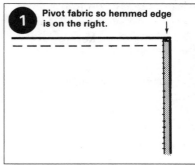

Pivot fabric so hemmed edge is on the right.

• Lay the needle along the unhemmed edge at the corner so the eye extends about 1″ beyond the fabric (Figure 2).

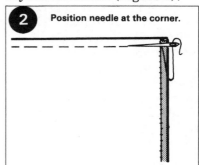

Position needle at the corner.

• Roll the raw edge over the needle (Figure 3). Pull the

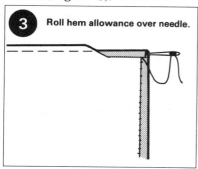

3 Roll hem allowance over needle.

needle out of the roll and hem the edge, working from right to left.

Some other tricks for better hand-rolled hems include:

• Machine stitch ⅛″ from the hemline in the hem allowance to stay the edge and provide a guide for an even hem.

• Trim away the excess hem allowance ⅛″ from the machine stitching, but to prevent excess fraying, trim only about 8″ to 10″ at a time.

• Dampen your left thumb and forefinger to roll a tight hem.

• Use a fine needle to hem with a slipstitch, felling stitch or overcast stitch.

JEANS JAM MACHINE

When I hem denim jeans, my machine practically comes to a halt as it approaches the flat-felled seams. How can I continue stitching over these bulky humps and keep the stitch length even?

Hemming denim jeans isn't easy, especially when crossing flat felled seams, where you're stitching through many layers of tightly-woven fabric.

To understand why the machine balks at stitching over the bulky seams, you should know that the machine's feed dogs move the fabric as you sew. The feed dog teeth can work effectively only if the presser foot is horizontal (Figure 1).

1 The feed dogs work best when the presser foot is horizontal.

If the presser foot tilts, as it does when it comes to the thickness of the flat-felled seam, the feed dog teeth can't grip the fabric and the machine stops feeding (Figure 2).

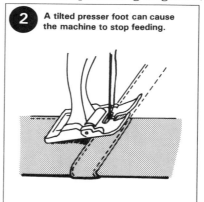

2 A tilted presser foot can cause the machine to stop feeding.

If you try to force the fabric through, you'll either break the needle or create a few, extra-long stitches.

The solution is as simple as placing a wedge of folded fabric under the back portion of the presser foot to keep it level and allow the feed dog teeth to grip the fabric (Figure 3).

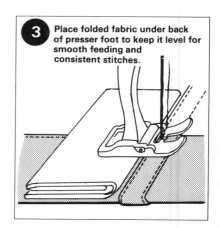

3 Place folded fabric under back of presser foot to keep it level for smooth feeding and consistent stitches.

It also helps to use a sharp needle or a size 100/16 denim/jeans needle, which has a special point engineered to penetrate tough fabrics. Treat the needle with needle lubricant before you stitch.

MENDING A MIS-CUT

I started to cut out a skirt, forgetting that I needed to add length to the pattern. Now I have a 2″ slash near the lower edge of my skirt. What is the least conspicuous way to repair this without shortening my skirt?

Everybody makes a similar cutting error at least once. If you're not fussy about the mend's appearance, you could simply apply a piece of press-on tape on the wrong side.

Or, use a piece of soft, fusible interfacing to hold the two slashed edges together.

For a more professional mending job, sew one or more rows over the repair with a serpentine or multi-step zigzag stitch (Figure 1). If the fabric has a design, choose a thread color that blends in or use several thread colors to hide the mend in a print.

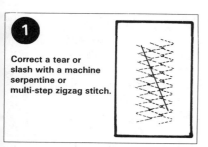

Correct a tear or slash with a machine serpentine or multi-step zigzag stitch.

Of course, no matter how skillfully you hide the stitches, it might bother you to know the repair's there. Judge the success of your efforts with the "3-foot rule" — if you can't see the flaw from a 3-foot distance, don't worry about it.

METAL BUTTON SECURITY

The metal buttons I sew on blazers break the thread and pop off, even though I use strong thread and wax it. Do you know an easy way to keep the buttons intact longer?

This frustrating problem is caused by the rough edges on the button shank which rub and cut into the thread during normal wear. To remedy, thread a metal, looped eye from a hook and eye set through the shank (Figure 1).

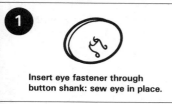

Insert eye fastener through button shank: sew eye in place.

Then, sew the eye in place by hand with doubled thread or buttonhole twist. The eye takes the wear and tear formerly inflicted upon the thread.

NARROW HEM TRICKS

I've been trying, with little success, to use my machine's narrow hem foot. Any tricks?

Like many timesaving devices, a narrow hem foot saves you time only after you take time to learn how to use it. But once mastered, the narrow hemmer is a foot you won't want to sew without.

A narrow hem foot has a scroll fitting (Figure 1) which

Scroll
Narrow Hem Foot

folds the fabric to produce a twice-turned edge as the machine stitches the hem. It's intended for straight or fairly straight garment edges, as it's difficult to ease in fullness as you narrow-hem.

Some machine brands offer several sizes of narrow hem feet; the narrower the hem a foot produces, the thinner and lighter weight the fabric should be. You might want to practice with the foot producing the widest hem since it's the easiest to use.

Starting the fabric on the scrolling process is the most challenging part of stitching with a narrow hem foot. Here's how to make this step easier:

• For the first 1″ or so, fold under the hem edge twice and press.

• Place this pressed, folded edge under the narrow hem foot and sew a few stitches. Hold the thread tails to help the fabric feed under the foot. Lower the needle into the fabric and lift the foot (Figure 2).

Sew a few stitches, then lower needle and raise foot.

• Hold the first fold firmly and guide it into the spiral scroll of the foot (Figure 3).

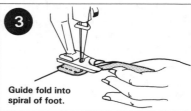

Guide fold into spiral of foot.

Lower the presser foot to stitch the remainder of the narrow hem. As you stitch, guide the fabric by holding it taut and lifting it slightly, since the fabric must feed in a straight line for an even hem (Figure 4).

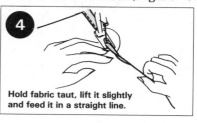

Hold fabric taut, lift it slightly and feed it in a straight line.

• An optional way to start a narrow hem is to first sew a 3″ square of tear-away stabilizer to the fabric, overlapping the edges about ¼″ (Figure 5).

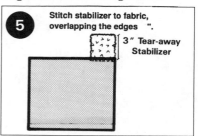

Stitch stabilizer to fabric, overlapping the edges ″.

3″ Tear-away Stabilizer

Fold and press the stabilizer to start the hem scrolling into the presser foot; by the time you reach the fabric, you'll be well on your way to a neat, narrow hem. Tear off the stabilizer when you've finished.

• If you're sewing in a circle, such as when hemming a sleeve or the bottom of a blouse, fold and press the hem to start sewing, as described on the previous page and shown in Figures 2 and 3. Hem around the circle until you come to within 1″ of the starting point. Remove the hem from the machine, finger press the unhemmed portion, and simply straight stitch to complete the hem.

NECKBAND LUMPS & BUMPS

Can you offer some suggestions for achieving a smooth finish on a shirt collar with a standing band? No matter how much I trim and clip, I still end up with lumps and bumps where the band meets the front edge of the shirt.

After stitching the collar section, follow these steps to sew the standing neckband:

• Staystitch the shirt neckline and clip to the stitching at 1″ intervals (Figure 1).

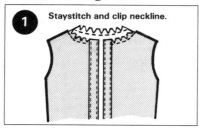
1 Staystitch and clip neckline.

• Interface the neckband. With right sides together, pin the neckband to the neckline, matching notches and construction symbols and allowing the ends of the neckband to extend ⅝″ beyond the finished front edge of the shirt.

• Stitch, then trim the seam allowances to ¼″. Press the band and seam allowances up, away from the shirt body (Figure 2).

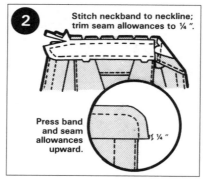
2 Stitch neckband to neckline; trim seam allowances to ¼″.
Press band and seam allowances upward. ¼″

• Pin the completed collar to the neckband, matching the notches and making sure the front edges of the collar are positioned at the center front on the neckband; machine baste (Figure 3).

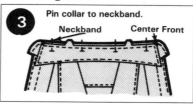
3 Pin collar to neckband.
Neckband   Center Front

• Machine baste along the lower edge of the neckband facing a scant ⅝″ from the raw edge. Using the basting as a guide, press under ⅝″ (Figure 4).

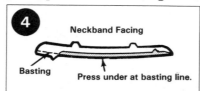
4 Neckband Facing
Basting   Press under at basting line.

• Right sides together, pin the neckband facing to the neckband over the collar. Beginning at the center front, stitch to the center back. To avoid a pucker, pull or lump where the neckband meets the front edge, use a slightly narrower seam allowance – start stitching the seam at the front end of the neckband ¹⁄₁₆″ from the front edge of the shirt.

Stitch the other half of the neckband/collar seam the same way, stitching from the center front to the center back, overlapping the stitches at center back (Figure 5).

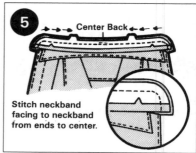
5 Center Back
Stitch neckband facing to neckline from ends to center.

Stitching in two segments this way insures that both halves of the neckband will look the same.

• Grade the seam allowances, notch the curves, turn and press.

• Turn the neckband right side out and pin the neckband facing in place, making sure the pressed edge is on top of the neckline stitching.

• Pin or hand baste as needed before edgestitching all edges of the neckband, catching the pressed edge of the neckband facing in the edgestitches (Figure 6).

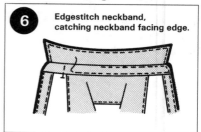
6 Edgestitch neckband, catching neckband facing edge.

NECKLINE GAPOSIS

My garments gap at the neckline. What causes the problem and how should I solve it?

The cause of a neckline that gaps may be a small neck, square shoulders, a small bust or a dowager's hump. Choose a basic pattern with a front opening and a classic, jewel neckline to work out the necessary alterations, then use them as a guide for fitting other pattern styles in the future.

To determine the pattern alterations you need:

• Cut the front and back bodice patterns from muslin or another test fabric. Staystitch the neckline and armholes. Sew the shoulder and under-arm seams.

• Try on the bodice and pin it together at center front. Clip the neckline and armhole seam allowances as needed for smooth fit. Ask a friend to help you remove the excess fabric in the neckline by pinning darts from the neckline to the bust point (Figure 1).

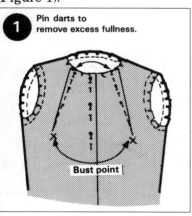

1 Pin darts to remove excess fullness.

Bust point

• Take off the bodice. Mark the dart stitching lines. Remove the pins from the dart so the bodice is flat.

• Transfer the dart to the bodice front pattern by covering the muslin bodice with the bodice front pattern and tracing the dart stitching lines onto the tissue. Using the bust point as the center, draw a circle with a 2″ radius; measure the depth of the dart on the circle (Figure 2). This

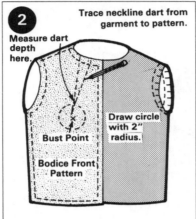

2 Trace neckline dart from garment to pattern.

Measure dart depth here.

Draw circle with 2″ radius.

Bust Point

Bodice Front Pattern

tells you how deep the dart should be 2″ from the bust point — useful information for pattern adjustments on future styles.

• Cut the bodice front pattern on one of the dart stitching lines almost up to the bust point. Also cut the pattern from the hem almost up to the bust point (if the pattern has a vertical dart at the hem, cut through the center of the dart almost up to the bust point). Match the traced dart stitching lines and tape them together; the hem cut will spread apart (Figure 3). Tape tissue underneath to fill the gap. Remove the excess width added below the bust by

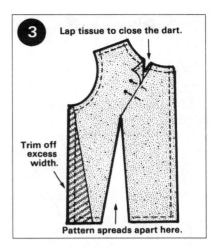

3 Lap tissue to close the dart.

Trim off excess width.

Pattern spreads apart here.

trimming the side seam or making the vertical bust dart deeper.

If you compare this adjusted pattern with the original, you will find the new neckline is smaller and the shoulder seam slopes less. The pattern should fit well. For future pattern styles, note that necklines vary; the depth of the fitting dart at the neckline decreases as the neckline is lowered, so adjust the dart size accordingly. Use the depth of the dart as measured 2″ from the bust point to help you alter future patterns accurately.

PANTS HEM DIP

When hemming classic pants, should the bottom of the legs be straight across or dip in back?

The style and length of the pants determines the hemline shape. In general, classic, straight-legged pants and men's trousers fall at the top of the instep or shoe in front. In back, the hem dips to the middle of the back of the shoe or the top of the shoe heel, according to personal preference. The hem is usually ½" to ¾" lower in back than in the front.

If the pants have very narrow, straight legs, the hem may dip as much as 1" in back. This type of leg style requires a separately-cut facing instead of a hem.

If you hem pants straight across instead of dipping the hem, you'll have a slight break in the fabric at the front of the pants leg. This is acceptable, although not quite as polished as a shaped hem. You can minimize the break by shortening the pants slightly or wearing shoes with a higher heel.

PANTS HEM PUCKERS

When shortening tapered pants, the shaping in the ankle area sometimes causes the hem to pucker. How can I avoid this pants hemming problem?

When sewing pants, be sure to shorten the pattern before cutting the fabric. Then, the shaping in the hem area will accommodate the tapered leg. To alter the pattern:

• Determine the required finished length by measuring from your waistline at the side, over the hip, to the desired length. Or, measure the side seam of a pair of pants that are the correct length.

• If your pattern provides no printed lengthen/shorten line below the knee, draw a line at right angles to the grainline at a point between the hemline and the knee, then fold to shorten the necessary amount. Blend the cutting and stitching lines at the side seams and inseams (Figure 1).

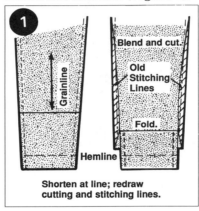

Shorten at line; redraw cutting and stitching lines.

Make matching length adjustments on the front and back patterns.

• Hem as usual.

Shortening tapered pants after you have cut and partially sewn them is a little more work. This method can also be used to shorten ready-to-wear pants:

• Measure the bottom of the pant leg at the hemline to determine the finished width.

• Cut away the excess pant leg length, leaving 1" for the new hem allowance.

• Turn the pants wrong side out and use tailor's chalk or a marking pen to draw tapering lines on the legs. Beginning just below the knee, mark to the hemline, removing equal amounts from the side seam and inseam so the width at the new hemline equals the original. To avoid a puckered hem, taper the stitching inward to the hemline, then outward to the bottom edge (Figure 2).

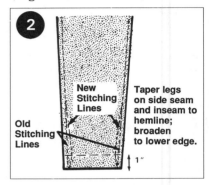

New Stitching Lines

Old Stitching Lines

Taper legs on side seam and inseam to hemline; broaden to lower edge.

1"

• Baste the alteration and try on the pants to check the fit.

• Stitch the new seams, remove the original stitches, trim the seam allowances if necessary and press.

• Turn up and press the pants leg hems. If the top edge of the hem is too narrow, causing puckers, let out the side seams and inseams in the hem allowance to add more width.

If the top edge of the hem is too wide, causing bulkiness, easestitch the top edge of the hem to control the excess fabric.

PANTS TOO TAPERED

Is there a general rule to follow for the width of pant legs when you don't have the figure for tapered-to-fit styles?

It's wise to recognize the importance of suiting a style to your figure, rather than being a slave to fashion. Whether pants legs are tapered or very full, a flattering and always "safe" width at the hemline is 20″ to 22″.

To adjust a pants pattern which is too tapered, decide how much you want to add to each leg, divide by four and add this amount equally to the inseam and the side seam at the hemline of the pants front and back patterns. Draw new cutting lines, tapering from just below the fullest part of the hip on the side seam and just above the knee on the inseam (Figure 1).

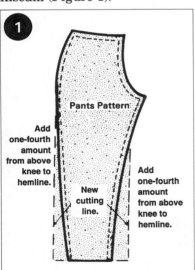

1

Pants Pattern

Add one-fourth amount from above knee to hemline.

New cutting line.

Add one-fourth amount from above knee to hemline.

PATTERN FABRIC ESTIMATES

Why do patterns always recommend more fabric than I seem to need?

Pattern layouts used to be worked out manually, but for several years they've been planned on computers. Computerized layouts are much more accurate and economical — there's less space allowed between pattern pieces. All fabric estimates are figured to the next ⅛ yard, not the nearest ⅛ yard; a layout that requires 3 yards 2″ will be rounded off to 3⅛ yards not 3 yards.

The computer is programmed with specific information. The fabric width is exact, the pattern is as it comes out of the envelope without alterations, the layout is simple, all seam and hem allowances are cut as printed on the tissue pieces and no seam allowances overlap.

If you consistently have fabric left over, it's because:

• You used a wider fabric. Even an inch makes a difference for some layouts.

• You reduced the pattern length or width.

• You omitted some pattern sections.

• You reduced the hem allowance.

• You allowed one seam allowance to notch into another to economize on fabric or to match a print.

• You refolded your fabric to save a few inches.

If you want to purchase exactly the amount of fabric you'll need, the answer is to plan your own layouts, but that takes time. In fact, dressmakers whose customers purchase less than the specified amount of fabric are justified in charging extra for this service.

PATTERN SIZE SENSE

Why do I need a size 14 pattern when I take a size 10 or 12 in ready-to-wear clothing?

You can't compare pattern size with ready-to-wear size — one does not relate to the other. In fact, garment manufacturers do not abide by an industry-wide set of size standards. Sizing varies from one label to another and might even change from one season to another. That's why you'll find higher quality and higher priced garments run larger than less expensive or discount brands. Some say this is a marketing ploy, since customers find it flattering to fit into a garment labeled with a smaller size number.

Fortunately, all pattern companies follow the same sizing standards. When you purchase a pattern, you know it was designed for and will fit a body with the specified set of figure measurements. You can depend on these size standards to remain consistent.

Note, however, that style of fit changes to keep up with fashion. Current trends may favor loosely-fitted, semi-fitted, or closely-fitted silhouettes — or anything in between. Keep on top of fit trends, as they affect the appearance of the finished garment, but select the pattern size that comes closest to your figure measurements.

Above all, don't worry about the number. Buy the pattern size that fits you best for faster, easier, better sewing. Pattern size doesn't define beauty or an ideal figure. Furthermore, the size you take is your secret when you sew.

PEN MARKS PERSIST

Water-soluble pen marks don't always dissolve, even though I avoid pressing over them. Can you help?

Every product has its advantages and disadvantages, and nothing is foolproof. Water-soluble ink works great on most fabrics, but it's important to test on scraps first.

The most critical test is what happens when you mark the right side of the fabric. If testing shows the ink won't disappear with a drop of water, substitute chalk. Marks on the wrong side of the fabric don't require removal, as long as they don't show through to the right side.

Fiber content might affect marking ink removal, but it's more likely that the fabric's surface texture will cause problems. Sizing and other fabric finishing chemicals can interact with the marking pen ink; preshrinking the fabric to remove the chemicals may be the best way to prevent persistent ink marks.

PERFECTING THE POINT

Waistlines that dip to a "V" in front are so attractive, but I cringe when asked to sew this style because I always have to rework that center point. Any secrets to reveal?

One key tip is careful marking of the bodice point and another is careful slashing of the inward corner on the skirt's seam allowance. Here's how:

• On the bodice front, mark the exact point where the seamlines intersect. Use a visible chalk "X" or a tailor's tack (Figure 1).

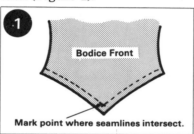

Mark point where seamlines intersect.

• Reinforce the corner on the skirt by adjusting the machine stitch length to a short 20 stitches per inch and stitching exactly on the ⅝" seamline. Begin and end this stitching 1" on each side of the inward corner.

Slash the corner to within a thread of the reinforcement stitching so you can spread the corner into a straight line (Figure 2). This slashing is so

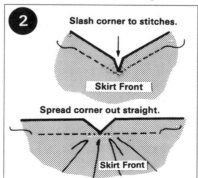

Slash corner to stitches.

Skirt Front

Spread corner out straight.

Skirt Front

crucial that if you don't slash far enough, the skirt won't fit smoothly onto the bodice point and you will experience stitching and pressing problems.

• With right sides together, pin the bodice to the skirt. Match the bodice point marking with the point of the inward corner on the skirt. Stitch from the skirt side.

• On extreme points, it's sometimes easier to pin and stitch the first half of the seam to the point. Leave the needle in the fabric. Pin the remainder of the seam, straighten out the point, pivot the seam under the presser foot and finish stitching the seam.

PLEAT HEM PREDICAMENT

How do you hem pleats that fall at a seamline? I'd like to know how to handle the bulk of all the fabric layers so the pleat lies flat.

Some special handling is required in this situation:

• Establish the hemline and trim the hem allowance to the desired width.

• Clip the pleat seam at the top of the hem area up to, but not through, the stitching; trim the seam allowance below the clip to ¼" and press it open (Figure 1).

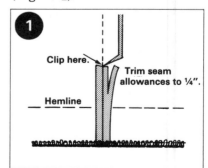

Clip here.

Trim seam allowances to ¼".

Hemline

- Hem the garment. Press.
- If the pleat doesn't hang smoothly, edgestitch the pleat fold within the hem allowance (Figure 2). Press.

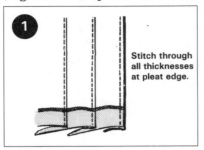

Hem

← Edgestitch pleat fold.

PLEAT RETENTION

I recently made a pleated skirt of wool flannel, a fabric suggested on the pattern envelope. The skirt wrinkles when I sit in it for any length of time and the pleats lose their crispness. Is there a remedy?

Unfortunately, the conditions created by long periods of sitting – heat and moisture – can cause fabric wrinkles. But, one of the beauties of quality wool fabric is its ability to shed wrinkles when allowed to hang overnight.

Lining pleated wool skirts can help. Cut a slip-style lining without the pleats. Make the lining fit comfortably and attach it to the skirt at the waistline seam only.

To keep pleats sharp and crisp and to make them easier to press when wear distorts them, edgestitch the inner fold of the pleats through all thicknesses, including the hem (Figure 1). The pleats will last

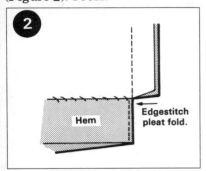

Stitch through all thicknesses at pleat edge.

longer, and you won't have to guess where to fold the pleats when re-pressing the skirt.

PRESHRINKING FUSIBLES

I've heard that fusible interfacings can shrink even though they're usually labeled "preshrunk." Is this true, and if so, how do you preshrink fusibles without damaging the adhesive?

All fabrics which are wrapped onto a bolt are held under tension. Most, including interfacings, will relax somewhat when removed from the bolt – you could consider this a type of "shrinkage."

Also, most fabrics will shrink when steam-pressed; fusing usually requires more steam-pressing than normal, so it's wise to preshrink fusible interfacings. Of course, it's equally important to preshrink the fashion fabric, too.

Do not attempt to preshrink fusible interfacings in the washer and dryer. Use one of the following methods:

- To preshrink fusible woven, knit or weft-insertion types, use the dip method.

Fill a sink with hot tap water and gently fold the interfacing accordian-style into the water. Allow it to soak until the water is cool to the touch.

Drain the water, letting the interfacing sit in the sink 5 more minutes to remove excess water. Carefully roll the wet interfacing in an absorbent towel. Drape the interfacing over a towel on a rack or shower rod to dry.

- To preshrink nonwoven types, use the steam method. Do not use the dip method.

To steam, press the fashion fabric to warm it and make it more receptive to fusing. Position the interfacing with adhesive side down on the wrong side of the warm fashion fabric; hold the steam iron about 1″ above. Steam, using the burst of steam feature if your iron has it. You may be able to see the interfacing edges drawing up slightly; this change in size won't affect the finished product. Apply the interfacing following the manufacturer's instructions.

> ### NO TANGLES
> To keep my thread basket neat, I use a felt-tip pen to mark the slit on the spool end where the thread begins so I can easily find and re-insert the thread end when I'm done sewing. It only takes a minute, but saves hours of frustration.
>
> *H. Brown,*
> *Spokane, WA*

RIBBING TOO SLACK

I serge T-shirts by the dozens. On some, the ribbing isn't tight enough, even though I stretched it while applying it. What went wrong?

When ribbing looks stretched out and doesn't control the shirt edge enough, the culprit is usually the ribbing not your sewing technique.

To avoid this problem, test ribbing resiliency before you buy. Stretch the ribbing firmly. If it doesn't return to its original size, buy another ribbing.

Some other helpful tips:

• Try ribbed bands. Cut the ribbing double-depth, fold in half with wrong sides together and serge the ribbing as a double layer.

• Because ribbings vary, applying them is not an exact science. Use the pattern cutting guides, but double-check the fit by trying the ribbing on the relevant body area. For example, for a crew neck shirt, test the ribbing fit around the wearer's head.

• Always cut the ribbing smaller than the garment edge and distribute the ease evenly. To distribute the ease, divide the ribbing and the garment edge into fourths with pins as markers. Note that on neck-lines, the pin-marks will not always fall at the shoulder seams.

Match the pins as you stretch the ribbing to fit the garment edge. Stitch with the ribbing on top.

RIGHT NEEDLE, WRONG THREAD

I'm sewing a christening dress of Swiss cotton batiste and am getting looped stitches. I switched to a fine needle in my machine but without success. What could be wrong?

Try using extra-fine or lingerie thread.

While it's important to match the needle and the fabric, it's also vital to match the needle and the thread. When sewing, the thread lies in the long groove in front of the needle (Figure 1). If the

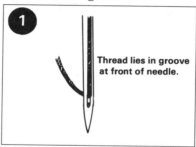

Thread lies in groove at front of needle.

thread isn't fine enough, it won't fit into the groove and you'll get faulty stitches.

RIGHT THREAD, WRONG NEEDLE

I'm sewing a wool coat. My sewing machine dealer sold me a special topstitching needle to use with buttonhole twist thread, but I still can't get my machine to sew with this heavier thread. What can I do?

A heavy needle thread causes much more friction among thread, needle and fabric. Try a larger needle such as a size 110/18; the larger needle eye and the larger fabric hole the needle creates reduces the friction.

Also, try tightening the needle thread tension. You often have to adjust the tension to get a balanced

stitch when using different threads in the needle and bobbin

ROLLED EDGE SANS SERGER

I don't own a serger. Is there a way to duplicate a fine, rolled edge on my sewing machine?

Although serging is the quickest way to sew a rolled hem, you can achieve a similar look with a simple zigzag stitch and a standard button-hole foot with a grooved sole. This method works best on the straight grain of soft fabrics:

• Use a medium to wide, short zigzag stitch. Loosen the needle thread tension slightly so the stitch will "wrap" the edge.

• Use a soft thread such as cotton or rayon embroidery thread.

• Use a fine size 70/10 needle.

• Trim the edge neatly. With the fabric right side up, position it so the edge is just to the right of the center under the presser foot.

Hold the fabric taut, not stretched, in front of and behind the needle as you zigzag along the edge. The fabric will roll up inside the stitch as the rolled edge "escapes" through the left groove under the presser foot (Figure 1).

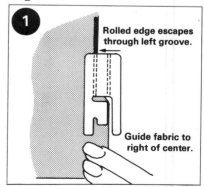

Rolled edge escapes through left groove.

Guide fabric to right of center.

ROUNDED BACK RESOLUTION

I have a rounded back because of osteoporosis, and this causes fitting problems. How should I adjust patterns?

Since every figure has its unique contours, you'll have to experiment a little bit. Try shaping a muslin square over the contours of a dressmaker's ham to help understand how to dart or seam fabric to fit this three-dimensional figure variation.

One key to fitting a rounded back is add a center back seam if the pattern doesn't have one. This gives you an extra opportunity to shape the garment back for your figure.

Another key is adding shoulder darts to the back bodice pattern:

• Draw a horizontal line across the upper back of the bodice pattern, at right angles to the center back and about 5" below the neckline; draw a vertical line from the center of the shoulder seam slanting down to the horizontal line (Figure 1).

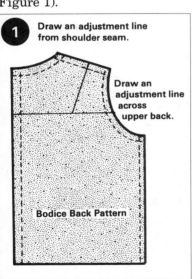

1 Draw an adjustment line from shoulder seam.

Draw an adjustment line across upper back.

Bodice Back Pattern

• Cut the pattern on the horizontal line from center back over to but not through the armhole edge; cut the pattern on the vertical line from the shoulder seam down to but not through the horizontal line.

• Measure your center back to find out how much to spread the pattern on the horizontal line to add more back length; spread the pattern on the vertical line 1" or more to create a dart (Figure 2).

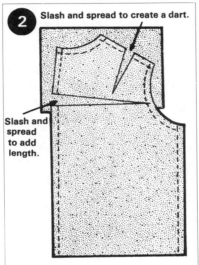

2 Slash and spread to create a dart.

Slash and spread to add length.

Tape tissue underneath to bridge the gaps. Correct the cutting and stitching lines, and draw in the dart stitching lines.

• Cut the adjusted pattern from muslin and sew a trial garment to test the fit.

Adjust the size, spacing and shape of the shoulder darts if necessary to accommodate your rounded back contours. The darts should point to the fullest part of the back, ending about 2" short of the fullest part.

If the darts are very shallow, consider easing the extra fabric into the shoulder seams instead of stitching darts. If the darts are very deep, consider dividing each large dart into two or three smaller darts for better fit.

• Adjust the armhole curve if it has become distorted.

• If you need additional shaping to fit rounded back contours, add darts to the neckline.

• Another option is lowering the neckline. A lower neckline can help to fit and flatter a rounded back.

• Sewing garments from textured fabrics or allover prints helps to hide the dart adjustments.

SERGER RIP-OUTS

What's the best way to remove serger stitches?

Ripping out serger stitches is simple. Slip a small seam ripper under the loops on one side to cut the threads. Pull the needle and looper threads on the other side of the stitch (Figure 1).

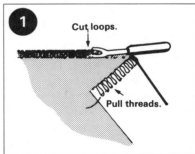

1 Cut loops.

Pull threads.

Two-thread serger chain-stitches are easy to remove, making them ideal for basting. Pull on the looper thread for instant removal (Figure 2).

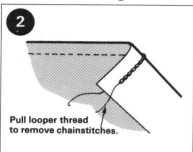

Pull looper thread to remove chainstitches.

SERGER THREAD BREAKS

The threads on my serger break continually. What's wrong?

Before you panic, run through this checklist:

• Open the front and side panels to make sure the needle and looper threads are in all the guides and are not tangled. Refer to the manual if you are uncertain about proper threading.

• Release any thread caught in a spool notch.

• Adjust the tensions. One or more thread tensions may be too tight.

• Replace the thread if it's old or of poor quality. Irregularities such as slubs can interfere with the thread path through the guides.

• Change to a new needle or a needle of a different size.

• If all else fails, remove the thread from the needle eye. Serge for a few inches (no thread chain will form). Rethread the needle, pulling the thread under the presser foot with the other looper threads, and try serging again.

• Consult your dealer.

SERGER THREAD ESTIMATE

How do I estimate the amount of thread I'll need for decorative serging with heavy thread, ribbon or yarn in the upper looper?

Use this formula: Measure the edges to be serged and multiply by 3½. In addition, allow extra thread for the essential steps of testing the stitch on scraps and adjusting the tensions.

SERGER THREAD MATCH

I use my serger extensively. Because I often need a thread color for just one garment, I don't want to invest in several large cones of thread and be stuck with leftovers. How can I minimize thread purchases and still obtain an acceptable match?

Unless your fabric is particularly sheer, you can use any color of thread in some of the loopers; use matching thread only when it might show.

For example, on 4/3-thread or 3-thread serged seams, only the needle thread color match is vital since this thread shows from the right side if the seam is strained. Similarly, the left needle and lower looper of a 4/2-thread stitch will show along a pulled seamline; the other needle and looper threads won't show.

If you want an exact color match for seams or finishing edges, purchase spools rather than cones for small projects. Use all-purpose polyester or polyester/cotton threads, or select extra-fine thread for more delicate seams and edges.

For spools that are parallel-wound rather than cross-wound, place the notched end of the spool down and use the spool caps that come with the serger for smooth thread feeding (Figure 1).

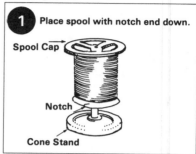

Place spool with notch end down.

Spool Cap

Notch

Cone Stand

SERGING SQUARER CORNERS

When I serge napkin corners with a rolled edge, they look too pointed, even through I carefully follow the fabric grainline to keep them perfectly straight. What's the problem?

Although it sounds odd, if you slightly round off the corners, they will look more square. About 2″ to 3″ from each corner, gradually angle the fabric so you are serging about ⅛″ in toward the corner by the time you reach the point.

Similarly, when you start to serge the edge on the other side of the corner, start about ⅛″ in, gradually returning to the straight grainline about 2″ to 3″ from the corner (Figure 1).

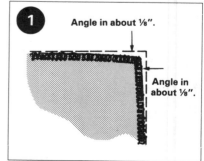

Angle in about ⅛″.

Angle in about ⅛″.

SEWING OVER PINS

I know sewing over pins isn't a good idea because you can break the needle, but is it really risky?

Sewing over pins can cause many kinds of damage to a sewing machine. Even if the needle never breaks, pins will make it dull, bent or burred; a damaged needle can snag fabric, break the thread or cause faulty stitching.

If the needle hits a pin hard enough, bits of metal can fly into your face or lodge in the machine's hook system, damaging the parts or causing faulty stitching.

If the needle bends the pin as it strikes, the pin and fabric can be jammed into the throatplate hole. You'll possibly damage the machine further when you struggle to release the jam.

If pins scratch the throatplate, this can lead to thread breakage as you stitch.

Those who sew over pins to save time eventually find out it's not worth the risk.

RING REMINDERS

I use large notebook rings to help organize my sewing notions. Buttons, needles, snaps and other carded findings store neatly on the rings. I just slide my stock around to the one I need and open the ring — no more searching through messy drawers.

S. King,
Grand Rapids, MI

SHEER SHADOWS

I've noticed interfacing tends to look like a shadow through sheer summer garments. Is there any way to avoid this?

Try using self-fabric as an interfacing. For example, to interface a front facing with self fabric:

• Cut the front facing pattern four times from fabric.
• With right sides together, stitch the outer, unnotched edges of two facing sections together in a ¼″ seam (Figure 1).

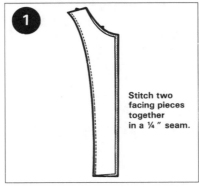

Stitch two facing pieces together in a ¼″ seam.

• Press the seam open over a curved surface such as a dress-maker's ham or a pressing board. Trim the seam allowances to ⅛″.
• Turn the facing right side out, press and edgestitch the seam (Figure 2).

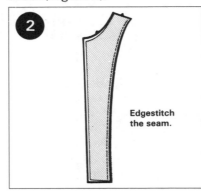

Edgestitch the seam.

• Repeat with the other two facing sections.

Or, choose the option of placing the two facing sections with wrong sides together and serging them together along the unnotched edge. Trim off ¼″ as you serge (Figure 3).

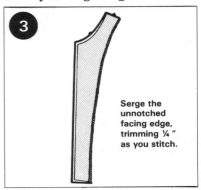

Serge the unnotched facing edge, trimming ¼″ as you stitch.

SHIRTTAIL HEM HELP

I've been unsatisfied with the appearance of the shirttail hems I've sewn. What is a good method for sewing this type of hem?

Shirttail hems can be tricky, but try serging them for a neat, smooth finish. The shape of the curve at the bottom of the blouse or shirt determines the sewing order you should use:

• For gently-curved shirt-tails, serge the side seams first. Then, serge the hem, trimming away ⅜″ of the ⅝″ hem allowance. Turn up the hem next to the serging stitches and topstitch on a conventional machine (Figure 1).

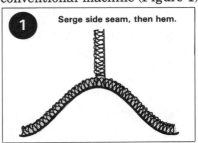

Serge side seam, then hem.

• For sharply-curved hems, serge the hem on the front and back garment sections separately, trimming away ⅜″ of the ⅝″ hem allowance. Turn up the hems next to the serging stitches and topstitch on a conventional machine. Serge the side seams (Figure 2).

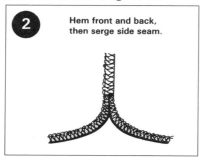

Hem front and back, then serge side seam.

If you don't have a serger, try ease-plus stitching, sometimes called crimping, to prepare the raw edge for hemming:

• Hold your index finger firmly behind the presser foot as you sew ¼″ from the raw edge. As the fabric piles up between your finger and the presser foot, the fabric will ease into a curved shape.

• Fold the raw edge under on the ease-plus stitching, then fold again (Figure 3). Baste by

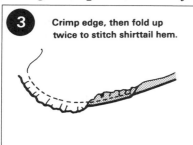

Crimp edge, then fold up twice to stitch shirttail hem.

hand, with glue stick or water-soluble basting tape. Hem by hand or machine.

SHOULDERS THRUST FORWARD

Sometimes my set-in sleeves wrinkle and pull at the shoulders, bind in the front armhole and feel tight across the upper back. What pattern alterations should I do to correct the fit?

Your shoulders probably thrust forward more than the pattern shaping allows. A key clue is if the shoulder seams follow a straight line from your neck, but then twist or curve toward the back at the armholes (Figure 1). This isn't

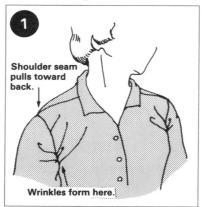

Shoulder seam pulls toward back.

Wrinkles form here.

an uncommon problem, especially with more and more women spending their days working at desks.

To alter the pattern:

• Add to the back shoulder seam at the armhole, tapering to nothing at the neckline; remove the same amount from the front shoulder seam (Figure 2). You are actually slanting the ends of the shoulder seams toward the front of the garment with this alteration. In the finished garment, the shoulder seams will appear straight.

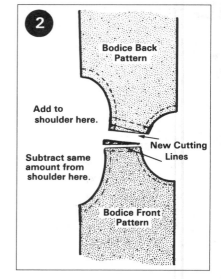

Bodice Back Pattern

Add to shoulder here.

New Cutting Lines

Subtract same amount from shoulder here.

Bodice Front Pattern

• The amount of alteration depends upon how far forward your shoulders thrust. Start with at least a ¼″ alteration, test the fit with a sample garment, then increase or decrease the alteration as needed.

• You may also need to rotate the sleeve forward in the armhole so the sleeve shoulder seam marking lines up with the new shoulder seam location. Baste the sleeve into the armhole and adjust if necessary.

SILKY BUTTONHOLES PUCKER

My machine sews beautiful buttonholes, except on silky fabrics. I use interfacing, but the fabric still puckers around the buttonholes. What can I do?

The soft interfacings generally used for silky fabrics may not stabilize the area enough to produce a pucker-free buttonhole, especially if the fabric is synthetic.

Use a small square of tear-away stabilizer under the fabric in addition to interfacing to stiffen the fabric while you sew the buttonhole. Simply tear off the stabilizer afterwards, leaving the interfacing in place to strengthen the buttonhole area.

SILKY STITCHES PUCKER

My machine has universal tension, but silky polyester fabrics still pucker when I stitch. Is this my fault or is there a problem with my machine?

Maybe neither. The textile industry has made great strides toward producing polyester fabrics with the look and feel of silk, but the finished garment often betrays the identity of the fabric. It just doesn't drape like silk. Synthetic fibers characteristically pucker at the vertical seams and darts if the garment is cut on the lengthwise grain as usual.

To minimize puckering:

• Cut the garment on the bias grain. As a second choice, cut it on the crosswise grain.

• To sew, think "fine." Use a fine, sharp needle and fine thread. Use a short stitch which allows less fabric to be drawn into each stitch, thus helping to keep the fabric relaxed.

• Try taut sewing – holding the fabric in front of and behind the presser foot so the fabric is taut as it feeds.

• Press as you sew. Press seams as stitched, then press the seam allowances open. Use a clapper to hold in steam and heat for a flatter press.

• As a last resort, try sewing over adding machine tape, tissue paper or tear-away stabilizer. Remove after you stitch and before you press.

SKIPPED ZIGZAG STITCHES

My machine sometimes skips a stitch when zigzag stitching, but never when straight stitching. What could cause this?

A dull, bent or burred needle is the most likely cause. Try a new needle.

If the machine still skips only when zigzagging, maybe your machine's needle height or hook/needle clearance needs adjustment. This minor adjustment can be made by a sewing machine mechanic who's trained to work on your machine model.

SLEEVE DIMPLES

My set-in sleeves always seem to have dimples instead of the smooth look I desire. Can you help me achieve more professional results?

Try this variation of the standard method for setting in the higher, more rounded cap on classic sleeves – use it on all but the most delicate fabrics and those that needle-mark easily:

• Make three rows of easestitches instead of the customary two rows in the sleeve cap from notch to notch. Stitch from the right side of the sleeve, using basting stitches. Easestitch ¾", ½" and ¼" from the raw edge (Figure 1).

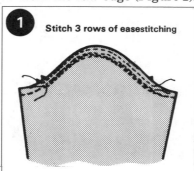

Stitch 3 rows of easestitching

• Pin the sleeve into the armhole, drawing up the bobbin thread to distribute the ease evenly and to fit the sleeve into the armhole. To keep the sleeve dimple-free and grain-perfect, draw up the ease from the front notches to the shoulder dot marking, then repeat from the back notches. Make sure the notches on sleeve and armhole match exactly.

• Keep in mind there's a small amount of ease allowed in the sleeve underarm between the front and back notches. Do not shift this ease toward the notches; keep it in the underarm area. Control the underarm ease with ample pinning.

• Stitch the sleeve into the armhole in a ⅝" seam, stitching between the two inner rows of easestitching so you can see exactly where you're stitching. You can readily control the ease for a smooth set.

• To finish, stitch the underarm section ⅛" from the first stitching, between the front and back notches (Figure 2).

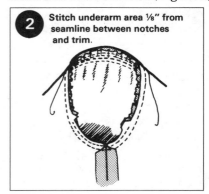

Stitch underarm area ⅛" from seamline between notches and trim.

Trim the seam allowances close to the second stitching. Remove the easestitching.

SLEEVE LENGTH PLEA

Can you help me figure out how to measure sleeve lengths for patterns with dropped shoulder, kimono, raglan and dolman styling?

There's no way to measure the sleeve length accurately on some pattern styles. However, you can establish your own, personal fitting guideline for use with such patterns:

• Ask someone to measure your arm from the shoulder bone to just below the bone on the pinky finger side of your wrist (Figure 1). Let your arm

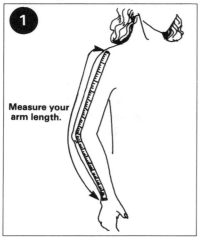

Measure your arm length.

relax at your side for measuring; many who sew have mistakenly taken this measurement with the arm bent at a right angle, resulting in a measurement that's too long.

• Select a classic, set-in sleeve pattern which fits your natural shoulders without shoulder pads. Measure the sleeve length between the seamline at the shoulder marking and the hemline, parallel to the grainline arrow (Figure 2).

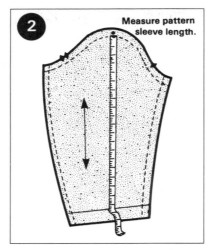

Measure pattern sleeve length.

• Compare the two measurements. The pattern sleeve length should be about ½" to ¾" longer than your arm measurement to allow for ease in the elbow area.

If the sleeve pattern is longer (or shorter) than your arm measurement plus elbow ease, lengthen (or shorten) the sleeve pattern the necessary amount.

• If desired, test the sleeve fit by making a sample garment.

• In theory, the amount you lengthen (or shorten) a classic, set-in sleeve is the same amount you would adjust any fashion sleeve style. In practice, you may have to fine-tune sleeve length a little bit with each new pattern style, However, once you have established your personal sleeve length standard, you will be able to cut and sew with confidence.

SLEEVE WRINKLES

When I set sleeves into jackets and coats, I occasionally end up with front or back wrinkles. Do you have a solution?

The wrinkles probably come from the way you've eased the sleeve into the armhole. Also, if your shoulder shape varies from pattern standards, you should adjust the sleeve cap easing for your shape. Some people need more ease in the back, while others need more ease in the front.

Try on the garment. If the sleeve wrinkles in the back, remove the stitches in the sleeve cap area and rotate the sleeve ease more toward the front (Figure 1). If the sleeve

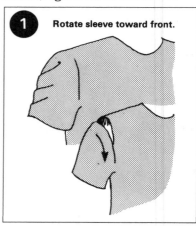

Rotate sleeve toward front.

wrinkles in the front, remove the stitches in the sleeve cap area and rotate the sleeve ease more toward the back. (Figure 2).

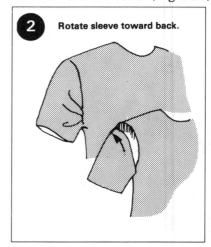

Rotate sleeve toward back.

STRAP STITCHES BREAK

Why do the stitches break when I turn narrow, tubular straps right side out? Also, how can I make tiny, firm straps?

The secret is to stretch the bias-cut strap as you sew. Then, the stitches won't break.

The finished size of the strap depends on the type of fabric you use. Straps made from soft, lightweight, smooth fabrics will be tinier than those made from stiff, heavier or textured fabrics.

To make very narrow straps:

• Cut a 1½″-wide bias strip of fabric. Cut it the desired length without seams. Fold it in half with right sides together.

• Shorten the stitch length to 20 to 25 stitches per inch.

• Begin by stitching a "funnel", tapering it close to the fold and stretching the fabric as you sew. As you stretch the fabric, the strip will become more narrow. You can stitch as close as $\frac{1}{16}$″ from the fold on very light-weight fabrics.

• Trim the seam allowances, making them equal to the distance from the stitching to the fold. (Figure 1).

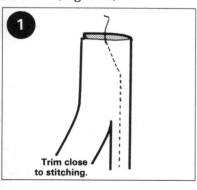

Trim close to stitching.

• Thread a blunt-tipped tapestry needle with strong thread such as buttonhole twist. Fasten the thread securely into the seam at the top of the funnel. Thread the needle through the strap to turn the strap right side out (Figure 2).

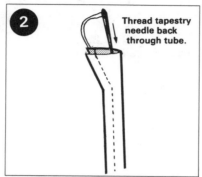

Thread tapestry needle back through tube.

• Pin the strap to an ironing board or dressmaker's ham in a stretched position to press. Trim off the funnel area.

TOPSTITCHING TROUBLES

My machine skips stitches when I topstitch. In addition, my topstitching doesn't look straight and sometimes the fabric ripples. Any tips to help me?

All of these problems can be solved. To remedy skipped topstitches:

• Start with a clean, well-oiled machine and a new needle.

• When using two threads for topstitching, use a needle one size larger than the size used to stitch the garment.

• If using heavy twist thread, use a larger needle or a topstitching needle which has a larger eye.

• Use a needle lubricant. For straighter topstitching:

• Follow a guide. For example, line up one presser foot toe with the edge of the garment. Or, mark with basting tape or chalk.

• When you must topstitch across seams, use a zipper foot.

• Shorten the stitch length slightly. Shorter stitches that are a little out of line are less noticeable than long stitches.

To prevent fabric ripples:

• Topstitch with the fabric grain if possible.

• Hold the fabric firmly in front of and behind the presser foot as you topstitch.

• Use an even feed, Teflon® or walking presser foot on your machine.

• Stitch slowly and at a uniform speed.

• Use the "stop and relax" technique for long stretches of topstitching – periodically stop with the needle still in the fabric and raise the presser foot to allow the fabric to orient itself smoothly, then resume topstitching.

ZIPPER BULGE

The zipper in my latest dress bulges out. What went wrong?

You probably used a zipper that was too long for the garment opening and you stretched the fabric to fit the zipper tape when you applied the zipper. In the future, you may want to ease about ¼″ to ½″ of fabric onto short zippers 7″ to 9″ long; for longer zippers, you can ease more fabric.

INDEX